A PHILOSOPHY OF SPORT

A Philosophy of Sport

Steven Connor

REAKTION BOOKS

Published by Reaktion Books Ltd
33 Great Sutton Street
London EC1V 0DX, UK
www.reaktionbooks.co.uk

First published 2011
Transferred to digital printing 2012

Printed and bound by University of Chicago Press

British Library Cataloguing in Publication Data
Connor, Steven, 1955–
A philosophy of sport.
1. Sports – Philosophy.
I. Title
796'.01-dc22
ISBN 978 1 86189 869 2

Contents

Introduction

Sport and philosophy do not, on the face of it, have a very natural affinity with each other. Philosophy, it is popularly supposed, and perhaps even supposed by a few philosophers, is the closest that one may come to the exercise of pure thought, typically, for example, involving the action of thinking about thinking itself. Sport, by contrast, involves the exertion of the body in something like its purest form. Sometimes this gulf between the cerebral and the corporeal can seem violent or tragic, but just as often the maladjustment of mind and body that has impelled so much philosophical speculation has also been the engine of comedy. The sometimes absurd distance of moral philosophy from practical issues is embodied in Tom Stoppard's play *Jumpers* (1972) by representing moral philosophy in terms of gymnastics, and the gap between the physical and the metaphysical is the source of the laughter in the Monty Python sketch that shows an Olympic final between soccer teams of philosophers representing Greece and Germany, the latter led out by their captain, 'Nobby' Hegel. (I should observe here that the game known to the world's billions as 'football', is given the rather prissy name of 'soccer' in this book, in order to distinguish it from the game played magnificently but somewhat more parochially in North America and one or two other places, for which no alternative designation that I can see exists.) As the whistle goes, the philosophers simply begin to stride around the pitch, taking no notice of each other, but extravagantly reasoning and expostulating to the air, the ball sitting undisturbed on the centre spot. Finally, after a sudden revelation bursts in upon Archimedes, the Greek sages put together an attacking move that scythes through the vapouring Germans and ends with

Socrates heading the ball into the German goal. The goal is vigorously disputed by the Germans, as the commentator excitedly explains: 'Hegel is arguing that the reality is merely an a priori adjunct of naturalistic ethics, Kant, via the categorical imperative, is arguing that ontologically it exists only in the imagination, and Marx is claiming that it was off-side.' The comic collision between soccer and philosophy has been enlarged upon in Mark Perryman's *Philosophy Football* and its sequel *Philosophical Football*, which offers transpositions of the intellectual careers of philosophers like Kierkegaard and Derrida (along with somewhat less obvious 'philosophers' like Dmitri Shostakovich and Paul Cézanne) into soccer terms.[1]

And yet, as the fact that the daft head-to-head imagined by Monty Python is played out in the Olympic Stadium may suggest, there are also some odd affinities and parallels between sport and philosophy, perhaps precisely because each is, to slump into philosophical lingo, so obviously the absolute other to the other. This has not always been the case. Sport and philosophy are held, for example, to have had their origin in Ancient Greece, which produced both organized sporting competition, in the form of the Olympic Games – the first taking place around 776 BC and continuing until their suppression by the Christian emperor Theodosius I in AD 393 – and systematized philosophy. In fact, a couple of centuries separates the establishment of the Olympic Games from the beginnings of Western philosophy, in the speculations about the physical world of Thales of Miletus (*c.* 624–546 BC), Anaximander (*c.* 611–547 BC), Anaximenes (*c.* 585–528 BC) and Heraclitus (*c.* 535–475 BC). But athletic exertion and intellectual enquiry nevertheless seem in this era not to be as obviously opposed to each other as they have become. Plato is said to have been not just a talented poet but also a notable athlete, his name having been changed by his wrestling coach from Aristocles to Plato, from *platon*, meaning 'broad-shouldered'. In his *Rhetoric*, Aristotle defined beauty in sporting terms, as 'having a body fit for endurance both on the racecourse and in contests of strength', and averred that 'pentathletes are most beautiful because they are equipped by nature at one and the same time for brawn and for speed'.[2] The Academy, where Plato taught outside Athens, was originally a grove of olive trees sacred to Athena, which was the site of ceremonial games and races, and many of the meetings of the Academy seem to have taken place in a gymnasium on the site. Plato's pupil Aristotle taught at the Lyceum, the site of another gymnasium, and the continuing use of the words Gymnasium and Lycée as names for schools in Europe is an ongoing reminder that for the Greeks PE would have stood for Philosophical as well as Physical Education. *Euthydemus*, a dialogue between Socrates and a couple of tricksy sophist philosophers, takes place in the locker-room of the Lyceum, which makes its own satirical comment on the fact that the sophists are said to be

> absolutely all-round fighters, not restricted to *physical* fighting as the pair of pancratiast Acarnanian brothers were. [The pancration was a brutal combination of boxing and wrestling.] Supreme physical skill at the sort of fighting which can overpower anyone is only the first of their attainments: they are expert fighters in armour, and can make others the same, for a fee ... [T]hey have now put the finishing touch to pancratiastic skill. They have now perfected the sole form of fighting they had neglected; they are utterly invincible, so formidable have they become at verbal battle – specifically, refutation of any statement, no matter whether it is true or false.[3]

There is more than a hint of mockery here, of course, but we can nevertheless accept Harold Tarrant's judgement that '[t]here was in fact a strong tendency in the classical period for philosophy to commend and encourage both physical health and the exercise needed to maintain it'.[4] In his *Antidosis*, the Athenian philosopher and orator Isocrates (436–338 BC) compared the teaching of the new discipline of philosophy to the competitive training undertaken by young athletes, affirming that philosophy and athletics

> are twin arts – parallel and complementary – by which their masters prepare the mind to become more intelligent and the body to become more serviceable, not separating sharply the two kinds of education, but using similar methods of instruction, exercise, and other forms of discipline. For when they take their pupils in hand, the physical trainers instruct their followers in the postures which have been devised for bodily

contests, while the teachers of philosophy impart all the forms of discourse in which the mind expresses itself . . . Watching over them and training them in this manner, both the teachers of gymnastic and the teachers of discourse are able to advance their pupils to a point where they are better men and where they are stronger in their thinking or in the use of their bodies.[5]

There are few who would make a similar claim now. Among them might be Michel Serres, who dedicates his book *Variations sur le corps* to 'my gym teachers, my trainers and mountain guides, who taught me how to think'.[6] There is also Heather L. Reid, who proclaims in her essay 'Socrates at the Ballpark' that

Aretē is the proper and ultimate goal of baseball and philosophy . . . Both activities seek knowledge, ask questions, require an admission of fallibility, encourage the constant and active testing of oneself, and include an obligation to challenge others. Furthermore, these connections are not just accidental or contrived. Baseball is an athletic competition, and like philosophy, it is directed toward the goal of *aretē*, or human excellence.[7]

For the most part, since the Greeks, and until recently, philosophy and philosophers have paid diminishingly little attention to sporting matters. Sport has not been a major or abiding preoccupation of the great philosophers of the Western tradition, or any other tradition, for that matter. Every now and then, of course, we come upon philosophers who happened to be interested in sport. Ortega y Gasset wrote a book on hunting; skiing makes a remarkable and extended appearance late in Jean-Paul Sartre's *Being and Nothingness*; Jacques Derrida was a goalkeeper, and dreamed in his youth of becoming a professional footballer, though never, as far as I know, referred to or made anything of this experience in his writing.[8] But, for the most part, the interest that philosophers have taken in sport is likely to be represented as a private or contingent thing, of no more philosophical significance than the state of the philosopher's liver or her taste in scarves. Ben Rogers's biography of A. J. Ayer notes his lifelong devotion to games, and the fact that at an early age 'he could recite from memory the list of all the English league football teams in the order in which they stood [and] what he took to be the strongest eleven for every one of the sixteen first-class county cricket teams (a mental list, excluding dozens of rejected players, 174 items long)'.[9] Ayer was also an accomplished cricketer and follower of his local cricket county Middlesex and not-so-local soccer team Tottenham Hotspur, though he stressed the arbitrariness of his passion for these teams – Ben Rogers hints at 'some connection here with his larger sense of the contingency of all our moral commitments – their ultimate groundlessness'.[10] Remembering this, the philosopher Lincoln Allison regrets the influence on him of Ayer's style of philosophy: 'I would compare him to the footballer Jimmy McIlroy of Burnley and Northern Ireland whose casual flicks and arrogant ball-holding made me want to be a genius footballer when my talents were more suited to being a clogger'.[11] Ben Rogers tells the story of a confrontation between Ayer and Mike Tyson, who was forcing his muscled attentions on model Naomi Campbell at a party. When Ayer encouraged him to desist, Tyson rounded on him with the words 'Do you know who the fuck I am? I'm the heavyweight champion of the world'. The 77-year-old Ayer replied: 'And I am the former Wykeham Professor of Logic. We are both pre-eminent in our field; I suggest we talk about this like rational men.'[12] But the point and purchase of such parallels between sport and philosophy is precisely the fizzling little sputters of comic incongruity they effect. Ayer's imprudent face-off with Tyson is perhaps to be seen, not so much as a sporting contest, as a contest between sport and some other kind of game altogether. It is hard to disagree with Paul Weiss's 1969 judgement that 'the opportunity to deal with sport philosophically was let slip away by the Greeks and their followers. From their time to our own, sports have not been taken seriously enough as a source or instance of large truths or first principles.'[13]

Oddly enough, even though sport has been a central preoccupation only of a tiny, if tenacious, minority of philosophers, Weiss's judgement was made just at the moment at which the philosophy of sport began to form and assert itself. There may be very little attention to sport among philosophers in the Western tradition, or Eastern, for that matter, but, since the 1970s, there has been a marked growth in what must be called, for it certainly calls itself, the philosophy of sport, even though much of it is a kind of second-order application of philosophical theories and arguments developed by philosophers who have not themselves been inclined to see sport in philosophical terms. The *Journal of the Philosophy of Sport* began publication in 1973 and was joined in 2007 by the journal *Sport, Ethics and Philosophy*. Among the many titles of the last four decades which hold out the promise of some kind of philosophical enquiry into sport are *The Philosophy of Sport* (1973), *Social Philosophy of Athletics* (1979), *Women, Philosophy, and Sport* (1983), *Sport in a Philosophic Context* (1983), *Toward a Philosophy of Sport* (1985), *Philosophy of Sport and Physical Activity* (1988), *A Philosophy of Sport* (1990) and *The Philosophy of Sport* (2007).[14] Recent years have also seen a growth in the number of writers promising to bring something like philosophical analysis to bear on particular games and sports, with the appearance of titles such as *Baseball and Philosophy* (2004), *Basketball and Philosophy* (2008) and *Football and Philosophy* (2008).[15] Sport has also been given systematic attention by other academic disciplines whose interest has sometimes also seemed in some sense or other philosophical, with the *International Journal of the History of Sport*, *Sociology of Sport Journal*, *Sport in History* and *Sport in Society* all into their third decades of publication.

Curiously, though perhaps I really mean unsurprisingly, the ways in which academic or philosophical writers have tried to bring serious attention to bear on sport have been rather predictable, in that they have tended to recognize in sport only those issues which already count as philosophical. Following Kant, these might be thought loosely to correspond to matters of pure reason (logical categorization), practical reason (morality and ethics) and aesthetics.

They are, I think, exemplified in the three dominant approaches to sport. The first, strongly impelled by Wittgenstein's theory of games, and exemplified in work by Bernard Suits, Graham McFee and Martin A. Bertman, considers sport as a problem of definition or categorization, and typically attends to problems of rules, norms and conventions.[16] Related to this, though it is conducted in a much less formalistic vein, is the substantial literature which has steadily accrued since the 1970s in the history and sociology of sport, which considers sport primarily as a social and historical fact, which is to be understood against the background of other social facts, political, economic, racial, military, technological.

The second way in which sport has been understood is as a sphere of moral action. This kind of work focuses on 'why sports morally matter', or the particular ways in which the sports and games seem to frame problems of justice, fairness and rights.[17] This way of thinking sees sport not as a social fact, but as a theatre of enacted ethical reflection,[18] a way of instancing and examining values, duties and responsibilities, in particular certain ethical problems – the involvement of animals in sport, for instance, or the development of genetic and technological forms of performance enhancement – that seem specific to sport.

Finally, sport can be understood in terms of aesthetics, in terms, that is, of the specific kinds of beauty or value-in-itself that may be held to characterize sporting activity, or specific kinds of response, admiration, joy, and so on, that they may be held to elicit. Hans Gumbrecht's *In Praise of Athletic Beauty* (2006) is a recent example of this kind of approach.[19] There has been very considerable debate about whether sport can in fact count as art, with writers like David Best being notably, and influentially, doubtful of the aesthetic view of sport, but in a way that has prompted some spirited defences of it.[20]

Naturally enough, there is much that is of interest and value in these three substantial areas of work. But I think it would have to be said that what they illustrate is the fact that no matter how earnestly or honestly philosophical thinking may be brought to bear on sport, the outcome is that sport tends to get reconstrued in philosophical terms. In the end, the tendency of this approach is to treat sport allegorically, as the exemplification or playing out of more general, fundamental or recognizably philosophical issues and implications.

I would like this to be a book that does something else with philosophical analysis. Perhaps because I am not a professional philosopher, and maybe not any other kind either, I have less at stake in making sure that my work is at all points recognisably and respectably philosophical. What I want to do is to bring to bear some perspectives and procedures from certain kinds of philosophy to try to focus as closely and interestingly as I can, and with as little precomprehension as possible, about the kind, or kinds, of thing sport is. This will involve me in not having to be, in fact in actively having not to be, too sure in advance about what sport is to be understood *as*: sport as ideology; sport as ethics; sport as art. This should help me write as though it were possible to provide an account of what sport is in its own terms, taking account of some of the things that are so apparent in sport that it is hard for them to become evident. I will have, I think, to cultivate an attitude that is at once quizzical and credulous. That is, I will want to suspend all the things I am sure I already know about what sport is and what it is for, and ask what this strange activity is, as though for the first time, as though I had never come across it before. And yet, and apparently cutting athwart this primly Martian outlook, I will also want to assume, a little perversely at times, the essential unity of what Americans call, plurally, 'sports': to assume, that is, that there is something, if not essential, then at least oddly insistent that runs through all instances of sport, despite the fact that it seems so hard to pick out precisely what it is that darts and skiing, Tae Kwondo and dressage, boxing and synchronized swimming, have in common. A philosophy of sport of the kind offered here is an attempt to articulate the meaning of sports – though the meaning of 'meaning' here is not that which might be expected. I do not, for the most part, aim to articulate what sport may represent, symbolize or stand for. I try to make out what sport means, in the sense of what it *means to do*, almost, one might incautiously say, what sport (in the mind it does not have) *might have in mind*.

I try thereby to try to find a way to ask what sport is and to try to swallow it whole, without having first decided to view it as something else that is more familiar and philosophically digestible. I want to use some kinds of philosophical analysis to capture more of the systematic strangeness of sport than has often been apparent to the 'philosophy of sport'. I try to show it as a weirdly coherent parallel universe, which is not so much a mirror for as an anagram of human life in general, and yet is becoming ever more definitional of what it means to be a human being. Where philosophical approaches to sport have been dominated by arguments that owe much to the analytic tradition, of careful and sceptical definition and discrimination of meanings and entailments, I would consent to my approach being characterized as a 'cultural phenomenology' – just as long as it were understood that I do not mean by this simply carrying over to the phenomena of culture the approaches developed by philosophers such as Husserl, Heidegger and Merleau-Ponty to classically phenomenological topics like the apprehension of time, the nature of self-consciousness and the experience of the body. What I hope to do in small part is contribute to the continuing reinvention of the philosophical tradition of phenomenology, the tradition of trying to understand the way in which things appear and are experienced, and in historically inflected terms suitable for making sense of external and collective phenomena rather than inner and individual experience, rather than trying to establish once and for all what they actually and in themselves are.

My approach will therefore be found to be at once highly particularized and highly generalized. I try to maintain a focus on the materiality of sport, on the elements of which sport is made, which commits me, especially in chapter Five, to trying to think carefully about the objects of sport, in both common senses: namely, the particular kinds of thing it characteristically makes use of and depends on – bats, balls, shin-pads, skates, posts – and the particular things that are its object, that is, the particular ways in which one can win or lose, scoring, coming first, lifting most, performing most elegantly, and so on. The single word 'goal' might draw these two dimensions of the object together, the goal as a particular physical object or structure, and the goal as the general aim of the game. I focus on these particular forms of equipment in order to think across and between different kinds of sports, trying to isolate certain recurrent features, that might together add up to something like a grammar of the nouns and verbs of sport, the objects and actions of which it consists.

There have been many attempts to define sport, many of which usefully isolate its different features. But, though it may be a mistake to try to identify a single principle of sport, I will maintain in this book the assumption that a sport is a game involving physical exertion. This definition will both run across and help to hold together all the topics I consider in the following chapters. The requirement for physical exertion, unlike other requirements for a sport that have sometimes been offered, such as the necessity of competition, or the display of physical prowess, distinguishes sports reliably from games, since games may be played virtually or abstractly, with no corporeal involvement at all. And the principle of exertion means more than just the involvement of the body. In essence, sports are *games that tire you.*

Nothing essential is missing from a game of chess played by telephone, instant messaging or even (a once common practice) correspondence by participants on different sides of the world. Sports that are played virtually, that is to say, without any corporeal involvement, are to that extent actually games. For this reason, sports must always involve material conditions; there must be a specific place in which they are played (the subject of chapter Two). They must also have a temporal dimension, which is considered in chapter Three, and one that is specific to the involvement of physical bodies, namely that they are subject to the inevitable increase of entropy, the horizon of all sporting exertion being fatigue leading finally to exhaustion. If games are subject to the first law of thermodynamics, which states that no energy can be created or lost, and therefore that time may be reversible, sports are subject to the second law, which states that all exercise increases entropy, and that time is irreversible. It is this condition, the fact that all exertion involves a striving in the lengthening shadow of exhaustion, which gives the tone and intention to the kinds of physical movement that are characteristic of sport, and which are discussed in chapter Four. My discussion of sporting objects in chapter Five offers an argument that the objects that feature in sport are themselves subject to a kind of exercise (from *ex-*, out of, and *arcere*, to bind or constrain), the unbinding or opening out of their possibilities. Sports resemble games most closely in having rules, the subject of chapter Six, but the agonistic nature of sporting behaviour means that one must always simultaneously play by the rules and test those rules to their limit. Sports are games that involve exertion, implying both constraint and the attempt to overcome it. The body is the very form of this ambivalence, since the body is both what constrains us, requiring us to live finitely in particular times, places and conditions, and also what seems to offer us the chance of overcoming or going beyond those conditions.

No definition of contemporary sport can ignore the indispensable element in it of competition, the focus of my final chapter. Sport involves striving, antagonism. Diverting, relaxing or sportive as it may be, these effects are the result of a concentration of purpose on winning. For Roger Caillois, this is not enough to justify a distinction between sports and games. 'It matters little', he writes, 'that some games are athletic and others intellectual. The player's attitude is the same:

he tries to vanquish a rival operating under the same conditions as himself.'[21] I think I must disagree here. For if a sport is distinguished from a game more generally on the grounds that it involves a specifically physical striving, then we can account for this by the fact that the idea of contention always in some sense implicates the body. For Gaston Bachelard, following Maine de Biran, mind itself must be conceived not as indifferently afloat in a bath of sensations, but as coming into being in a certain manner of being at odds with the world, which is never simply there for it; it is a 'cogito of striving'.[22] Being-in-the-world is always being-up-against-the-world. It is the body that is the medium of this contention – of striving against other bodies, human and non-human, or striving against the body itself. Perhaps we can go further even than this, to say that the body is the principle of resistance. To be embodied is to be limited in place and time, to be condemned to a have a particular perspective on things – which is also to say that it is to have a place from which to wish to move. If the body is, as Sartre suggests, always in advance or to the side of itself, it is because it is striving against itself. For Sartre, I cannot simply transcend my body, because I am it; but this makes it my 'coefficient of adversity'.[23]

All sports involve some kind of disabling impediment, in the form of rules that restrict the ways in which one can achieve the object of the game. Bernard Suits has identified this kind of restriction as an essential feature of all sports, in his assertion that 'Playing a game is the voluntary attempt to overcome unnecessary obstacles'.[24] One of the oldest games of which we have knowledge, the ball game played by pre-Columbian peoples, forbade the use of any other part of the body to move the ball but the hips, with a Mayan version of the game requiring the players to propel the ball with their chests.[25] The objects of sport are often the signs and vehicles of these prohibitions. The restrictions offered by the particular forms of projectors and projectiles, like all the other strictly limiting circumstances of sports, such as times, places and rules of behaviour, are not mere background conditions for the exercise of freedom. They are, like the body itself, both a restricting necessity and an enabling form of limit that is necessary for me to be able to assert my freedom. My freedom can never be absolute and unconditioned, and never purely a *freedom to*: the only kind of freedom it is possible for me to have is a freedom *from* particular kinds of constraint, which means that it is never absolute. My freedom can never itself be free of conditions. The objects and instruments of sport are the means both of imposing and surpassing disability, of imposing disability in order for it to be possible partially to overcome it. It is for this reason that there is no real difference between able-bodied and disabled sports, since all sports are means towards the exertion of freedoms through the imposition of impediment. Disabled sports deserve our interest and support, not just in order to give us an opportunity to be condescendingly generous with our attention, or because they solicit our respect for the spirit of striving they exemplify, but because sport is not possible without the assumption of disability, which means that disabled sports are *the only kind there are.*

For Sartre, we may not choose the disability which is our physical being, but we may – in fact, we must – choose our comportment in relation to it.

> Even this disability from which I suffer I have assumed by the very fact that I live; I surpass it toward my own projects, I make of it the necessary obstacle for my being, and I can not be crippled without choosing myself as crippled. This means that I choose the way in which I constitute my disability (as 'unbearable,' 'humiliating,' 'to be hidden,' 'to be revealed to all,' 'an object of pride,' 'the justification for my failures,' etc.) But this inapprehensible body is precisely the necessity that there be a choice, that I do not exist all at once. In this sense my finitude is the condition of my freedom.[26]

The body, which must always be implicated in sport, is not merely one locale or occasion of striving among others. The body is implicated in the very notions of resistance, aspiration and contention. It gives leverage, impetus and definition to every form of *agôn*. Sport requires the exercise of the body, because in sport, the body is always up against, and going beyond, itself.

Philosophy is not history. Philosophy strives, like the mathematics that it has sometimes sought to emulate, to be more than historical, more than just the intellectual idiom of its time and place. History produces opinions, philosophy aims at truth. There is, of course, such a thing as the philosophy of history, of which one of the leading concerns is what it means to be essentially historical creatures, that is, creatures whose essence is to live in time, able to recognize this condition, yet never able completely to command it. But philosophy has typically striven to articulate the general truth about this condition – the general truth for instance of always having to occupy and speak from a particular historical moment, which prevents the articulation of general truths – which always means in part attempting to suspend or set aside the condition. The condition of historicity, the impossibility of transcending one's historical situation, is common to all historical periods and conditions, and so cannot itself be regarded as merely historical. An account of the conditions attaching to this particular time is historical, an account of the general force of this particularity is philosophical. Philosophy must always have Olympian ambitions. But we will need, as a prelude to the enquiries to be undertaken later in this book, to grasp the historicity of sport. Why should such an unnecessary activity have become such a defining necessity for human beings? In what sense is sport natural, or, at least, part of 'our' 'nature'? If these sound like philosophical questions, they are questions that are perhaps best come at through a consideration of the history of sport.

one
History

Disporting

Why play? For a multitude of reasons. For exercise, for diversion, to pass the time, to exercise and even exorcize an obsession, and, we are sometimes told, for fun. Sport is from disport, itself formed from *dis-* away or apart and *portare*, to carry. This suggests that a sport is a way of being carried away from serious duties and purposes, a view confirmed by the closeness between sport and diversion, since to divert is literally to turn away. The core sense of disporting and diversion is contained in the prefix dis-, which derives ultimately from Greek *dis*, twice, from *duo*, two, the primary meaning being 'in two'.

Probably the reason that sports have at various times come under suspicion is that, in contrast to the idea that they offer some kind of 'recreation', and are therefore formative, they pull one apart, draw one aside and asunder. They are dubious, duplicitous, even, as we will see before long, diabolic. Where the life of an individual body or a collective entity depends upon its continuing coherence, or holding together, early understandings of sport saw it as the urge to spread and propagate, which seems linked to and may ultimately lead to the dissolution that is death. Philémon Holland's translation of William Camden's *Britain* (1610) speaks of the river Ex 'growing bigger, and sporting himselfe, as it were, with spreading into many streames'.[1] The English expression to 'sport away', suggesting idle or wasteful behaviour, seems to echo and redouble the *dis-* that has been eroded in the word sport.

A story has come into my mind, told me by my friend Jack Nicholas, and then frequently told back to each other, when we were at university together. Two friends were doing fielding practice, the one hitting a ball with a cricket bat for the other to catch. But they didn't have a ball, so were using an apple. Eventually, inevitably, the apple split in two as it was hit; but, not having or giving himself time to consider the matter, the catcher launched himself upwards and backwards and, spreading his arms cruciform, succeeded in catching both halves of the apple, even though he also succeeded in dislocating both shoulders. Distraction is here literalized, since to distract is literally to draw or pull apart. The danger of sports is that they will amount to no more than a dissipation, a scattering of concentrated human will and purpose. But the glory of this story is that, after all, both halves of the apple were caught. Sport is an attempt both to scatter and to capture. Sport spreads out, splits up and gathers in.

Indeed, modern sport has been something more than pure disporting for some time. For one must also observe in early usages of the term sport a reflexive tendency, or turning back on oneself. Another aspect of the dubiousness of sporting pleasure is that one disports *oneself*. So perhaps the full meaning is that one withdraws or deports oneself away from serious occupations in order to give pleasure purely to oneself. A writer in 1691 evokes scapegrace souls in their 'Masterless sporting themselves in the wide Sea of *Libertinism*'.[2] In such early usages of the idea of sport, there is a strong sense of the contrast between human or godly purpose and natural wantonness. It is natural to sport, because the essence of nature is itself to sport, in the sense of to ramify, propagate, to divert into diversity. The idea of a 'sport of nature', meaning an accidental or spontaneous mutation, buds out from this association between sport and undirected propagation. The things that are said commonly to sport, to carry or be carried away, are natural rather than human and, if human, are imitative of these natural entities. 'When the sun shines, let foolish gnats make sport', says Shakespeare's Antipholus (*Comedy of Errors*, III.ii.30). Sporting in this sense often refers to sexual play, which, when separated from the duties of reproduction, may be regarded as both aimless and propagating. The singer of the English folk song 'The Bonny Black Hare', which represents sexual dalliance as the hunting of a hare, asks his enthusiastic partner 'Have you had enough of my old sporting gun?' Sporting in this sense usually has no object or antagonist, though there are usages in which natural processes, especially chaotic or turbulent ones such as the movements of wind and wave, are said to 'sport' with something as its object, or plaything; the seventeenth-century preacher Thomas Adams calls dust 'the sport of the winde, the very slaue of the beesome'.[3]

Sporting could be thought of, not just as natural, but also as devilish. Adams condemned solicitors as 'Petty-foggers, *Satans* fire-brands, and mortall things; *which he casteth abroad, to make himselfe sport*'.[4] The devil was associated with sports and games during the seventeenth century, not because of a general disapproval of pleasure, but more specifically because sport suggested idle, profitless and fundamentally unserious action, action without a point or purpose, other than to propagate itself. It is not just that sport was sinful because it was pointless: sin and evil were themselves sportive because of their essential frivolity, their lack of seriousness. The devil was a sportsman because he was a trickster. The word 'devil' derives from *diabolos*, meaning literally to throw across, from *dia-* through, across and *bollein*, to throw. The devil throws curve balls, he is a seam bowler. He promulgated the illusion of evil (the devil was held actually to have no power except that given to him by permission of God) and therefore the greater evil of illusion.

Adams draws these ideas together in a sermon entitled 'The Foole and His Sport'. 'The *Foole* is the wicked man: his *Sport,* pastime, or babble is *Sinne. Mocking* is the *medium* or connexion, that brings together the *Foole* and *Sinne:* thus he makes himselfe merry; they meete in *mocking. The foole makes a mocke at sinne.*'[5] The greatest sin is failing to take sin seriously, sporting with sin, taking sin as its plaything; in fact, this is probably sin itself. The fool is most sinful when he mocks at the very notion of sin. Foolishness, sinfulness and mockery caper together in a grinning swirl.

Purposeless sport is not without cruelty. Adams stresses the fact that Satan will often create rivalry and violent contention between his followers.

> There may be *Dissention* betwixt the wicked and the wicked; and hereof also is *Satan* authour. He sets his owne together by the eares, like cockes of the game to make him sport. Hereupon hee raised these great Heathen warres, that in them millions of soules might goe downe to people his lower kingdome.

Hereupon hee drawes ruffian into the field against ruffian: and then laughes at their vainely spilt bloud.[6]

In this, the devil again resembles nature, which could equally be thought to look on indifferently, or with amusement, at the suffering caused by human contention. Here the sporting consists, not of divagation, but of the idle pleasure in the viewing of such processes. This is a violence that is hateful and sinful because it has no other point than to provide sport, the futile and foolish relish of pure disorder. As Adams says in his sermon 'Inwardly', alluding to Proverbs 26.18 *'dum ludunt, laedunt* [when they play, they pain], *'He casteth firebrands, and arrowes, and death; and sayth, Am I not in sport. As Solomon sayth, Their very mercies are cruell:* so their very iest is killing earnest'.[7] Against this, there is the clearly articulated and sustained purpose of the godly life, in its struggle against sin, which is to say, against unseriousness. Adams contrasts this play-violence to the steady and resolute martial purpose of the convinced Christian, in his battle against sin, the world and the devil:

> to this *War* euery *Christian* is a professed *Souldier:* not onely for a spurt, for sport; as young Gentlemen vse for a time to see the fashion of the warres: but our Vow runnes thus in *Baptisme*; that euery man vndertakes to *fight manfully vnder Christs Banner against Sinne, the World, and the Deuill; and to continue his faithfull Souldier and Seruant to his liues end*.[8]

The problem for Adams, even though it is the very feature of his remarkable language that makes him still worth reading today, is that he is so tempted at every turn to enliven and variegate his grim and menacing religious message with sportive puns and plays on language – such as the characteristically prankish jet of wit that gives the quibble on 'spurt' and 'sport' in the quotation just given.

During the eighteenth and nineteenth centuries, and, for a time, as it remarkably seems, almost entirely in England, sport changed its meaning, and came to designate particular pursuits involving forms of physical competition governed by rules. This meaning of sport, and the values that came to be associated with it, took time to spread elsewhere in Europe and, as late as 1844, the entry for 'Sports' in a German dictionary explained that as there was no German word for the activity, it was necessary to adopt it from English.[9] These two kinds of sport, sportiveness and rule-bound competition, correspond broadly to what Roger Caillois distinguishes as *paidia* and *ludus*, where *paidia* signifies the basic freedom of the instinct to play, as indicated in activities involving improvisation and the delight in various forms of tumult, agitation and disorderly, unpredictable movement, and *ludus* signifies the development of rules in what we call organized sports.[10] But Caillois is offering a classification that would hold good across the whole field of human games, amusements and diversions, including, slightly oddly, the field of simulation and pretend-games that, in their institutionalized forms, constitute theatre and performance. Within the general horizon offered by *paidia* and *ludus*, and the tendency for the former to develop into the latter, Caillois distinguishes two specific kinds of game which may correspond to the contrast between sportiveness and organized sports. There is *ilinx*, which describes those kinds of games in which the pleasures of vertigo and disorientation are paramount, and which consist of 'an attempt to momentarily destroy the stability of perception and inflict a kind of voluptuous panic on an otherwise lucid mind'.[11] Then there is *agôn*, characterized as 'a combat in which equality of chances is artificially created, in order that the adversaries should confront each other under ideal conditions, susceptible of giving precise and incontestable value to the winner's triumph'.[12]

Even if the practice of the kind of reasoning we call philosophical does seem to have arisen at the same time and place as organized sports, there are strong reasons to see organized sport as tied up with the development of the kinds of societies we call modern, that is, societies that have become highly self-conscious and rationally self-directing. The development of sport, in the movement from free and effervescent sportiveness, governed by the principles of *paidia* and *ilinx*, into the formalized competitions of *ludus* and *agôn*, may be seen as part of this process. Sport is, and has been for some time, something very different from free, divagating 'sportiveness'. We may perhaps see a steady development, in step with the move from *paidia* to *ludus*, from *ilinx* to *agôn*, from the scrambling struggles of the melee through to the whirling scrimmages of the medieval game of football, day-long, stravaging, almost unbound by rules, to the formalized, if no less crunching, confrontations of American football, in which violence and technicality interpenetrate.

The Unnecessary Animal

Modern societies define themselves in terms of the break they make (self-deludingly, some have thought) between a natural condition, characterized by the struggle against necessity, and a cultural condition, in which humans are both enabled and required to make choice of their own histories. This freedom to choose is a gift and a burden. Man is free to choose, and not free not to choose, because he is, so he likes to tell himself, the unnecessary animal. This is not to say that there is no necessity for him to be, for that is true of all animals and probably all forms of being. Even if there is a need for there to be being of some kind, there is never a need for any particular being to be the being in particular that it is. I did not have to be; if there had to be being, it did not have to be me; in fact, it had to be this way, that it did not have to be me. But man, so he is wont to tell himself, is the creature who has made a necessity of his non-necessity, the creature defined by the possibility of aware acceptance of the necessity of his non-necessity.

As usual, man assures himself of his distinctiveness in this respect, as in so many others, by claiming that in this he is distinct from all other animals. Animals too are unnecessary, but they are not formed in such a way that their non-necessity can become a necessary condition of their being. As we might put it, they do not have a relation to their non-necessity. Man is formed in fact from the question he asks himself of his being, born and borne out in what Giorgio Agamben has called the 'anthropological machine' of this self-questioning.[13] Though the whole being of man turns on and forms around the question 'what kind of being might be mine?', philosophers have tended to find a particularly intense and defining expression of this self-questioning in the exercise of privileged kinds of non-necessary action, such as art, sport and the cultivation of style. It is commonly said that the realm of the aesthetic is constituted as this paradoxical necessity of that for which there is no need, this arbitrariness which is essential to our being, and some have included sports and games in this category. Jean-Paul Sartre writes that the goal of the actor or sportsman is not to possess himself as an object but rather 'to attain himself as a certain being, precisely the being which is in question in his being'.[14] In a sense, the antagonism or grotesque sense of the scraping of gears involved when philosophy comes together with sport conceals a deeper affinity between the two. Philosophy, like sport, inhabits and exemplifies non-necessity, even arbitrariness, even if, like sport, it may have as its vocation the disclosing of the necessary conditions of things. When philosophy considers sport, it may in part be considering a kind of mirror to itself, a competing form of play with necessity.

The human practice of hunting foregrounds these questions of the necessary and the gratuitous. Philip Stubbes spoke for many Puritans in his condemnation of all kinds of sports and pastimes, including hunting, in his discussion of which he distinguished clearly between the necessary killing of animals, and the gratuity of hunting:

> If necessitie or want of other meats inforceth vs to séek after their liues, it is lawfull to vse them in the feare of God, wt thanks to his name: but for our pastimes and vain pleasures sake, wée are not in any wise to spoyle or hurt them. Is he a christian man or rather a pseudo-christian, that delighteth in blood?[15]

Stubbes did not mind the occasional use of hunting for recreation, but was appalled by

> the continuall vse therof daylie, hourly, wéekly, yéerly, yea all the time of their life, without intermission. And such a felicitie haue some in it, as they make it all their ioye, bestowing more vpon hawkes and hounds, and a sort of idle lubbers to followe them in one yéer, than they will impart to the poore members of Christ Iesus in vij. yéers, peraduenture in all the dayes of their life.[16]

This question of necessity recurs in the discussions of the recent British legislation regarding blood sports. The Hunting With Dogs Act which came into force in 2005 banning foxhunting in Britain was aimed principally at outlawing the infliction of cruelty on animals, which was often defined as 'unnecessary suffering'. As Emma Griffin has argued, the focus of this legislation, like that of previous efforts to ban or mitigate the hunting of animals, is not on the suffering or well-being of animals as such, for, if that were the case, there are many other arenas in which the suffering inflicted on animals would have to be regarded as far more intense and systematic and that therefore would make much more deserving targets. Rather it is on the moral offensiveness of the taking of pleasure in, or deriving of sport from the suffering of animals: the need for humans to kill animals is accepted, but the line is drawn 'at making sport out of the process'.[17] It seems to be this which makes the suffering unnecessary, and therefore offensive – though this rests upon the uncomfortable assumption that other kinds of suffering are in fact necessary. But necessary according to whom, required by whom? I think of Belacqua Shuah's horrified discovery in Samuel Beckett's story 'Dante and the Lobster' that lobsters are boiled alive: 'it was going alive into scalding water. It had to.'[18]

Animals have been removed from sport, as part of the process whereby sport has become more and more the means of marking man's way of standing out from nature, that is, his willing acquiescence with his condition as the unnecessary animal. In one sense, this is to protect animals from the indignity and humiliation of being treated as mere playthings. But by the same token, it quarantines animals from the sphere of play, from the anthropogenic privilege of nonnecessity, for this is reserved by and for the animal that gives itself the unique right to put itself in play (and for that reason squeamishly forbids itself the vulgar self-indulgence of playing with its food). Cruelty to animals is also sometimes known, tellingly, as 'abuse'. But to abuse an animal is not to use it in the wrong way or for the wrong purpose; rather, it is to do something other than merely use it, implying as a normative background that human use is what animals are essentially there for.

One of the awkward obstacles to this way of thinking is the fact that animals are not in fact excluded from the realm or possibility of play. One of the most influential theories of play, first articulated at the end of the nineteenth century in a book by Karl Groos (1898), was that it is to be regarded as a means by which an animal can rehearse or enhance skills under simulated conditions that will be necessary for it to sustain its life.[19] Such playful behaviour in animals may stop well short of the putting of oneself in play that is thought to be uniquely characteristic of human animals. It may be in the nature of certain animals to play; but it is only the nature of the human animal to want to play with its nature, to put its nature in play. And yet there have been those who are less certain of this categorical distinction, like Michel de Montaigne, who famously asked himself, in a marginal annotation to his 'Apology for Raymond Sebond' in 1588: 'When I play with my cat, how do I know she is not making a pastime of me rather than I with her?' – '*Quand je me joue à ma chatte, qui sçait si elle passe son temps de moy plus que je ne fay d'elle.*'[20]

The expression 'blood sport', the earliest usage of which is recorded from 1895, does not, as we know, refer to a sport in which blood may be spilled: otherwise football, rugby and even table tennis, at which I once got a nasty nick from the edge of the table, could be regarded as blood sports. It refers to a sport in which the spilling of blood, or the harming of living creatures for which it is the synecdoche, is the aim (and it is for this reason that boxing can sometimes be said to qualify as a blood sport, for, in this sport uniquely, the infliction of injury is the intended aim and not the accidental outcome). The point of the expression 'blood sport' is that it seems oxymoronic, since the taking of pleasure in suffering has come to seem the very opposite of sport. However, this is the outcome of a very long process, in which the idea and practice of sport have slowly become unpicked from its association with aggressive or cruel actions. From its earliest usages in English, to 'sport' has meant both to 'disport oneself', and to mock or make merry at some object other than oneself. The word embodies an ambivalence: to make sport out of suffering is a scandal, and yet sport has been strongly identified for many centuries precisely with this process: as Shakespeare's Gloucester complains, 'As flies to wanton boys are we to the gods: they kill us for their sport' (*King Lear*, IV.i.36–7).

The notion of sport always held within it some element of duplicity and simulation, some internal departure from actuality. For hunting to provide good sport it is necessary for there to be a kind of extended uncertainty, a playful lengthening out of possibility.

Many noted the analogies between hunting and sexual dalliance in this respect. The writer of a late sixteenth-century popular romance says 'I can most fitly compare louers to hunters, that likes better of the sporte, then they doe of the game it selfe when they haue it: or like him that would needs goe a fishing, though hee caught but a frogge.'[21] Indeed, we might say that the very turning, deporting or perversion of sense that is involved in deriving pleasure from pain is at the heart of sport. While seemingly unable to participate in that process, the animal has nevertheless been indispensable to it, precisely because it is its suffering that is required.

In order to understand this, we should take note of a fundamental ambivalence that is involved in the sport of hunting. Defenders and advocates of hunting have for centuries represented it as being natural to man, or a sign of the continuity of man and nature. Even Montaigne, who was revolted by cruelty to animals, remarked that 'We go out to hunt animals: lions and tigers go out to hunt men; each beast practises a similar sport against another: hounds against hares; pike against tenches; swallows against grasshoppers; sparhawks against blackbirds and skylarks' – though we should note that the English translation I am here quoting forces the issue a little, for Montaigne writes, not precisely of animals who practise sport, but *ont un pareil exercice les unes sur les autres*, 'exert themselves similarly one against the other'.[22] But the sport of hunting involves a complex mixture of the natural and what might be called the paranatural, the natural minimally nudged into the 'natural'. We might perhaps discern this in the expression 'a sport of nature', a translation of *lusus naturae*, a joke or freak of nature, which came into use in the early seventeenth century to signify an accidental or anomalous departure from natural law, or, as it were, a game that nature plays with itself. (The word 'freak' itself originally referred to a whim or trick rather than a deformity – the OED suggests that it is perhaps cognate with Old English *frícian*, to dance.)

There is a fundamental ambivalence in the act of hunting. Its primary aim is the promise and proof of the subjugation of nature. It therefore involves not just an action – the action of pursuing and killing an animal – but a performance, which is to say an enactment of the meaning of an action. The hunt is both a form of action, and something acted out. As Matt Cartmill observes, the meaning of the hunt is that it is 'an armed confrontation between humanness and wildness, between culture and nature'.[23] In the hunt, the human recognizes itself as an active exception from nature. But the hunter is not simply or straightforwardly outside or on the other side of nature. For what characterizes hunting is that one hunts nature *with* nature, typically with the accessories of hounds, hawks and horses, though sometimes with more unexpected animals, such as cheetahs.[24] The animal is necessarily a participant as well as an opponent. Not only this, but the mythology and symbolism in which hunting is so richly laden frequently construct the pursued animal as the mirror as well as the other of the hunter.

The animals which are subject to the sport of hunting have entered a forest of signs. The most important feature of this symbolism is the fact of reversibility and repeatability. Each individual hunt, though always deliciously unpredictable in its itinerary, is also reliably repeatable in its irrevocable outcome, the death of the animal. Each slain hart is both itself, and the figure of the Hart which it embodies. Indeed, a central part of the mythology attaching to the hart is the belief in its extraordinary longevity and even power of magical self-regeneration. There is a story of a stag killed in the forest of Windsor in the fifteenth century that was found to be wearing a collar reading '*Julius Caesar quant jeo fu petis / Ceste coler sur mon col ad mys*' – 'Julius Caesar, when I was young / Around my neck this collar hung'.[25] Death is here undone by the symbolic order: indeed, one might say that, in so far as it is other or outside of the symbolic order, death is what the hunt aims symbolically to transmute and neutralize.

This is not the only reversibility that is evident in hunting. Hunting in the seventeenth century produced an efflorescence of technical and ceremonial terms, which one mistook at one's social peril. Nature is both captured and ramified by these luxurious orgies of designation and discrimination, in their form resembling the arboreal branching of the antlers which were themselves among the features of the deer subject to this meticulous naming of parts. Each stage of the action was carefully choreographed, making the hunt the meeting place of the scripted and the unpredicted, the necessary and the contingent. Values were both invariant and yet reversible. A particularly telling example of this is the ritualistic attention paid to the dung of the stag, which expert trackers conned as attentively as the haruspicator his entrails. George Gascoigne provides a telling image of a selection of stag's faeces – or fuments, as they were known – being reverently presented to the young Queen Elizabeth (who would remain keen on hunting throughout her life, being prepared to spend all day in the saddle even in her late sixties): 'For if you marke, his fewmets euery poynt, / You shall them finde, long, round, and well annoynt, / Knottie and great, withouten prickes or eares, / The moystnesse shewes, what venysone he beares.'[26] Excrement, animality and royalty here seem perfectly reversible and comfortably compatible. What is true of the animal's excrement is also true of its corpse once it has been despatched. Hunting codes called for an elaborate and painstaking ritual of unmaking, with the placing of the cuts, the ordering of the dismembering and the distribution of different portions of the carcass being carefully discriminated.[27] It may be that the ostensible or public reason for this ritual is to display due reverence for the body of a noble opponent: but it also seems designed to prevent the dead body of the animal from slipping underneath the net of signification into the condition of undifferentiated surplus, or mere matter. The vast amount of literary writing devoted to the hunt has ensured that it was as much poesis as predation, a matter of wordcraft as well as woodcraft.

We should not forget the persistent and abiding link between blood sports and aristocracy. Aristocracy here refers to more than the shifting fortunes of a particular class. For we can see at work in blood sports a desire for what philosophers from Nietzsche onwards have identified as an absolute sovereignty, which extends far beyond actual political power. The sovereign will wishes to transcend nature, including and especially its own nature. It is this dynamic which explains the peculiarly intimate mixture of identification and antagonism in hunting, and what Donna Landry approvingly calls the 'identificatory loss of human distinctness in the chase'.[28] The animal must be the hunter's own 'natural' self that is put at stake, and put to the stake. The animal is the external bearer of this internal psychomachia. More than this, sovereignty means the power to command the sign, and to effect the reversals of meaning that are characteristic of the hunt. The hunter affirms and assures his nobility, which is to say his absolute distinctness and autonomy, through the relay of the animal, through the fact that the animal can be made to mean anything. The polymorphousness of the hart, the hare and the fox depends upon the capacity of the human partner in the transaction to put the meaning of everything in that transaction in play. But the power to effect reversal is radically non-reversible. Sport is a kind of playing with life – playing with the forces of life that might otherwise seem to make you their plaything.

Writers on hunting have rightly observed its 'sacramental' nature, depending as it does on a language of the body, a play of signification that is enacted not principally through abstract symbolism, but through the forces and forms of bodies in motion. But, as the word suggests, the sacramental is founded upon a sacrifice. Ultimately, what has come to be seen as the offensiveness of hunting does not depend upon the charge of cruelty, though it may indeed involve considerable pain and distress for the fox or hare. For it is not so much that the animal is put to death through hunting, as the fact that it is simultaneously given its death and deprived of it, the fact that its pain and death are sported with, that is, deported into meaning, into play, into performance. What has become nauseating is that, like Ted Hughes's black rhino, in the poem of that name, the hunted animal 'has blundered somehow into man's phantasmagoria, and cannot get out'.[29]

So the most obscene thing about hunting is its status as scene or spectacle. The hunted animal is made to seem to be a willing actor on the stage of its passion. Animals provide sport when they put up a fight, thus delaying and diversifying what is nevertheless felt to be the inevitable outcome of the hunt. In this, they seem to join with the humans who sport with them, in putting their own natures into play, in entering the sphere of the gratuitous rather than the necessary. The cruelty and violence towards animals of the hunt is the pretence or simulation of the fact that they are freely offering sport to the hunter – the sporting with the pretence of their freedom. Animals are play-antagonists; the agony of the animal in hunting comes from the mock-*agôn* that it is made to seem to offer, and the cruel mockery of their unfreedom that results from it. In reality the sport of hunting is a sport of spectacle, which allows man to relish the fictional contest, in just the same way as, according to Pliny, nature looks on and enjoys the bloody play of human antagonism. Philémon Holland's 1601 translation of Pliny's *Natural History* asks, of the supposed vicious rivalry between elephants and dragons, 'What reason should a man alledge of this so mortall warre betweene them, if it be not a very sport of Nature, and pleasure that she takes, in matching these two so great enemies together, and so euen and equall in each respect?'[30]

The staging of atrocity thus becomes the atrocity of staging. One thinks of the story of the nineteenth-century German theatre, the strict regulation of which included a ban on all kinds of improvisation or non-scripted action. One evening, an actor was performing with a live horse, which suddenly dropped a spattering load of dung on to the boards. 'What are you doing!' protested the actor. 'Don't you know we are forbidden to improvise?' Improvisation is as impossible for the hunted animal as for the performing animal, for its every twist and turn has been scripted in advance by hunting's theatre of cruelty – though this term here has a sense that is precisely opposite to that intended by Antonin Artaud, the originator of the phrase,[31] in that here, theatricality is not made more actual and immediate through the passions of the body, but rather spirits away the suffering of the animal even as it insists on it.

Up to the end of the nineteenth century, the word 'sport' continued to refer to various forms of hunting and the forms of horse-racing (the 'sport of Kings') and dog-racing that were their spectator equivalents. The *Sporting Life* newspaper, which began publication in 1859, testifies to this usage. The melancholy beginning of a review of 1899 of *The Encyclopaedia of Sport*, edited by the Earl of Suffolk and Berkshire, makes it clear that the identification between sport and hunting was both very strong and also beginning to wane at the end of the nineteenth century: 'The spread of civilization is the bane of wild sport. Colonization, conquests, annexations and spheres of influence, with firearms approaching to perfection, have been exterminating the wild animals or hunting them from their immemorial haunts to less accessible retreats.'[32] This accounts for the many late nineteenth-century books with what might seem like unlikely titles like *Sport in Somaliland*, *Sport in the Crimea* and *Sport on the Tibetan Steppes*, which are none of them ethnographic studies of local games and pastimes; similarly, an 1893 article on 'Sport in the Snow' turns out to be about bear-hunting in Russia.[33]

It is possible to make out an argument that the steady urbanization of the population, along with an ever more distanced and instrumental view of nature and animals, are in part responsible for the growing unease with hunting from the early nineteenth century onwards, which has matured in Britain into the majority opposition of recent years. Another of the effects of urbanization has been the growth of mass-spectacle organized sports in which animals feature less and less. We can date the change in the word 'sport' to a very short period, beginning at the end of the nineteenth century, which is precisely the period when humanitarian and anti-vivisection groups began to exert their most powerful influence. In the early 1890s, 'sport' still usually meant hunting. By the teens of the twentieth century, 'sport' was much more likely to refer to organized and intrahuman team games. This reverses a change which took place in the other direction between the mid-seventeenth century and the mid-nineteenth century, in which rural sports became known as games, and sport came to refer ever more exclusively to hunting.[34] The change in the meaning of the word 'sport' to refer to organized competitive recreations between humans was brought about by the steady growth through the twentieth century of sports in which the relay of the animal is dispensed with, except sometimes as partner or participant, for example in archaically aristocratic sports like polo. Sport is still a way to formalize and make graspable man's sense of his unnatural nature, but a dominative dreamwork of identification between man and animal has given way to a melancholy recognition of the epistemological fissure between them, which means, in part, between man and himself. In modern sport, man must be his own other, relayed back to himself by objects rather than other beings.

Modernizing Sport

Since the 1970s, when historians and sociologists began to pay serious attention to the development of sport and its place in cultural and political life, it has become clear that mass spectator sport was one of the most salient and defining features of urban modernity. Sport was not merely modernized in the twentieth century: in a sense what we now mean by sport was the invention of the twentieth century, and, reciprocally, sport was one of the most distinctive ways in which the modernity of the twentieth century was produced. The attention of philosophers too, especially those with an interest in the development of modern forms of social and economic life, has been increasingly drawn to sport during the twentieth century, the period in which it took its modern, organized forms. The question asked by many of these philosophers is whether sport is to be seen as opposed to or expressive of the mechanical, regulated, urban mass society that became common during the twentieth century. Many conservative, organicist and fascist writers who identified sport with energy, impulse and dynamism saw in it an indignant protest against this mechanization. One of the most emphatic of these was José Ortega y Gasset, whose *Meditations on Hunting*, first published in 1943, affirms the aristocratic transcendence of or contempt for the realm of social necessity.[35] In a later essay of 1940, Gasset provided a restatement of the opposition between sport and rationality, in the form of a bizarre speculation on the origins of the State itself. The central principle animating Gasset's essay is the irreducibility of life to utility. Where utilitarian considerations bring about adaptation and the meeting of means and ends, life consists essentially in excess: 'the first and original activity of life is always spontaneous, effusive, overflowing . . . in the beginning there is vigor and not utility.'[36] Gasset identifies the sportive instinct with this joyous excess, rather than with labour: 'Sportive activity seems to us the foremost and creative, the most exalted, serious, and important part of life, while labor ranks second as its derivative and precipitate. Nay more, life, properly speaking, resides in the first alone; the rest is relatively mechanic and a mere functioning'.[37]

Gasset proposes in his essay an intriguing variation on Freud's account in *Totem and Taboo* of the inauguration of neurotic guilt in the murder of the patriarch in the primal horde; Gasset's focus is on the erotic drive which leads young males in the horde to begin to covet females of alien hordes. Since these other hordes are unlikely to give up their women for rape without demur, it is necessary for these libidinous young adolescents to band together and submit to collective planning and discipline in order to effect their purpose. For Gasset, it is these collective structures, physical as well as institutional, that constitute the beginning of the State:

> The first house built by man is not a home for the family, still nonexistent, but a casino for young men. Here they prepare for their expeditions and perform their rituals; here they indulge in chanting, drinking, and wild banquets. Whether we approve of it or not, the club is older than the family, the casino older than the domestic hearth.[38]

From this, Gasset can conclude that 'It was not the worker, the intellectual, the priest, properly speaking, or the businessman who started the great political process, but youth, preoccupied with women and resolved to fight – the lover, the warrior, the athlete.'[39]

Others saw in sport not just a general impulse that was contrary to or in excess of the utilitarian, but a specific response to the cramped instrumentalism that characterized the modern world. This line of thought perhaps finds its beginning in Hegel's *Philosophy of History*, which argued that

> Sport itself is opposed to serious business, to dependence and need. This wrestling, running, contending was no serious affair; bespoke no obligation of defence, no necessity of combat. Serious occupation is labor that has reference to some want. I or Nature must succumb; if the one is to continue, the other must fall. In contrast with this kind of seriousness, however, Sport presents the higher seriousness; for in it Nature is wrought into Spirit, and although in these contests the subject has not advanced to the highest grade of serious thought, yet in this exercise of his physical powers, man shows his Freedom, viz. that he has transformed his body to an organ of Spirit.[40]

It was in Germany more than anywhere else that, as John Hoberman has argued, 'sport emerged as nothing less than a modern style in which an ideologically diverse collection of temperaments found an issue of sociological significance and, in not a few cases, a locus of value in a value-starved world.'[41] Heinz Risse wrote in his *Soziologie des Sports* of 1921 that '[m]echanized man has no other form in which to manifest this will in everyday life but in the domain of physical culture'.[42] He found in the marathon runner

> a strange expression of our entire world-feeling, which wants to dominate everything both backwards and forwards in time, for which there are no limits and which is always straining beyond itself. Always, we are men of the day before yesterday and the day after tomorrow. Temporally and spatially, we are are always standing with one foot in the beyond. Sport is in absolute accord with this world-feeling.[43]

Karl Jaspers wrote in 1931 in his *Die Geistige Situation der Gegenwart* (translated as *Man in the Modern Age*) that '[s]port is not only play and the making of records; it is likewise a soaring and refreshment'.[44] As such it is 'a defiance to the petrified present. The human body is demanding its own rights in an epoch when the apparatus is pitilessly annihilating one human being after another'.[45] Johan Huizinga similarly saw sport as liberating ecstatic energies that were otherwise at risk from administered forms of play and entertainment: 'Why is a huge crowd raised to a frenzy by a football match? This intensity of, and absorption in, play, finds no explanation in biological analysis. Yet in this intensity, this absorption, this power of maddening lies the very essence, the primordial quality of play.'[46]

But there was another current of thought, more identified with Marxist and leftist critique of culture, which saw in sport, not the ecstatic assertion of life, impulse or spirit, but a false and feeble compensation for the authentic joys of the bodily life, and thus actually a means of extending the mechanization of man. Lewis Mumford summed up this line of critique when he wrote in 1933 that 'sport, which began originally, perhaps, as a spontaneous reaction against the machine age, has become one of the mass duties of the machine age'.[47] Robert Musil, himself an ex-athlete, saw the subordination of art to sport, in the fixation upon athletic bodies, as 'without doubt a great victory of sport over spirit'.[48]

The most developed form of this critique is to be found in the work of T. W. Adorno. In *The Dialectic of Enlightenment*, Adorno and

Horkheimer see sport as part of the apparatus of rationality, which they compare with pornography:

> What Kant grounded transcendentally, the affinity of knowledge and planning, which impressed the stamp of inescapable expediency on every aspect of a bourgeois existence that was wholly rationalized, even in every breathing-space, Sade realized empirically more than a century before sport was conceived. The teams of modern sport, whose interaction is so precisely regulated that no member has any doubt about his role, and which provide a reserve for every player, have their exact counterpart in the sexual teams of *Juliette*, which employ every moment usefully, neglect no human orifice, and carry out every human function. Intensive, purposeful action prevails in sport as in all branches of mass culture, while the inadequately initiated spectator cannot divine the difference in the combinations, or the meaning of variations, by the arbitrarily determined rules.[49]

Elsewhere, Adorno associates music with popular music, which

> seems imaginatively to restore to the body some of the functions which in reality were taken from it by the machines – a kind of ersatz of physical motion, in which the otherwise painfully unbridled motor energies of the young, in particular, are absorbed. In this respect the function of music today is not so very different from the self-evident and yet no less mysterious one of sports. In fact, the type of music listener with expertise on the level of the physically measurable performance approximates that of the sports fan. Intensive studies of football habitués and music-addicted listeners might yield surprising analogies.[50]

Adorno approved of Thorstein Veblen's view of sports as 'not so much a relic of a previous form of society as perhaps an initial adjustment to its menacing new form'.[51] This is precisely because sport regulates and industrializes the free bodily pleasures it seems to offer:

'Modern sports, one will perhaps say, seek to restore to the body some of the functions of which the machine has deprived it. But they do so only in order to train men all the more inexorably to serve the machine. Hence sports belong to the realm of unfreedom, no matter where they are organized.'[52]

Adorno is certainly right to see sport as part of the modern world, or as caught between the modern and the archaic. During the twentieth century, the very notion of sport became subject to some of the famously liquefying effects of modernity, as, during the early years of the twentieth century, sport started to become more and more organized, professional and commercial. Sport was no longer a rural, aristocratic pursuit, but an urban and working-class one. The opening of Philip Larkin's 'MCMXIV' captures something of this new status of sport as mass entertainment:

Those long uneven lines
Standing as patiently
As if they were stretched outside
The Oval or Villa Park,
The crowns of hats, the sun
On moustached archaic faces
Grinning as if it were all
An August Bank Holiday lark.[53]

The lines are however not for a Test match or cup-tie, but to enlist in that other form of modern mass action, and one that modernists dignified with much more attention: war.

An essay of 1900 by H. Graves entitled 'A Philosophy of Sport' provides an indication of the minor turbulence which characterized understandings of sport at this time. The essay begins by observing that '[t]here are few words in the English language which have such a multiplicity of divergent meanings' and looking forward to the illumination promised by 'Dr Murray . . . when he works down to the later ages of the letter S'.[54] Acknowledging that 'some sportsmen of the old school seem disposed to restrict the term sport to such non-competitive recreations as involve killing, thus restricting the term to hunting, shooting, fishing and so forth' (878), Graves nevertheless makes out three broad meanings in the dictionaries he consults, namely simple pastimes, the pursuit of animals, and gambling: 'Starting from the simple notion of sport as an amusement, we come down to the curiously specialized uses of the word which tie it down on the one hand to pursuits of killing and on the other hand to games in which a money stake is involved' (878). In what follows, Graves makes a determined effort to defend the idea that sport is a competitive pastime undertaken for its own sake, and in particular the idea that sports 'must be undertaken purely for the sake of recreation as distinct from business' (879). The threat to this definition of sport comes, not at all from the tally-ho classes, but from a tension that would come to define sport in its modern form, namely that between *le sport pour le sport* and the economic and commercial powers that began to be focused on it. Graves insists that sport must be amateur: 'In so far as a pursuit is followed as a means of livelihood it ceases to be a sport, and becomes merely a matter of business. Sport is followed for no other end than to afford pleasure to those participating in it, and a sportsman follows sport for no other reason than to enjoy that pleasure' (880).

The most important development here is mass spectatorship, for it is this which turns a participative absorption in the game into something mediated. In part this is because it opens the prospect of making a living from sport, and '[o]nce the idea is imported into sport that a man's subsistence depends upon it, then the pleasantness of sport as a recreation ceases, and we import into it the bitterness of the world's struggle for existence' (883). Spectator involvement encourages gambling of course, though Graves is less concerned by this, since, as he observes at the beginning of his essay, betting had become inextricably linked to the 'sporting life' during the previous century and perhaps even before, so that there was nothing wrong with betting 'provided it be conducted by gentlemen or, what for the purposes of sport is synonymous, by sportsmen' (888). The real threat to the sporting ideal, however, comes from the rationalization of competition:

> there is a strong feeling among the more thoughtful lovers
> of sport that the competition of to-day is overdone, that the

desire for individual distinction is carried to an excess which is harmful to sport, and that the complex organization thereby necessitated acts as an incubus, and being too much of the nature of a business, robs sport of its natural character as a recreation. (890)

Graves linked what he oddly calls 'the Cambridge tripos system of play, of carefully grading clubs and competitors in order of merit' (891) to the creation of

a curious class of spectators – men often incapable of appreciating the beauties of a fine game, yet inspired by the wildest enthusiasm for the success of the side which they "support", men who know nothing of the sport beyond the method of the computation of the championship table and are ready to mob a hostile team should they defeat their favourites. (891–2)

There is one sport in particular which focuses these issues, the sport which had become most thoroughly systematized, namely soccer, or round-ball football. Graves enunciates a socio-economic contrast that would hereafter run through the folk sociology of British sport, that between the aristocratic and public-school sport of rugby and the working-class sport of soccer:

Most men are agreed that truer sportsmanship is to be found among the adherents of the Rugby Union than among those of the Football Association, or still more of the Northern Union [the semi-professional clubs who broke away from the Rugby Football Union in 1895] or of the Leagues. There is something brutalizing in a competition which is bound to result in the expulsion of great and historic names from the ranks of 'first-class' football. (891)

The growth of the spectator both made modern sports possible and also, as it seemed to many, fatally compromised sport as such. Commentators on the first modern Olympic Games in Athens in 1892 were perplexed and affronted by the noisy partisanship of the

American spectators, their numbers boosted by sailors on shore leave from the cruiser *San Francisco*.[55]

As they became more popular, sports were ever more precisely and elaborately codified. As we have seen, the most emphatic transformation that this brought about was the removal of animals, or of animals as objects or victims, from sport, and an almost exclusive concentration on intra-human competitions, even if animals might sometimes be used as accessories, as in residual sports like show-jumping or dressage. This was the most important part of the process whereby sports began to approach the condition of pure play, of *sport pour le sport*. Animals here might be taken to include human beings, since what characterizes the animal is that it is a mere object or instrument. As soon as one ceases to aim at the death or physical destruction of one's opponent, then the human as animal, or the reduction of the human to a mere animal, may be said to have been removed from sport. During the twentieth century, sport, like art, increasingly could only be sport if it were unreal, or real and unreal at once. Sport, in other words, has undergone something like its own modernist transformation, and sport as we understand it is very largely the legacy of that modernization. Indeed, perhaps one of the reasons for the inattention of aesthetic modernists to sport is that, unlike other forms of mass entertainment, sport could not simply be represented as part of the ugliness, triviality and commercialism of modern life. Sport, in short, represented a rival aesthetic to art, or might have done, had it occurred to modernists to allow its claims. In a sense, sport can be seen as an anagram or anamorphic mirror of modernism.

In the light of this, it is not at all surprising that certain avant-garde writers should have begun to look back on the earlier forms of blood sport, not as an atrocity or vulgarity, but as a desirable self-image for the boldly unconstrained artist. The praise of hunting could become a proof of the anti-modernity of the modernist, as, for example, in Wyndham Lewis's 'Our Vortex', published in the first issue of *Blast!* in 1914, which oddly associates the hunt with a machine aesthetic: 'We are proud, handsome and predatory. / We hunt machines, they are our favourite game. / We invent them and then hunt them down.'[56] Associated with the privilege given to the hunt is the fascination of a range of very different modernist artists and writers, including

Hemingway, Picasso, Dalí, Bataille and Leiris, with the so-called sport of bullfighting. (You can tell from my sniffy qualification how thoroughly I am myself recruited to the modern assumption that the use or abuse of animals invalidates any claim that the activity in question can be regarded as a sport.) In a world in which competitive sports were identified with democratic modernity, bullfighting seemed to offer modernist writers an identification with aristocratic values. Where sports had become mere games, bullfighting could be represented as tragic drama. These are the terms in which Michel Leiris offers his defence of 'tauromachy', which he says is

> something more than a sport, on account of the tragic element inherent in it – doubly tragic since there is a death, and a death entailing an immediate risk to the life of the celebrant . . . tauromachy can be regarded as a sport augmented by an art in which the tragic, made explicit as it were, is particularly affecting.[57]

On the one hand, Leiris regards sport as not enough of an art. On the other, he regards it as too aesthetic, in the sense of not real enough, since it does not really risk death or injury, does not encounter perversity and violence. The aim is not 'to banish death or hide it behind who knows what architecture of timeless perfection' but rather '[t]o incorporate death in life, to make it in some way voluptuous'.[58] Mere sport is buffered by its framework of rules from the reality of death and suffering, while bullfighting offers a ritual bursting of the frame:

> Whatever the risks and challenges it implies, no sport will cross the boundary that separates the profane from the sacred, because none is conceived in its essence as perdition or as a defiant provocation of perdition. In sport everything is wholesome; everything is straight; deviation appears only in the base form of cheating, crookedness in the rudimentary guise of a purely physical chanciness, a hazard to be reckoned with but not the basis and condition of the activity itself. Never will a boxer (however fierce his fight and formally beautiful his

gestures) see his brow crowned with a storm cloud instead of the academic laurel. Never will a swimmer (no matter how at one he may be with the world summed up by the wave in which he moves, and no matter how imminent the danger that his skill enables him to escape) come as close to the crucial point as the torero does, the poet or the lover whose entire action is founded on the tiny but tragic flaw by which the unfinished (literally infinite) part of our condition shows itself. Only the acrobat – and particularly the aerial acrobat, who moves in the void and whose body seems abstracted from its environment, or at least held only by a thread – sometimes communicates his sacred vertigo, inasmuch as his work presents itself as a succession of supernatural feats running parallel to a series of provocations.[59]

It is tempting to see in this panting after the ecstatic, which is so marked in others who were, like Leiris, associated with the Collège de Sociologie, such as Georges Bataille and Roger Caillois, a kind of cultural-political hinge or chiasmus. Henceforth the exaltation of force, impulse and intensity would be the signature not of the fascist right but of the libertarian left, though the frank athleticism of futurism and fascism would modulate into the libidinal and epistemological energetics of Lyotard, Derrida and Deleuze.

Perhaps the best proof of the definitional indifference to sport in modernism is the fact that sport has lately given leverage to various forms and definitions of the postmodern. Modernist and postmodernist arts are sometimes distinguished as between a focus on game and a focus on sport. Vladimir Nabokov, who was keenly interested in mountaineering, seems modernist in the intricate forms of ludic preoccupation and structure in his work. The frank interest of Don DeLillo in (American) football (*Endzone*) and baseball (*Underworld*), or Peter Handke in soccer in the *Goalkeeper's Fear of the Penalty Kick* seems like a postmodernist riposte to this kind of modernist sport. Claes Oldenburg's 1970 manifesto 'I Am For An Art' includes in its catalogue of anti-aestheticist affirmations 'I am for art that coils and grunts like a wrestler' and 'I am for the art of sailing on Sunday'.[60] American post-war fiction seems particularly hospitable to sporting themes or forms, for example in the work of Updike, Mailer, Roth, Malamud and Ford.

Critics like Roland Barthes began to pay serious attention to sports such as wrestling and cycling, both in his *Mythologies* and in *What is Sport?* (2007), the text he was commissioned in 1960 by the Canadian Broadcasting Corporation to write for a documentary film by Hubert Aquin. Paying this kind of serious attention to sport was a central part of the irritation that Barthes's panoramic criticism caused for certain writers. Alain Finkielkraut complained in 1987 that

> Not only must Shakespeare be humiliated: the bootmaker must be ennobled. It is not just that high culture must be demystified, brought remorselessly down to the level of the sort of everyday gestures which ordinary people perform in obscurity: sport, fashion and leisure now lay claim to high cultural status.[61]

We may suggest that as game is to modernism, so sport is to postmodernism. Perhaps this is an effect of that dedifferentiation of spheres that is said to be characteristic of postmodernism, though the equation can also work the other way round; just as postmodernism can gain a kind of self-definitional edge by going in for sport, so sport, or at least writing about sport, can gain extra philosophical dignity by going in for postmodernism.

Giving the World to Men

Whether wedded to an aesthetics of force or an aesthetics of grace, whether impelled by energy or form, modernist reflections on sport have centred on the imagination of the mass. As Susan Sontag observed, the fascist imaginary emphasizes the fusing and subordination of the mass to the will of the leader, or the charismatic Idea. Sontag points to the use in Leni Riefenstahl's *Triumph of the Will*, of

> overpopulated wide shots of massed figures alternating with close-ups that isolate a single passion, a single perfect submission; clean-cut people in uniforms group and regroup, as if

they were the perfect choreography to express their fealty. In *Olympia*, the richest visually of all her films . . . one straining, scantily clad figure after another seeks the ecstasy of victory, cheered on by ranks of compatriots in the stands, all under the still gaze of the benign Super-Spectator, Hitler, whose presence in the stadium consecrates this effort.[62]

Athletic displays allow for the gathering in or disciplining of the mass:

The rendering of movement in grandiose and rigid patterns is another element in common, for such choreography rehearses the very unity of the polity. The masses are made to take form, be design. Hence mass athletic demonstrations, a choreo-graphed display of bodies, are a valued activity in all totalitarian countries; and the art of the gymnast, so popular now in Eastern Europe, also evokes recurrent features of fascist aesthetics; the holding in or confining of force; military precision.[63]

Many modernists saw in sport – and recoiled from – precisely the subordination of individuals to the undifferentiated mass – the club, the tribe, the class, the nation. In both cases, there seems to be no way of conceiving the crowd except in terms of the strict dichotomy between the differentiated individual and the undifferentiated crowd.

What has happened to sport in the years since the Second World War? In many ways, it seems as though the use of sport to enforce mass discipline through the mesmerism of spectacle has proceeded uninterrupted. In fact, though, sport has undergone a subtle shift. It has begun to provide a way to conceive of a new kind of imagina-tion of the mass, different because it is also a massified imagination.

Barthes saw sport as the domain of myth, and most especially the myth of life against matter:

What is sport? Sport answers this question by another ques-tion: who is best? But to this question of the ancient duels, sport gives a new meaning: for man's excellence is sought here only in relation to things. Who is the best man to overcome the resistance of things, the immobility of nature? Who is the best to work the world, to give it to men . . . to all men? That is what sport says.[64]

It is not so much the mythic making of the human as the giving of the world to all men that I am struck by in Barthes's words. Walter Benjamin seems to have a rather similar intuition in his essay 'The Work of Art in the Age of Mechanical Reproduction', which first appeared in 1936, the year of the Munich Olympics, noting that 'in big parades and monster rallies, in sports events, and in war, all of which nowadays are captured by camera and sound recording, the masses are brought face to face with themselves'.[65] In a thoughtful essay, which he begins by pointing out that among the spectators at the Munich Olympics was one Jacques Lacan, who would observe, in his essay on the mirror stage that 'the formation of the I is symbolised in dreams by a fortress, or a stadium', Alan Meek has spoken of the role of media in producing new versions of the 'fascistic subject'.[66]

But I am not persuaded that this is still the effect of the complex forms in which sport is mediated. The ways of participating in sport have become more and various and ramified – as player, manager, administrator, investor, fan, spectator, viewer, game-player, commentator, academic – just as sports themselves have multiplied and the ways have multiplied in which sport is meaningful or makes other things so. Sport has therefore become progressively depolarized, despecialized. Sport less and less represents a particular concretion or repository of value or meaning, or a particular kind of hinge or moment around which things may be turned or cultural force exerted. One might say of sport something similar to what Fredric Jameson has said of the sphere of culture after the Second World War, namely that it has undergone a prodigious expansion, so that everything has come to seem, in a sense, 'cultural'. Sport has equivalently radiated and ramified to such a degree that, if everything has become cultural, then everything in that culture is tending to the condition of the sporting. The two meanings of performance – achievement and imposture – have come close together.

Perhaps the most important feature of sport in the modern world is not that it embodies this or that aspect of the modern, not that it is the sink or carrier of this or that set of values; but that it would become the first of the great globalizing forces. It has sometimes been suggested that sport is, like some forms of narrative or performing art, a way of worldmaking, and that different sports 'are capable of creating new and original worlds'.[67] But sport operates on the scale of The World. It is not just accidentally a world phenomenon; it is a way of inventing the world, bringing the world into being as a world. World champions make of the world a *champ*, a Kampf, a field of striving. It is a converter of scales, a converter of times and a converter of values. (That is why sport can also be 'camp'.) Triumph and disaster; everything, nothing; important, unimportant. Sport is a second nature that has become entirely natural to us, both unnecessary and indispensable to the kind of sport of nature into which human beings continue to form themselves.

two

Space

Space of Play, Play of Space

Sport can take place anywhere – on tracks and field and pitches, in pools, and in or on courts of different kinds. But the place of modern sport has come increasingly to be identified with one particular kind of structure, the special kind of enclave or space apart represented by the stadium. Such structures suggest an historical link with the practices of sport in ancient civilizations such as Greece or Mexico, which can inhibit our recognition of the distinctively modern nature of organized sports. One might compare sport in this respect with music, for both have tended to move from outdoor and unbounded spaces to indoor and enclosed spaces. All modern music is in this respect chamber music, designed to resound within walls and interior spaces, rather than to diffuse into space. Sport too, takes place predominantly within enclosed spaces or structures. And yet something has happened to these enclosed spaces, rendering them both enclosed and expansive, able, because of the particular forms of their spatial concentration, to be spread everywhere abroad. By becoming sequestered, sport has been able to approach ubiquity. It is no accident that musical performance often takes place in the very same arenas that allow for the coalescence of the local and the global in sport.

This chapter will consider the relations between architecture and the spaces of play, gaming and sport. What is play space, I will ask, and what might be the spatial grounds of play? Can one say that when space is set aside for play, space itself must always then come into play?

There are two architectures of sport. One is the kind with which we are all-too-familiar; the rising, resounding hollow O of the classical sports-stadium, its tiers of seats hemming the space of contention marked out below. On the outside, such edifices routinely effect some kind of compromise between high and high-visibility technology and the fluency and grace of 'natural' formations, an habituated conversation between girders and swerves that duplicates the two features of industrialized sport-as-entertainment. As stadia are required to deliver more and more functions – restaurants, accommodation, office facilities, communications, commerce – the stadium has become a playspace for architects and civic bodies.

But the space constituted by the physical stadium is ultimately accessory to another space, a space that by definition it contains, and with which it must of necessity be conjoined, but from which it must also be not only physically but also ontologically separated, namely the space in which the play occurs. The role of the stadium is to allow and control access to this space, to open this space to view, and to accent, enhance and amplify it, while also standing apart from it, most particularly by preventing encroachment. The stadium both opens and enframes the space of play, both discloses it, and closes it off.

On the one hand, then, there are what I want to call the spaces of play – stadia, arenas, sports grounds. On the other, there is the play of space that is initiated within the space of play. Let us see if we can understand some of the traffic between these two. There are other such arenas, where space is set off in order that space may be in various ways be put into play – courtrooms, cinemas, dancehalls, art galleries, theatres – but, as the prominence in such discussions of the word 'arena' might itself suggest, the spaces formally set aside for playing as such may have a particular salience and command. Indeed, as we will come to see, such spaces may be beginning to impinge upon whatever space is left that is not in play.

Maurice Merleau-Ponty uses the markings of a soccer pitch to exemplify the way in which the field of play is never a mere object, 'which can give rise to a multiplicity of perspectival views and remain equivalent under its apparent transformations'. Rather, it is drawn into a play of space that includes the bodily intentions of the players, just as those intentions are pervaded and orientated by the space in which they are to be enacted. So, for Merleau-Ponty, the soccer field:

is pervaded with lines of force (the 'yard lines'; those which demarcate the 'penalty area') and articulated in sectors (for example, the 'openings' between the adversaries) which call for a certain mode of action and which initiate and guide the action as if the player were unaware of it. The field itself is not given to him, but present as the immanent term of his practical intentions; the player becomes one with it and feels the direction of the 'goal', for example, just as immediately as the vertical and horizontal planes of his own body.[1]

For Merleau-Ponty, the field of play is never prior to or separate from the way in which, as the expression has it, it 'plays', or is modified according to the play undertaken upon it:

It would not be sufficient to say that consciousness inhabits this milieu. At this moment consciousness is nothing other than the dialectic of milieu and action. Each maneuver undertaken by the player modifies the character of the field and establishes in it new lines of force in which the action in turn unfolds and is accomplished, again altering the phenomenal field.[2]

For Merleau-Ponty, these conditions are actually not specific to the soccer field or any other sporting arena, but serve to illustrate the inseparability of environment and action in any space whatever. But the particular aptness of the soccer-pitch metaphor suggests that, under these sporting circumstances, the habitual distinction between space as mere object or merely given environment, and the dynamic space formed and transformed by action, is much weaker than under other circumstances.

Decisions

The space of play is carefully patrolled, to the millimetre. For there can be no mid-space, no space between secular space and the space of play. Either the ball has wholly crossed the line, and it is a goal, or it has not, and play will continue from where it left off. If a lace from the cricket fielder's boot is in contact with the boundary rope when he takes the lofted catch, it will be four runs; if not, the batsman is dismissed. If the ball is deemed to have clipped the line – betrayed by the puff of chalk or detected by the automatic sensor – there may be a new grand slam champion; if it misses, the player's chance may have receded forever. In this sense at least, in its implacable abhorrence of the middle way, its intolerance of any *tertium quid*, there seems to be no room for play in the space of play.

These boundary decisions are not just effected at the extreme edges of the field of play. Similar caesuras shear through the play itself, the play being textured by the alternation between states of play and suspensions of it, playtime and time-out. Thus the space of play is not entirely spatial. Rather it is the place where the space and time of play are decided on. There can be endless reopening of the case of the dubious leg before wicket or penalty decision among the spectators in their seats and in their subsequent generations, but there can be no two minds, no equivocation, no agreement to differ, no fancy *Aufhebung* lifting and preserving the thesis and antithesis in a new synthesis, on the field of play. Even when the the process of reaching the decision is protracted, as it may increasingly be with the involvement of officials off the pitch with access to video replays, this is aimed at establishing a single and incontestable truth about how things happened. Play solicits and precipitates decisions at each moment, in forking paths that mimic and confirm the anterior and ultimate deciding on the space of play as a space of decision – from *caedere* to cut, which engenders a sizeable clan of similarly incisive words in English, including *scissors*, *abscission*, *circumcision* and the sadly obsolete *occision*, providing a passage to the many words that link *deciding* with *cutting down* or *cutting off* – *homicide, suicide, genocide*, and so on. For, oh, yes, there is fatality in play. The stadium effects the opening, the admission without access, to this arbitrary and absolute space of irrevocable arbitrations. In play: that is to say, in crisis.

Yet it is for precisely this reason that the crisis of play runs quietly and cleanly through the middle of it, that, in the space of play, space is neither given nor fixed. Instead, it is absolutely in play, which is to say, the subject of continuous contention. Although teams have their own territories, their own end-zones, the point of every game is that such ground is dubitable, debatable, impermanent. The space of play is a mutable product of the play itself. In rugby, for example, the two team's territories slide back and forth like the shuttle of a loom, as determined by the 'gain line', or front feet of the attacking team. *In extremis*, the defending team's territory may have diminished to a desperate ribbon of ground fifty yards across and one foot wide. The difficulty of explaining the offside rules in rugby and more especially in football arises from the fact that it requires just this Einsteinian jump from absolute to relative space.

In thinking of the space of play, we will repeatedly have to cope with the following contortion. The space of play is set off, by an act of pure decision, by the simple decision to mark out a space in which to decide the matter. In this space of play, space is decidedly *in play*, in a way that it is not in spaces not so marked off. And yet the play of space is not always limited to the space of play. Space will increasingly prove to be in play not just within the designated spaces of play, but also between those spaces and the other spaces that adjoin, administer and attend on them. Wherever there is a space of play, there is a chance for the play of space within it to propagate beyond and across that constitutive division. Kicking the ball 'into touch' derives from the rule in nineteenth-century football that, when the ball left the field of play, possession went to the team who were first to touch it off the field. The space of play is a semi-conductor, a black box, which is closed off on one side and open on the other.

This complexity unfolds in a number of different dimensions, of which I will distinguish four: interiority, orientation, height and proximity.

Inside-Out

Interiority and exteriority are particularly in play in a sports arena. The arena itself is a surrounding, an environment, a setting, a local habitation and an enclosure for the field of play. It is the *within-which* within which the sporting action plays out. If an open space is necessary for any kind of game, the bounding of that open space is also requisite. Play needs space in which to occur, but even more fundamentally, play is agoraphobic. The enclosed space of play is itself intensive, an interiority with respect to the quarantining clinch of what surrounds it. When the ball leaves the space of play, it is called 'out', and the lookers on in the enclosing stadium are an indeterminate outside to that which they have as their inside.

And yet the inverse also seems true: the game transpires in an open enclosure, which is usually unsheltered, subject to the vicissitudes of rain, wind and sun, compared to the spectators, who will usually have immediate access to the facilities characteristic of the indoors – lavatories, electricity, catering, communications and so forth. Thus the teams 'come out', and the action transpires 'out on the field'. The most striking feature of a stadium is the fact that it really has no interiority. When one enters a stadium, one finds at its innermost core aperture, exposure and expanse. A stadium has two exteriors; the outside that bounds and surrounds it, and the open expanse which it itself bounds and yet, for that reason opens on to. The field of play and the stadium which surrounds it are at once each other's inside and outside. The interior portions of a sports arena lie between the outside and the evacuated middle, in a compact zone or *périphérique*, the rind that separates the outside of the stadium from the pitch or ground that constitute the outerness at its heart.

There is a tendency to regard the enclosure of modern sports as part of the creation of passive spectacle out of participative action. According to this view, the sports activity which had previously consumed or spread out into an open space, taking over a market square or even whole villages, is split between players and spectators, which turns the entire activity of sport into a form of display or exhibition rather than a melee, a mixed or mingled striving. As we saw in the last chapter, an important accessory feature of this newly restricted economy of sport is the almost total concentration on human action – for the medieval world, sport was unthinkable without the involvement of animals, as quarry or accomplice, in hunting, hawking and so on.

The removal of the spectators from the action is equivalent to the isolation of the spaces of sport, which detaches them from the spaces of ordinary life and work. If it is true that in one sense sport seems more diffused than ever before – with runners a familiar sight on the streets of almost every major city (even those, like Tokyo and Amsterdam, that call for the greatest powers of alertness and endurance), and sport ubiquitous in print and electronic media – it also seems more insulated, or partitioned off than in previous eras, as sports facilities have become more and more 'artificial worlds'.[3] There can be no doubt that an important factor in the enclosure of sports was the possibility of charging for admission that it brought. But the commodification that went with enclosure also encouraged the expansion of the enclosed space of spectatorship into other locations.

The separation of protagonists and spectators is often seen as equivalent to the great enclosures – of infants, the insane, the infirm, the criminal, the animal – that, according to Foucauldians, have sliced and diced the plenitudinous hurly-burly of the pre-modern world. John Bale has tried to bring alternative evidence to bear, pointing out that, for every sport in which spectators have become more sedentary and sedate, there may be another sport – cricket and tennis would be good examples – in which spectators are becoming more raucous and assertive.[4] However, the degree of apparent involvement between players and spectators is only an accessory symptom. For in fact, in any game played before a crowd of spectators, the game is always suffused from top to bottom with this condition of *being-for* its spectators. Young boys who develop the skills of commentating on their game even as they are playing it exhibit an intuitive understanding of this inter-involvement of player and spectator. Players are nowadays increasingly required by TV and radio broadcasting to offer commentary, in some games actually during the course of play. To play is nowadays to be inside and outside the game, to be player and spectator at once. The space of play thus begins to put the space between it and the space outside it into play.

Orientation

The space of the stadium is theatrical, in the sense that it is both literal and ideal, both particular and general, both this place, *hic et nunc*, and an any-place-whatever. We may say of modern sport that, as John Donne wrote of love, it 'makes one little roome, an every where'.[5] There is always some kind of home advantage in any stadium (though many stadia are in fact not owned and occupied by particular teams or even particular sports). But the actual field of play is in fact the paradoxical particularization of a general set of relations – between service line and net, corners and touchlines, goalposts and penalty spots – which ensure a layout that is in essentials exactly the same whether the teams line up in Brighton or Beijing. This is the first of many intersections that characterize the stadium – between place and space, here and anywhere. Sport-space depends upon the invention of geometry, said to date from the discovery of Thales of Miletus of the principle of equivalence that allowed one to measure the height of a pyramid by comparison of its shadow with that of a man of known height. Geometry means literally the measurement of the earth, but sport-space depends upon the abstract equivalences that make every pitch or court both earthly and ideal.

Sports arenas evolve as a circling of squares, a smoothing out of corners, and an ensphering of edges. The resilient rectangle of the oxymoronic 'ring' in boxing is the obvious exception to this tendency. Bullfights in southern Spain originally took place in the central square, overlooked on four sides by high buildings, with spectators stationed at the windows and balconies. As the bullfight was relocated to a sandy arena, the area of combat became a circle, with the seats arranged tightly around it. Soccer stadia exhibit the same evolution. A lowly non-league club will usually only run to one stand, either on the left- or the right-hand side of the pitch. As the club's fortunes increase, stands may be added at either end, and gradually the awkward spaces at the corners grouted in. Finally, the most successful clubs will aspire to a purpose-built stadium, in which the pitch will be circumscribed by an unbroken torus, maximizing seating and visibility on the inside while closing it off from the outside. Sports stadia tend, in other words, towards the creation of sealed or introverted environments, in an instance of the generalized air-conditioning that, according to Peter Sloterdijk, characterizes modern spaces.[6] As the form evolves, it tends towards the dome or the globe, in which there is no priority of viewpoint, in which orientation gives way to omnispectivity and opacity is purged in ostentatious appearance. Everyone can see and everything can be seen. This transcendence of locality is extended with the aid of large screens to the overcoming of distance. The dome is supplemented by the technological enhancements which ensure that all viewers have access to the authoritative view provided by the video cameras. The promise of the dome is that one can be everywhere at once. Its ritual enactment is the Mexican wave, traditionally performed as a sardonic protest against a boring match, but which is also a utopian assertion of the identification of the crowd with the energetically rotary forms and motilities of the stadium.

Stadia are all designed to look cosmic, or at least extraterrestrial. They imply circuits, orbits and zodiacs, rather than a topology of positions. The form of the stadium is mimicked in the running-track, which doubles the stadium's enclosing form, and yet is part of the space of play. According to John Bale, the running track helps confirm the stadium as a 'non-place' or 'placeless plane'.[7] The enclosed, perfectly level, precisely calibrated running-track is the endpoint of an evolution 'from being an unspecialized, unsegmented and non-territorialized place to becoming close to an isotropic plane surface'.[8] For this reason, says Bale, track athletics are 'one of the most placeless of sports and in few, if any, other areas of life is there so much pressure for one place to be the same – exactly the same – as any other of its kind'.[9] The closed loop of the running track epitomizes the tendency towards placelessness in modern stadia more generally, confirming Bale's judgement that '[t]he modern sports landscape can be described as tending towards "placelessness" in its geographical sense of places looking and feeling alike with "dictated and standardized values."'[10]

This flaunted surpassing of the phenomenological requirement of oriented perspective must purge or suppress the archaic or surviving traces of orientation. This became strongly apparent to Arsenal football club supporters when they moved from their traditional four-square stadium to the new Emirates stadium in 2006. The rivalrous versicle and response that used to be exchanged between parishioners of the North, South, East and West Stands at Highbury suddenly had no purchase in a stadium where there were no breaks in the continuity of the seating. One is never likely to build up loyalty to the *genius loci* of the Orange Quadrant as one has done to the North Stand, the Kop at Anfield or the Shed at Chelsea.

But, as they persist through time, stadia may decay back into orientation, become susceptible once again to the experiental drag of listing, orientation, laterality. The uniform space of the stadium becomes pulled out of shape, as the open space of sensory awareness is pulled out of shape in the sensory homunculus, with its massive puffy lips and clownish hands. The uniform distribution of temperature becomes a meteorological landscape, in which hot-spots of attentiveness and intimacy are sprinkled across dark zones of indifference or abandonment.

Of course, the greatest obstacle to the alateralism of the stadium is the game itself, in which the antagonism of the two sides is indispensable and irreducible. But this is an antagonism which aims to reproduce the white uniformity of the stadium not by abstracting space, but by saturating it with movement.

At the beginning of the game, there is the immaculate, moist, geometrical green of the pitch, the wicket, the court. It represents possibility, it is possibility itself, like a wind-razored dune or the white witness of a field of fresh snow. Its laser lines are out of Euclid, abstract, absolute, unearthly, as though they were lines of light, or the luminous inscription of the idea of lines. When the actual lines are doubled by electronic lines that enable one to determine absolutely whether a line has or has not been crossed, as in the Hawk-Eye system in use in tennis, cricket and other sports, the line moves even further towards the condition of electronically absolute geometry. Anything can happen in a space like this. The form of the stadium mimics and substantiates this dwelling in possibility. When we say that we 'draw a line in the sand', we mean to dignify the act of establishing some *arché*, some absolute, originating, governing distinction between that and this, then and now. But the real *arché*, the real *archi-tecture*, is the condition of absolute openness, allowing any and every line to be drawn, of any breadth, in any direction, but before any line, any direction, has actually appeared.

The moment play begins, this perfection, this pregnant vacancy, will be ruined irretrievably. With the first moment of play, the equilibrium of possibility is broken in on by choice, or hazard: will I kick long or short, serve wide or narrow, cut, glance or drive, pitch the ball up or try a bouncer? I am absolutely free in the space of play, that is to say, absolutely constrained to make a move to inaugurate the play of space. The only choice not available is the choice of remaining in the condition of being able to choose anything. As the play develops, it will leave its traces in the pitch, to the bitter Platonic rage of groundsmen the world over. The open space will become striated by the play, deeply rutted in certain areas, like the goalmouth or the service line, relatively untouched in others. The unearthly apparition of essence will decay into a scarred cartography of accidence.

The space is now no longer topographical, but rather topological. It is folded and refolded, its fixed distances subject to stretching, twisting, tilting and contraction. But this then creates the possibility of a passage beyond orientation. We can understand this in terms of the distinction that Michel Serres draws between the 'scenography' and the 'ichnography'. In the scenography, space is broken up, differentially distributed. It is diacritical, allowing for *fort* and *da*, over there and right here, locking one in location, in fixed intervals and distances. The ichnography is a mapping not of spaces, but of passages, itineraries and traversals and reversals, all of them more or less lateralized, off-balance, or like the Earth in Milton's *Paradise Lost*, 'Mov'd contrarie with thwart obliquities'.[11] For Serres, the ichnography approximates to 'the ensemble of possible profiles, the sum of horizons . . . It is the complete chain of metamorphoses of the sea-god Proteus, it is Proteus himself'.[12] The ichnography is an aggregate of all actual and possible movements, a white totality, not because it is blank and therefore open to any possibility, but because it is a white noise, a brass rubbing as opposed to a blueprint, a spectrum compounded of every colour, a map at once obliterated and reconstituted in the scribbled blizzard of directions.

The practice of changing ends, to ensure that both teams suffer the same advantages and disadvantages of any variation in the pitch or other imbalance, belongs to the logic of the ichnography, for it creates equality, not by erasing the space, but by maximally overwriting it, creating an equivalence between the logic of *neither . . . or* and that of *both . . . and*. The tendency of sports practised in the 'fourth-generation' arenas and stadia described by Rod Sheard of the giant architectural firm HOK Sport,[13] which is to say practised amid the networks of communications that such structures imply and implicate, is to move further towards this integral, for example, by action replays, that overlay unique instants, aggregating different angles, or by the data that integrates the action of this particular game with others elsewhere or in the past. So there are three stages of orientation. Before the game begins, the stadium is an anorientated space of pure play. The beginning of the game forces a lurch away into orientation. But then the play of space begins laboriously to engender the return to an anorientated condition.

Denied physical access to the space of play, the crowd participates in the play of space largely through sound. There is of course an element of location and laterality in the singing and chanting of the crowd, which aims to enlarge the space of play and enhance the fortunes of one side or the other. But, like the game played on the pitch, the game of sound is played out in the attempt to annihilate the very space in which the play is taking place. The crowd aims at saturation, and the form of the stadium amplifies the tendency of sound to go in all directions, minimizing sound's occasions and maximizing its powers of expansion and propagation. Simultaneously a megaphone and the amplifying ear it lends itself, the stadium is an auto-auditory apparatus. The stadium prolongs and accelerates sound, giving encouragement to the ambition to make of the sound a kind of architecture or textured mass in its own right, a muniment of din to crush the opposing team. The victory at which orientation – one side opposed to another – aims is not that of one side over another; it is the obliteration of laterality as such, and the assertion of the one-and-all. This second neutrality or 'no-side' resembles the neutrality of the opening of the match, except that it is a uniformity not of vacancy but of assimilation. As Serres writes:

> The cause and goal of a squabble are the taking of a place, and noise occupies space. The whole point is to hold, occupy, or take a place . . . Noise against *noise*. Noise against weapon. Noise is a weapon that, at times, dispenses with weapons . . . And noise occupies space faster than weapons can.[14]

As on the pitch, the play of sonorous space is formed from the desire to put an end to the play, and the space of sonorous strife is preserved and renewed by the contrary efforts of the rival supporters to extinguish space by cramming it with sound.

Up and Under

Perhaps the most important instance of orientation is the relation to gravity. There is a certain aspiration to height in nearly all games.

The cup is raised high above the winning captain's head, while the losing team measure their defeated lengths on the pitch. Typically, the stadium rises sharply above the pitch, receding at as steep an angle as is necessary to optimize both visibility and comfort. In a stadium, one essentially looks not at but down on the play. But there is a zone of height that the spectators do not occupy, namely the indeterminate area of play above the pitch. The dimension is unlike the other dimensions of play in that it is both invisible and infinite. There is usually no theoretical limit to this zone. The ball can be struck or kicked as high as a player is capable, and will remain in play. A few years ago, an aerial camera was introduced to cover rugby internationals at Paris's Stade de France. The camera shuttled along a line strung over the pitch, diagonally from corner to corner. The plan seems to have been abandoned, not just, one may surmise, because the straight-down coverage it offered lacked all dynamism, but also because a camera in the apparently spare and untenanted space above the pitch was in fact a trespass into the limitless but included dimension of the upper air. It was as intrusive and in the literal sense transgressive, stepping across a line, as a camera on the pitch would be. A similar sense of incursion attaches to the roofs, girders and lighting bars of some indoor tennis arenas.

There is much that is resistant to upwardness in a stadium. Greek amphitheatres often took advantage of natural slopes or gradients, and were carved out of the side of hills. The fact that, before the Hillsborough Stadium disaster of 1989, the term 'terraces' was the favoured synecdoche for the soccer stadium itself suggested that the space was excavated from earth rather than constructed upon it. The stadium is always a kind of pit or declivity, scooped or gouged out. Although many stadia do rise high, the effect of the elevated perspective is to suggest looking down into the earth, rather than down on to it, as would be the case from a tall building. The habit of filming or photographing stadia from above assists this sense that they are to be thought of as volcanic craters, giving vent to subterranean forces, rather than eminences.

There is evidence that what David Larmour calls the 'agonal space' of Greek theatrical and athletic events was often synchronized with the passage of the sun across the sky,[15] a practice recalled in the 'day-night' cricket matches, inaugurated at the Sydney Cricket Ground by Kerry Packer in 1978, which begin in early evening and are concluded under floodlights. This is, in the strict sense, an 'orientation', inaugurated by the rising of the sun in the east, but the lateral passage of the sun also involves a sinking into the west. One of the effects of the closed circle of the stadium is to mitigate the ill effects of the low sun, though it remains enough of a factor in cricket grounds and tennis arenas to function as a distributor of advantage. For all its celestial annulations and concentricities, the stadium has a stronger affinity with the gorge, chasm or quarry, and other spaces of chthonic excavation, than with the heavens. Hence, perhaps, the favouring of the rainbow or arch form in stadium architecture, which seem to emblematize the up-like-a-rocket-down-like-a-stick parabola of all sporting aspirations.

Although the crowd has a kind of perspectival advantage in looking down on the pitch – for seats at ground level rarely afford a very animated or informed view of the game – they are actually marooned in their elevation, which represents a fundamental exclusion from the field of play. Although players may occasionally climb into the crowd at the end of the match, most notably in the old Wembley, when players had to undertake a long climb up to the Royal Box – a tradition mimicked by Pat Cash who climbed through the crowd to greet his girlfriend after winning the Wimbledon title – the domain of the players or athletes is the underworld. They come out of what is usually called a tunnel, as though from under the earth, and the management team will typically spend the match in a 'dugout', like goblins or other burrowing elementals.

The throwing of light materials like balloons and streamers on to the pitch and their slow drifting to the ground also emphasizes the inexorably gravitational pull to which the stadium is always subject. The floodlights slanting down at the field of play suggest that in the stadium, even brightness falls from the air. The very word *arena* seems to have some reference to this insistent declension. For *arena* means simply sand. Unlike grass, which, though porous, is tightly textured and therefore relatively impenetrable, sand was strewn in gladiatorial arenas primarily to provide drainage, for blood and other bodily issues. In fact, good drainage is still a desideratum of the very best grass pitches. What blood remained to stain the surface could be removed simply by turning the sand over it, thus visibly inhuming the last traces of the slaughtered beast or mauled combatant. The fact that most stadiums are open to the sky in fact emphasizes this lowering tendency of the bowl, which can resemble a sink or sump, and its implicit evocation of the swirling away of wastes. In the days of closely packed soccer terraces, where one was in constant danger from the weight of the crowd behind and above one, there used to be a very literal signalling of this at the Kop end of Liverpool's Anfield stadium. Since fighting one's way to the crowded lavatories during the match or even at half-time was such an ordeal, many would relieve their bladders, distended by lunchtime pints, *illico*, by rolling their copies of the *Liverpool Echo* into a cone and using it as a funnel. The lower down the terraces you were, the more important it was to have galoshes or gumboots to deflect the cascade.

On the Spot

Stadia offer some strange distortions of scale. In most stadia, the players and the action they unfold are much more vividly visible and seem much closer than they in fact are, as though the space of play acted as a magnifying lens. A player on the pitch a hundred yards away seems clearer and better-defined than a member of the crowd just a couple of rows below.

There used to be a time when proximity to the action was determining. Thus, in theory, nobody could be better placed to make a ruling than a referee, who is in the thick of the action. The supplementation of human vision with automatic sensing devices and with replay facilities is in the process of changing all this. Nowadays, when there is uncertainty about whether a try has been scored in an international rugby match, we may hear the commentators say 'We'll have to go upstairs for a decision on that', meaning that the referee is about to invoke the advice of an external official who has access to replays of the action provided from a number of different viewpoints. It would be perfectly possible for this fourth official to be sitting in front of his monitors on the touchline, or even under the pitch – and, come to think of it, he may well be, since the point is that it is entirely mysterious where he is. When the referee speaks to him via wireless headset, he never looks in any particular direction, as though to indicate that the fourth official in fact does not inhabit the visible space of the arena at all. He certainly may as well be in the car park as in the gods, for at this point somebody on the other side of the world watching the replays to which the television audience are privy will see and know more, and more quickly, than the players and referee. The privilege of proximity here yields place to the ecstasy of the panoptic.

World-Objects

Peter Sloterdijk has suggested that the spatiality of the contemporary world must be understood as a multiplication and diversification of the unifying images of the macrocosm that had reach and purport for previous eras. His three-volume work *Sphären* reads human history – philosophical, religious, artistic, political – as the elaboration of different kinds of spheres, or spaces of introversion. The three volumes of *Sphären* track the movement towards and then away from global or world-sized enspherings, leaving us in a polyspheric condition that Sloterdijk characterizes as an 'assemblage of assemblages, a semi-opaque foam of world-making constructions of space'.[16]

The stadium seems to be an anachronistic defiance of this global movement away from centring, presence and concentration. The stadium has become the most representative form of secular monument, a space of ludic reflexivity in which cities, nations and cultures offer to image themselves and draw themselves to a focus. Arenas are microcosmic, magnifying, monomaniac, monarchical. They feed and famish the craving for the absolute. A stadium is a pompous omphalos, which proclaims itself the centre of the world. This is perhaps another reason why stadia always suggest a depression in the ground; the omphalos was the navel of the world because it reached down into its heart. The most famous omphalos stone in the ancient world marked the place of the oracle at Delphi, the spot where two eagles released by Zeus to fly round the world met, where Apollo defeated the earth-serpent Pytho, and where, according to a later legend, the Pythian priestess was inspired to prophecy by the mephitic vapours rising from the interior of the earth. The braggadocio profile of the stadium makes us understandably uneasy about it. There is something dangerous, hubristic, barbaric in this attempt to mass the whole world together into one place. There is much in it of the concentration camp – what is a camp, after all, but a *champs*, with champions those who command the field of tourney or battle? All stadia are dangerous places that, whatever the safety measures in place, are much harder to get out of than into. The only way to make stadia completely safe would be to have exits every few rows. But the effect of this would be to diffuse the very cramming and cramping, the very time-trap, from which the energy and excitement of being part of a stadium crowd derive. Many American stadia, which are provided with much more in the way of food and other franchises to tempt the spectators away from their seats, lack the pressurized interiority of the European stadium for this reason.

Stadia connect back to the tradition in which they functioned as microcosmic concentrations, presumptive worlds; the point of the Roman circus in particular was to emphasize both the reach of the Empire and its capacity to oversee it as though its compass were no more than that of the coliseum, super-vision being precisely the mode of observation requisitioned by this kind of superbowl. And yet emperors and dictators are not always at their ease in the stadium, for it is not entirely clear from what position one may dominate it. A story from the beginning of the modern period of stadium experience makes this point. When the Austrian Emperor Joseph II visited Verona, the Governor of the town laid on a bullfight for him in the town's Roman amphitheatre. The Emperor was led to his seat, and, in the contemporary description offered by the Prussian historian Johann Wilhem von Archenholz,

> all at once he arrived via a small opening at his seat, and saw in this confined circle all the inhabitants of the town and its neighbouring areas, filling the amphitheatre from top to bottom, who all immediately rose and applauded him. It was a sight that quite knocked the Emperor sideways [more specifically, '*ein Anblick, der den Kaiser ganz außer sich setzte*', 'a sight that set the Emperor quite outside himself'].[17]

His displacement finds its modern equivalent perhaps in the dilemma of the occupants in the Royal Box: do they join in the Mexican wave pulsating round the stadium and thus surrender their distinction, or do they abstain from it and thus in a sense endure their eviction from the space? Interestingly, stadium rock usually wrenches the round space of the stadium into a scenography, setting the star and the audience in a more familiar and governable face-to-face relationship.

And yet, stadia help constitute and are themselves taken up in a play of space that throws this microcosmic mirroring off-centre. Not only is the space of play put into play by the fact of its *being-for* the crowd in front of whom it transpires, this play of contention is itself increasingly drawn into relation with a set of other audiences, near and far, in space and time. The stadium has become what Michel Serres calls a 'world-object'.[18] For Serres, a world-object is distinguished by two features. The first is that it is not restricted to any one culture, tradition or locality, but spreads throughout the world, and therefore, itself transported everywhere, provides a kind of portal or *passe-partout* to all parts of the world. The second is a consequence of the first. Serres reminds us that, according to the medieval understanding, an object is that which is 'thrown before' the subject: 'Held by a subject, a technical object acts on other objects, sometimes even on other subjects; all these elements inhabit a spatiotemporal ensemble that is restricted in space and relatively invariant in time.'[19] But, since they are everywhere, and provide passage to anywhere, world-objects (such as the 'World Wide Web', for example) are not merely items set out in a world-space. Rather than being disposed in front of us, in the relation of availability signified in Heidegger's relation of *Gestell*, they form a habitat, an *Umwelt*. They are world-objects because we inhabit them as we inhabit the world. The difference between this and other kinds of habitat is that it is not a specific location or coordinated niche in space. Rather it is the opening into the generalization of environments, the pantopic and panchronic ubiquitization of man that Serres has called 'incandescence'.[20]

There have always been games which are open to the physical world, and perhaps none more than cricket. Whereas most games strive for the perfection of a perfectly even playing surface, that offers no advantage in any direction to either side, cricket assimilates the imperfection of the ground, building entire strategies out of the variable and inevitably entropic state of the wicket. Unlike most other sports, cricket often allows spectators to graze over the pitch during the lunchtime interval; the wicket remains roped off, but one can approach close enough to inspect it and form one's own judgement as to the likelihood of its taking spin on the fifth day. Until it was blown down in a gale in January 2005, a lime tree grew inside the boundary of the Kent County Cricket Ground in Canterbury, requiring the formulation of special local rules: a ball hit into the tree scored four, and a batsman could not be caught off it. Rather than attempting to close itself off from the contingencies introduced by meteorology, cricket allows itself to be impregnated by them, the better to be able to draw them into play. Is there another game in which fortunes (along with the ball), can swing so dramatically as a result of a cloud covering the sun, and in which players need to pay so much anxious attention to the sky? This provides a match for the careful specifications for playing dice given by Gerolamo Cardano in his *Liber de Ludo Aleae*:

> Set the round gaming boards in the middle; if they incline toward your opponent, then the dice box will incline in the opposite direction, and this is unfavorable to you. Similarly, if there is a slope toward you, then the box will be out of plumb in your favor; but if the dice box is not moved, then this does not matter. Similarly, if the board catches the light from the side opposite to you, then this is bad, since it disturbs your mind; on the other hand, it is to your advantage to have the board against a dark background. Again, they say it is of benefit to take up your position facing a rapidly rising moon.[21]

Games like cricket in which the world enters into the play contrast with games which spill out into the world. Perhaps the game in which worldhood is most in play is baseball. But baseball is unlike most other games in one important respect. The dimensions of the infield, the diamond whose principal apex is the home plate, are absolutely fixed. There must be 90 feet between bases, with 13 feet arcs around each base. The distance from the apex of the pitching mound to the home plate must be 60 feet and 6 inches. But the outfield, which radiates from the central point of the diamond, can be and is, different in every ball-park.[22] When one asks for a 'ball-park figure', this play between exactness and approximation is summoned up.

This makes baseball the perfect enactment of the ambivalently open-closed condition of the space of play in sport. Don DeLillo's *Underworld* (1997) exploits and forms itself on this quasi-aperture. The opening scene is set in the Polo Grounds, the stadium where the New York Giants won the epic final game of a three-match pennant-deciding series against the Brooklyn Dodgers on 3 October 1951. The game was won by a home run hit by the Giants outfielder Bobby Thomson. In DeLillo's novel, the ball is caught by a skinny, truanting kid called Cotter, who carries it away in secret triumph amid the elation and lamentation of the two teams' supporters. The home-run became known as 'the shot that echoed around the world', partly because of the number of serviceman in Korea who listened to the match. But DeLillo also reminds us of the fact that news broke during the Giants–Dodgers play-off of the first nuclear test by the Russians. The purloined ball will pass from hand to hand throughout the novel, a perfect enactment of what Michel Serres has characterized as a 'quasi-object', an object that, in its passages from hand to hand, acts as a distributor of meaning and subjectivity.[23] DeLillo gives us J. Edgar Hoover's reflections on the proliferations of secrets:

> This is what he knows, that the genius of the bomb is printed not only in its physics of particles and rays but in the occasion it creates for new secrets. For every atmospheric blast, every glimpse we get of the bared force of nature, that weird peeled eyeball exploding over the desert – for every one of these he reckons a hundred plots go underground, to spawn and skein.
>
> And what is the connection between Us and Them, how many bundled links do we find in the neural labyrinth? It's not enough to hate your enemy. You have to understand how the two of you bring each other to deep completion.[24]

The home run will be both closed and open, complete and incomplete and the peregrinations of that uncompleted home run will come to constitute the entire 'underworld' of DeLillo's novel. At once closed and open, the stadium is beginning to constitute and participate in the same play of space. No longer either ancient or modern, it is a new-old transformer and transmitter of times. The stadium may continue to have the archaic look of a mimic world, exorbitantly entire and autistically closed upon itself. But stadia no longer enclose and surpass the world, they suppose and open into it. Where stadia used to be presumptuous imitations of the world, they are now its intimations.

In this, they indicate the double movement of sports in the modern world they have partly made. First, there is a secluding movement inwards, in which certain spaces are marked off as exceptions to the contingent, chaotic conditions of ordinary space, cross-written as they are by so many different perspectives and experiences. But then there is the movement outwards from these delimited spaces of play, to include observers and locations everywhere in the world. This play of space seems to be in the process of creating from the whole human and nonhuman world a space of play.

three

Time

Let us roll all our strength and all
Our sweetness up into one ball,
And tear our pleasures with rough strife
Thorough the iron gates of life:
Thus, though we cannot make our sun
Stand still, yet we will make him run.[1]

Absolute and Immanent

There are essentially two kinds of temporality in sport, which I will call absolute and immanent. We will see that this distinction corresponds to the distinction between the space of play and the play of space introduced in the previous chapter. Games which must be played out within a given amount of time are subject to external, absolute temporality. A game of basketball is played over two halves of fifteen minutes, a game of rugby over two halves of forty minutes, a game of soccer over two halves of forty-five minutes and a game of ice hockey over three twenty-minute periods. In such games, the time within which the game is played is to be imagined as a pure and neutral exteriority, a colourless and frictionless medium. In such games, the time available is both a resource and a constraint, which applies equally and is equally available to both sides. Like the pitch, the ball and the framework of the rules, the time allotted for the match is part of the general environment of the game, the framework or condition of possibility of its playing. For such games, time must be regarded as absolute and invariant.

Sport takes time. This is to say that sport doubles time. To play a sport is to enter a second duration, which does not however merely displace primary duration, but coexists with it. Participating in a sport means participating in these two interpenetrating temporalities, of real time and game time. In certain games, officials or players can declare time out, or stop the clock. In reality, though, this suspension allows ordinary time to reassert itself, starting up the clock of the quotidian. Real time is not of course uniform; it has its own concentrations, fractures and distensions. But the effect of entering game time is to push real time into the background, and to give the latter thereby the monochrome homogeneity of mere succession, one moment after another, in comparison with the heightened, impassioned, iridescent time of the game.

Game-time does not simply elapse. The fact that most games involve an interval, followed by a change of ends, gives playing-time time a double character; time ticks onwards, and yet also can seem to flow first in one direction, and then back on itself. One of the cliches of soccer managers is that it is 'a game of two halves', an expression meaning that a pattern established in the first half can easily be reversed in the second. It can often be hard to maintain the momentum that one has established during a half of play, and every break in the flow of game-time provides an opportunity to deflect or reverse the flow of advantage.

The time to which games are subject is both exterior and interior to it. On the one hand, time is simply duration, the relentless ticking away of the seconds, which go no faster or slower for the game being played than for the boiling of an egg or a railway journey. In games that are subject to absolute temporality, the duration of the game has nothing to do with the playing of the game and cannot be affected by it in any way. The wisest soccer players know that a goal only takes about fifteen seconds to be scored, whether it is scored in the first or the last minute, even though time may feel much more squeezed and hurried in the final minute. Though this means that in principle all games of soccer will involve ninety minutes of play, in fact of course it will take varying amounts of time to play out those ninety minutes, since various kinds of stoppages will always intervene and need to be compensated for. One of the characteristics of game-time is that it is discontinuous, meaning that time cannot simply be allowed to pass. In this, watching a game resembles the act of reading a book or, increasingly, watching a film, more than the act of watching a play or listening to a concert. So, in this sense, the time to which play is subject is not independent of the game at all, but subject to its contingencies. When the clock is running, its dominion is absolute and independent; but precisely when the clock is running and when it is suspended is determined by what happens in the game – what injuries and other interruptions there may be.

In certain games, there is a requirement that the game cannot end until some particular sequence of play has been completed. This makes for a game which is temporally determined in every respect except in its ending. Thus international rugby is played strictly to the clock, with the referee deciding and announcing when the clock starts and stops. But once the eighty minutes of play have been completed, the game cannot in fact be declared over until the ball goes dead, usually by going into touch. This period will not usually last for more than a few minutes, since the side that is in the lead will have an interest in ending the game as quickly as possible. But, in principle, if the side that is attempting to avoid defeat succeeds in keeping possession, or if the scores are level and both sides have an interest in keeping the game going as long as they still have a chance of victory, the game could go on indefinitely beyond the stipulated eighty minutes. In fact, even in games where there is no such requirement, it is usual for referees to wait for a moment at which there is no conspicuous advantage to either team before blowing for time. If referees really ended the game at the precise moment that time was up, we would expect the whistle to blow occasionally at crucial moments – as the ball hangs in the air from a corner kick in soccer, for example. But it almost never happens, perhaps because there is a tendency to want the game to have some role in shaping time to its contours, forming it into what, at the end of the game, is expressively known as 'full-time', rather than being subject to absolute and objective temporal determination.

Not only can one only play during the periods when the clock is running, it is a requirement that both teams in fact *play* – hence the penalties imposed in many sports for various forms of time-wasting. The culpability of wasting time, along with the quite complex protocols that determine in different sports the different ways in which time may fairly and unfairly be consumed, discloses an essential principle of sport time: namely that its time should be at all times fully occupied, never allowed merely to pass. The game must be played in time; as soon as the game and its time become detached, as soon, in other words, as a player or team will seem to be doing something else, while time merely passes in the background, an offence has been committed.

But there are also games in which the length of time the game takes is not externally determined, or only partially so. Sports characterized by immanent time last as long as it takes for a particular goal to be attained or situation to arise. Games of immanent time may be said to generate their own durations. The differing speeds, compressions and stretchings of time seem to be produced out of and dependent upon the actual patterns of play of the game. The alternation between external and internal time in games may be compared to the distinction between metre and rhythm in poetry, metre applying to the abstract rhythmical pattern to which the poem confirms, and rhythm accounting for the variations on and syncopations of that underlying pattern. No game has fully immanent time, but the patternings of time generated by games like cricket, baseball and golf make them equivalent to a kind of free verse, which is unregulated by exterior frameworks.

Sometimes the time of play can seem to create a sense of seclusion, of time drawn into a self-referring circle. Murray Ross sees baseball as creating an 'expanded and idle time' which, for all the excitement and climax it contains and allows, is fundamentally the time of pastoral, a genre which proposes 'a timeless world of perpetual spring, and . . . does its best to silence the ticking of clocks which remind us that in time the green world fades into winter'.[2] This may well have something to do with the fact that the time of baseball is internally rather than externally determined; like certain forms of cricket, it takes as long as it takes. Ross distinguishes baseball, which 'dissolves time and urgency in a green expanse' from football, which he believes converts space into time.[3] In football, the field of play offers no such leisurely synoptic perspective, but encourages zeroing in on the particular hotspots where play is concentrated, and the game is played against the clock rather than within a time that shrinks and swells obediently to accommodate itself to the unfolding of the game.[4]

Games that are played strictly against the clock, that is to say, that are subjected to a time that is not isomorphic with the play, tend to be indifferent to the time that is passing external to the game – for example in the cycles of light and darkness and variations of weather. Sports that are tightly synchronized to clock-time are therefore more homogenous and therefore more transferable from clime to clime and time-zone to time-zone. The regularization of the playing-times of many sports during the nineteenth century went hand in hand with the process of rendering them compatible with each other, and therefore transferable from context to context. The same timings helped sport to be played in many different places. For many years it was traditional for soccer matches in Britain to kick off at three o'clock on a Saturday afternoon, but now soccer matches can be played and watched at almost any time of the day or night that a crowd or a TV audience can be mustered.

The external time of the ninety minutes is therefore an abstract, purely quantitative time. By contrast, sports like cricket and golf, which tend to draw time into themselves, forming their own time imma-nently, and establishing their own patterns of tension and relaxation, also tend, somewhat paradoxically, to have more significant relations and interchanges with diurnal, meteorological and even celestial rhy-thms. There is perhaps no sport of which this is truer than cricket, and no sport which is more structured around mealtimes in par-ticular, those conjunctures of bodily and circadian rhythms. Scarcely anyone in Britain still regards mid-afternoon tea as an occasion for a sit-down meal, as opposed to a snatched break, but in cricket, the tea interval has considerable symbolic and strategic importance. So one of the rhythms that ripples across the play during a game of cricket is that of hunger, repletion and digestion. The commentator John Arlott was given to quoting *Julius Caesar* as the clock moved round towards 1 p.m., remarking that a bowler displaying particular avidity had developed, like Cassius, 'a lean and hungry look'. The period just before lunch is fraught with danger, for the batsmen dis-tracted by thoughts of gravy and custard, and lurid with opportunity for the bowling side. The end of the day is also subject to this flagging of concentration, as the shadows lengthen, and the engine of the day's events begins to run down.

But there are many other ways in which cricket, especially in the classical form of the five-day Test match, adapts itself to and therefore assimilates to itself the slow cyclings of conditions during the day, from the morning and evening dew, especially at the beginning and end of the season in England, to the changeable gradient of the sun, with its effects on light and shadow, visibility, temperature and humidity. Chapter Two suggested that cricket put more in play than most other sports and cricket is also a game that, more than any other, is made of, and played with, time or what may be the same thing, the weather (time and weather being the same word for speakers of French). So it is not for nothing that the emblem of Lord's cricket ground is the weather-vane showing Father Time as an umpire with a sickle over his shoulder removing a bail from (or perhaps replacing it on) the wicket.

In sports in which draws are not possible, and which must therefore continue until a winner emerges, the commonest form of open-endedness with regard to the ending of the game is the convention that a player or team should demonstrate a clear advantage – typically by gaining a lead of two, whether goals or points. This can lead to extraordinary prolongations of play, most notably in recent times the first-round tennis match at Wimbledon played between the American 23rd seed John Isner and the French qualifier Nicolas Mahut, which lasted 11 hours and 5 minutes, fought out over three days from 22 to 24 June 2010. The final score was 6–4, 3–6, 6–7, 7–6, 70–68. The most astonishing thing about the match was the fact that the final-set endgame, in the uncharted region beyond the score of 6–6 at which a tie-break would come into operation in earlier sets, and which rarely lasts more than four or five games, itself lasted longer than the rest of the entire match. In fact, when play was suspended at 59–59 in the fifth set at ten past nine in the evening on the second day, there had already been nearly twice as many games played in this endgame period (106) as in the whole of the rest of the preceding match up to that point (57). This is like a book whose epilogue is two or three times as long as the preceding chapters, or a symphony whose climactic cadenza outlasts the work itself by some hours.

There have been occasional attempts to achieve a kind of absolute immanence of sport-time, in which the length of the game is entirely determined by the game itself. The most famous version of this was the Time-less Test played at Durban between England and South Africa in March 1939, which was designed to be played until both teams had batted through two innings, however long it took. After ten days, England were in a strong position, with five wickets remaining, and within 42 runs of victory. At this point, the match had to be broken off, in order that England could take the train to get them 1,000 miles to Cape Town to catch their boat home. Cricket's capacity to draw different temporalities into itself, or to expand its rhythms out into those different temporalities, is suggested by the rhyme between lifespan and length of innings, both of them exceptionally producing what are called 'centenarians'. I am in fact writing these words on 7 August 2010, which it is pleasing to discover is the 99th birthday of Norman Gordon, the oldest surviving Test match cricketer, who played in that match in Durban. He was 0 not out in both South African innings, and got 1 wicket for the loss of 174 runs hit off his bowling.

Whether internally or externally determined, all sports involve a more or less intense complication of regular clock-time. The two extremes are the attempt to run down the clock on the one hand, and the attempt to force an outcome in a short time on the other. In some sports, these alternatives are distributed differentially between the adversaries. A team that gains a precious lead in a close-fought match may seek to appropriate and expend all the available reserves of time. To have a large lead is in effect to have stockpiled reserves of time, since, even if you concede points, games or goals, your opponent still has a great deal of work to do in what, from their point of view, is a challengingly short time. In fact, to win or achieve dominance in a match is nearly always to corner most of the reserves of time. The struggle against the other team is really a struggle against their time. One side struggles to accelerate time by gaining advantage. If I am 3–0 ahead, I will have wound the clock forward, starving the other team of the time available to them by increasing the work that they must do in it. The other team responds by trying to distend time; to defend is to defer, to hold time open, to maximize the reserve of time that remains.

Ordinary, elapsing, progressive time has no place in the experience of sport. This is not because time is here stalled or suspended, nor because one is unconscious of the passing of time, even if this may be the experience of the players and spectators. Rather, it is because in the playing of the sport, time is so remorselessly and exceptionlessly materialized. Everything now is time, time solidified, materialized, made palpable and therefore put into play. The game, whatever it may be, from hockey to tennis to volleyball, is a choreographed meteorology of speeds and durations, with the ball, puck or shuttlecock as the switcher and transmitter of these speeds.

Far from being a timeless space, the space of play is gravid and engrained with time. Time here has no transcendence, for it is nothing but its measurement, and everything measures it out. Rather than standing behind or having to be inferred from changes of physical form, time is here absolutely immanent in physical form, which is to say visibly displaced into it. Just as certain medical conditions produce the phenomenon of 'referred pain', pain felt in some other place than the site of an injury, so the space of play produces 'referred time'. For is not pain indeed the primary index of time in play? In sport, time is forced into embodiment – the body becomes the very physiology of time, its lineaments the contours of time, its speeds and angles time's very enfleshed profile. The body not only acts in time, time is also acted out through the body.

All the time, though, the time is running out. But there are moments of recoil and resilience, pockets of time in which time is remanded. We had a boy in my school called Nigel Gallop, who played fly-half. He had the ability, at the moment he received the ball from his scrum-half, to hold time up as he leaned, say, to the right, suspended like Aphrodite amid the foam on the tip of his right toe, drawing both his team and the opposing team in the direction of his expected pass, as though with a nudge of his left hand he had tipped up a tray of marbles. But then, as the rest of the field of play slewed away to his right, he would suddenly pivot to his left, to run or kick through the corridor momentarily opened up by his feint. Just as the theory of relativity shows us that light is bent by gravity, so here the space of play was puckered together in one point and stretched out in another. By taking a stitch in time in one part of the field, he purchased for himself a precious rent in time in another. Gaps in space and gaps in time are entirely equivalent. In any sport, an *epoché* or aperture of this kind is a wormhole in time, a *lusus temporis*. The field of play winks and shimmers, opening and closing, actual and virtual, with these wrinkles and pockets of opportunity. The play of space worked within the space of play is nothing but the fluctuation of these chronotopological compossibilities.

And there are moments in the game at which something like the plenitude of original possibility can be restored. To wait to receive serve, or to try to save a penalty, is to be prepared to move in any direction whatsoever. Michel Serres has evoked this suspension of space-time:

> Have you ever kept goal for your team, while an opponent rushes in to take a clean, close shot? Relaxed, as if free, the body mimes the future participle, fully ready to unwind: toward the highest point, at ground level, or halfway up in both directions, left and right; toward the center of the solar plexus, a starry plateau launches its virtual branches in all directions at once, like a bouquet of axons. This is that state of vibrating sensitivity – wakeful, alert, watchful – a call to the animal who passes close by, lying in wait, spying, a solicitation in every sense, from every direction for the whole admirable network of neurons. Run to the net, ready to volley: once again, a future participle, the racket aims for all shots at once, as if the body, unbalanced from all sides, were knotting a ball of time, a sphere of directions, and were releasing a starfish from its thorax.[5]

Serres sees this as nothing less than the figuring of the soul, as an 'unfurled omnitude'. As opposed to the necessary Dasein, or having to 'be-there' of the animal, soul is 'the kind of space and time that can be expanded from its natal position toward all exposures'.[6] But, in this space and time, the time-held-up-as-space of play, one cannot remain in play, that is, in potential. For the space of play is one in which you are always having to make your play, to move to left or right, to stretch or dive. In the space of play, time is always being divided into, decided as space.

Time will always be liable to stretching and contraction, attenuation and thickening, cooling and incandescence, as a result of the patterns of the play. The time of play is a mutable medium, sometimes sluggish and viscous, sometimes fleet and fluent, sometimes smoothly uniform, sometimes spasmodically convulsive. All play winds time up into a kind of narrative, gives time a more or less determinate shape. Robert Perinbanayagam sees the playing of games and sports as one of the most powerful ways of living one's mortal relation to time: *games are poetic and narrative structures that enable a human being to conceive time and experience it.* Watching games or playing them, a "reader" experiences time in its three-dimensional complexity – attending, remembering, and anticipating.'[7] Indeed, sports reveal that our principal relation to time may be that of play: 'One plays with the time of one's life – in games and in everyday life.'[8] The principle and purpose of sport is, like that of other human activities, to give a shape and significance to temporal experience that it would not otherwise or in itself possess. It is to give one's time scansion, direction, variation and, most especially, finality:

> While time in everyday life structures indefinitely into a future – with an agent's anticipating various stages in it, including his or her demise – in games, time has a refreshing finality to it. A game begins, runs an appointed course, and ends at a particular moment. It is all final, cut and dried, neat, and not subject to doubts, debates, and reruns.[9]

And yet, paradoxically, the player of a sport has often to learn to lift himself or herself out of the intensely patterned time that is built by sport in order to be able to succeed with it. Notoriously, a player who may be propelled on an irresistible forward current of success towards victory may suddenly find taking the last few steps to winning impossible – the phenomenon known unkindly as 'choking'. If sport-time powerfully binds stretches of time together in tightly chained patterns of protention and retention, succeeding often depends upon being able to separate, even to atomize, time, rigorously shutting out everything but what is happening in what is known, not entirely intelligibly, as 'the moment', and keeping at bay anticipation, apprehension, fear, desire and regret. At what we call crucial moments, different alternatives seem to be crushed together in a single crossroads. The player serving for the match at Flushing Meadow or stepping up to take the crucial penalty kick in a World Cup shoot-out is well-advised to try to clear the moment of this concentrated consequence and implication. This is perhaps the greatest paradox of sport-time; that, in order to win, one must set aside all the most important ways in which sport structures and intensifies time. Most of all, one must surrender all the forms of anticipation, the anxious straining to weigh up, work out and second-guess, that it is natural to experience at such moments. It is at such times that one is most at risk of trying to override one's habits and mechanisms, even though it is at such times that one most needs to allow one's responses to be simple, immediate and uncomplicated by doubt or hesitation. One can perhaps force or trick oneself into such a state, but I suspect that the players who are most able to succeed at such times are not those who can consciously control their responses, but those who can find a memory of animal joy in the achievements of play, the kind of joy in which one is so taken up by the time of play as to be unaware of it except as a kind of radiance. This is in itself a paradox, though perhaps a familiar one; in order to unravel oneself from the complex knot of time, it can be helpful to surrender to a kind of bodily time, the sort of memory that is stocked up in nerve and muscle and brain during hours of training.

Calendars

The kind of time I have so far been considering is internal to sport, since it concerns the temporal conditions under which sport is played and the temporal effects to which it gives rise. This kind of time is largely focused on questions of duration and its variations – on how long, how fast. Another kind of sport-time concerns the ways in which sport enters into personal memory and social history. This kind of time is less focused on duration than on periodicity and patterns of recurrence – on how often, on what kinds of cycle.

The sporting calendar is the equivalent to the ecclesiastical calendar. Even in the world of year-round sports, and even in sports that no longer even have the pretence of a 'season', the sport is still subject to cyclical sequences. Just as the ecclesiastical calendar was integrated with the astronomical calendar, so the sporting calendar is too, with different phases or periodicities creating astrological conjunctions and oppositions. The basic pulse is annual. In tennis, the four Grand Slam tournaments are spread unevenly through the year, with the Australian Open in January, the French Open and Wimbledon in May and June and the US Open in September. The syncopated beat of these four events is further variegated by the long, winding, world-wide trail of the ATP tour, with a new event starting up somewhere in the world every three or four days. This annual sequence is keyed into the quadrennial metre of the major world sporting events. The two largest global sporting events, the Olympics and the soccer World Cup, each take place once every four years, but alternating with two years between them. Since 1987 the Rugby World Cup has run on a four-year cycle too, being held in the year following the soccer World Cup.

It is tempting to see the time of sport as a special kind of time, and there are reasons to identify it with two ways of thinking about special or exceptional time: *kairos* and sacred time. In Ancient Greek, *kairos* was distinguished from *chronos* in marking a moment of decision or fulfilment, a moment at which the empty and meaningless succession of events (*chronos*) suddenly concentrates into significance. The *kairos* is a moment out of time, but a moment that nevertheless gives meaningfulness, continuity and direction to the whole of what comes before and after it. It is used by theological writers to account for the entry of the sacred or divine into history, most notably in the incarnation of Christ, and by extension to name moments of special inspiration or revelation. Sport too seems to involve the instinct to force time into crisis, for games, or at least our ways of watching them, seem similarly to distinguish crises or turning-points – the penalty, the break-point – from the simple succession of events that characterizes the ordinary passages of play.

Yet, for all this, sport itself is probably not best thought of as constituting, or even orientated towards, *kairos*, since *kairos* involves the suspension of time, and sport, even as it is set aside from *chronos*, always nevertheless realizes itself through it. Sport does not give experiences of *kairos*, because sport involves the effort to coincide with time in its passing, rather than to suspend or surpass it. Sports and games are sometimes called 'pastimes', and we may take this in a stronger sense than is usually meant. In Beckett's *Waiting for Godot*, Estragon meets Vladimir's cheerful remark that a little routine in which they have been engaged 'passed the time' with the sour rejoinder that 'it would have passed in any case'.[10] But sports do not simply allow us to forget or distract ourselves from the ongoingness of time. Far from turning away from the passing of time, sports attempt to inhabit and exactly coincide with that passage. Since time is nothing other than pure passage, all it can do is pass. But sport represents a kind of free and active willing of the necessity of this passage. When one passes the time in a pastime, one makes transitive an intransitive action, in something of the same way that Jean-Paul Sartre suggests we may be said to 'exist' our bodies, meaning, not to cause our bodies to exist (for they anyway cannot but exist), but to give them their manner of existing.[11] The active immanent passing of the time, rather than the suspension or transcendence of that passage, is of the essence in sport.

Mircea Eliade proposed that religious peoples and persons experience a kind of sacred time that is different from profane time. Profane time simply passes, relentlessly, but meaninglessly. Sacred time is actualized in the festivals that recall world-forming events that took place in a mythical past. '[S]acred time is infinitely recoverable, indefinitely repeatable. From one point of view it could be said that it does not "pass," that it does not constitute an irreversible duration. It is an ontological, Parmenidean time; it always remains equal to itself, it neither changes nor is exhausted.'[12] There is no doubt that, just as sport has a claim to be called 'the religion of the twentieth century', sporting events do have striking similarities with religious festivals, and may supply many of the same kinds of excitement and satisfaction.[13] As Dennis Brailsford notes, although the links between religious holidays and sporting activities have been eroded, 'the rhythms of the old holiday still continue to beat beneath the smooth metallic surface of today's sporting calendar'.[14] Like the liturgical calendar, the sporting calendar 'flows in a closed circle'.[15] As with religious festivals, sporting events seem to bring about an intersection of different levels of time, or an irruption of 'primordial time, which is always the same, which belongs to eternity', into historical time.[16] In such festivals, Eliade suggests, 'religious man periodically becomes the contemporary of the gods'.[17]

But the timing of existence, the existing of time, in sport should be distinguished from Eliade's 'sacred time'. The aggregate of Christmases, or Easters, or Diwalis is a kind of nonprogressive simultaneity. There is no expectation of any kind of historical progression through this sequence, since what matters is that these festivals move human beings temporarily from the profane time of sequence to the sacred time of cyclical recurrence. But the calendar of sports is ongoing and progressive, a matter of incremental building as well as of recurrence, if only in the obsession with record-breaking achievements of various kinds. Sacred time turns on itself; but the sacred moments of sport never succeed in holding time back.

Allen Guttmann sees sport as the mark of the passage from sacred to secular, maintaining that

> The bond between the secular and the sacred has been broken, the attachment to the realm of the transcendent has been severed. Modern sports are activities pursued for their own sake, partly for other ends which are equally secular. We do not run in order that the earth be more fertile. We till the earth, or work in our factories and offices, so that we can have time to play.[18]

All sports come into being in the antagonism between absolute and immanent time, governed by the desire to convert the former into the latter, in other words, to take the time to which one is subject and convert it into a time of which one is the subject. Playing sports involves the attempt to live time intensely rather than merely living in and through it. Sport is not alone in this, of course. Almost any purposive human action can be said to bring about this attempt to move time inwards and to move oneself inside time, rather than simply being shunted along by it. But there is a particular feature of sport which gives it a claim to effect this coincidence, namely the fact that it often involves an intensely agonistic relation to time. All sports, even those which do not involve the direct activity of racing, pit themselves in some sense against time, if only because all sports involve expenditure of energy and therefore fatigue. This is why it is necessary to insist on the simple but absolute definition of a sport as a game that makes one physically tired. Sports are always played within the encroaching horizon of the fatigue that would ultimately bring them to a standstill. All sports are game-like, in that they play with time, but only those games that synchronize themselves with the movement of time towards exhaustion can be called sports.

Synchrony

The historical tendency has been for immanent time to give way to external time, as a result of the pressures exerted by commercialization, TV scheduling and professionalization – all of which exert pressure to make the time taken to play out fixtures predictable. This is part of a long historical process whereby the expansive and unregulated festivities of the ancient and medieval worlds have gradually been subject to more and more regulation, especially in terms of their times and places.[19] In contrast with medieval sports, which would often occupy a whole day, modern sports are nowadays nearly all governed in some way by the clock. Where traditional sports and pastimes, including not just football but also bell-ringing and even 'leaping', were condemned by Puritan divines as both a sinful deflection of attention from godliness and a waste of time that could be put to productive use, leisure and sport in particular have steadily been not just constrained by the time-disciplines of capitalist production, but also made a productive part of the economy, as more and more ways have been found to make playing pay. The old opposition between commerce and sport survived only in the distinction between the amateur and the professional, and only up until the 1980s.

Modern sport is characterized by growing standardization of temporalities and durations, both within and across individual sports. Television schedules have exerted very great pressure in this respect. The defining case is probably cricket, the game that held on for longest in the era of fast sporting turnarounds to the leisurely, unfolding time of ancient pastimes and entertainments. Indeed, the possibility of playing out a cricket match that could be completed even in the span of a single day had to wait until 1962 to be actualized among English county teams and the first one-day international was not until ten years later. Recent innovations have included twenty-overs-a-side matches that typically last for three hours – in fact, in Twenty20 cricket, a team that has not begun bowling its twentieth over within 75 minutes incurs penalties. The railway had a particular importance in standardizing sport-time in the nineteenth century. Just as the railway brought about standardized or synchronized time, so it also allowed players and spectators to be transported to more and more widespread venues, this encouraging further uniformity of start-times and durations.[20] Among other things, it helped produce the conventional distinction between the working week and the sporting weekend. The mobility of players and spectators strengthened communication and communication created both the possibility and expectation of comparability and commensurability. Communication and codification went along together.

For the most extreme critics of this process, such as Jean-Marie Brohm, who has maintained an unbroken critique of organized sport for more than 30 years, sport has become part of the process of ordering and controlling the rhythms of social work and life under capitalism. It is 'a product of the reduction of working hours, or urbanization and the modernization of the means of transport. Sport *itself* turns the body into an instrument which it helps to integrate into the complex system of productive forces.'[21] Sport's concern with records and statistics constitutes a kind of 'quantophrenia', in which Brohm sees 'a deep analogy with the administrative formalism of lists, questionnaires, account, balances and relations in totalitarian systems'.[22] The striving of human against human in ancient sporting competition gives way to the pitting of individual human beings abstractly against the clock: the *agôn* thereby becomes the test.[23]

As sporting events became shorter and faster, with more emphasis on skill and speed than on endurance, so interest grew in the pitting of like against like. The growing need for sports events to provide entertainment to paying customers brought about a new interest in closely matched and exciting finishes. National and then international competition began in the 1870s, with touring cricket and baseball teams. One might almost say that the modern concept of fairness and of the sporting chance was closely attuned to this growing synchronization of times. With speed and proximity came recurrence and repeatability. In prize fighting and other drawn-out sports in the eighteenth century, what Dennis Brailsford calls the 'long agonies of the vanquished' could be excruciatingly protracted (we might recall that sporting occasions often provided the venue for public executions and punishments such as floggings well into the nineteenth century).[24] In the new era of evenly matched contests, one expected the loser to be able to fight another day, and that day not to be far distant. Institutions such as the annual Oxford vs Cambridge and Eton vs Harrow cricket matches became more popular, and the annual Oxford vs Cambridge boat race still commands an interest and audience far beyond its intrinsic importance.

The regularization of sport-time, the growing commensurability of codes and the increasing competitiveness of players made for much more regular fluctuations of fortunes. As more matches were played, individuals and teams had more opportunities to bounce back from defeats, victories became less absolute and reverses became more easily and regularly reversible. What mattered was not the victory but the fixture, a word that became common in sporting parlance during the 1860s. The regular fixture stabilized variation and reversibility and the ethic of participation as opposed to winning began to arise in tandem with this endlessly revisable, reversible temporality.

Since Records Began

In one sense, the generalization and synchronization of sport-time led to a stalling or thickening of progressive time into a sort of perpetual, endlessly renewed present, in which it was more difficult than ever before to demonstrate continuing dominance – not least in international competition, in which England, the *fons et origo* of so many games, promptly began losing matches to other countries on a regular basis. At the same time, the new sense that sports were played in the 'same time' also made it possible and desirable to begin comparing the performances of athletes and competitors at different historical moments. Increasingly, the rivalries between different competitors were cut across by a more abstract and general struggle for high performance, and a battle against limitation as such. The focus in all of this started to become the record. The nineteenth century saw the beginning of sports statistics and the keeping of records. The use of the word 'record' to mean not just a document, report or piece of evidence, but a standard or measure of a superlative, dates from the 1860s. For the first time, records were not just for keeping, but also for breaking, a usage that first appears in the 1880s. Record-setting and record-breaking and the acts of score-keeping and statistical analysis that were necessary to them created a new, secondary kind of historical time.

Until the middle of the nineteenth century it was not possible to measure short periods of time with any accuracy, which meant that races over short distances tended to focus on competition rather than absolute achievement. The development of ever more accurate devices for measuring short amounts of time brought about an increasing emphasis on sprint events. John Bale considers the relentless drive towards improvement of athletic times as a parallel to the general compression of global time and space.[25] The pursuit of records accelerates and decelerates at the same time. The drive to maximize performance and the growth of sport mean that more records are broken (sometimes, as sceptical commentators pointed out, by multiplying the number of very similar different events and therefore opportunities to set and break records, especially in swimming), even as the amounts that are shaved off record times get smaller and smaller. Bale suggests that, as records get stuck at certain points, there will be pressure to develop the technology that will allow them to be timed to ever smaller fractions of a second. This will mean that '[t]here is, in theory, no limit to the speed that can be run', a bizarrely unlooked-for adaptation of Zeno's paradox of Achilles and the tortoise.[26]

The most important kind of record is the world record, and we can say that the very idea of the record tends naturally to the *ne plus ultra* of a kind of universal world-time. But there are also spots of syncopated time, in the form of local records, which do not move as uniformly or at the same pace as world records. 'Slower' nations might therefore also seem to be further back in abstract sport-time than others, while their records may be very slow to be improved on, making as John Bale puts it, for 'nations where time has stood still'.[27] The Indian record time for the men's 5,000 metres would only have represented an improvement on the world record time in 1965, while the equivalent date for the current Albanian record over the same distance is 1932.

This agonistic time, in which time itself has been the antagonist, is not homogenous, but clotted and clustered. Improvements in running times over the twentieth century for instance have not been equally distributed across different events; they have been proportionately much greater in the marathon and other distance events than in sprints. Only a second, or 10 per cent, has come off the 100 metres world record, which, as I write, stands at 9.69 seconds, compared with the 10.40 record set by Charles Paddock in 1921; whereas the world record time for the marathon has gone down by almost 30 per cent, from 2.55:19, set by John Hayes in 1908, to 2.04:26, set by Haile Gebrselassie in 2007. Not surprisingly, there has been a dramatic narrowing of the gap between men and women in certain events. But the fastest ever women's time for the 100 metres, Florence Griffith-Joyner's time of 10.49, which has stood since 1988, is still slower than the men's record set in 1921, whereas Paula Radcliffe's world record time of 2.15:25 for the marathon is faster than the men's world record set in 1954.

In racing, in which timekeeping is more important than anywhere else, the battle against time itself comes increasingly to matter much more than the struggle to outrun one's rivals, leading to the strange spectacle of events in which two different kinds of race are being run simultaneously – the race to be first on this occasion and the race to be the fastest ever. For Allen Guttmann, a record is 'the marvellous abstraction that permits competition not only among those gathered together on the field of sport but also among them and others distant in time and space. Through the strange abstraction of the quantified record, the Australian can compete with the Finn who died a decade before the Australian was born.'[28] For the potential record-breaker, the race in which they are participating may be no help at all, and even in fact constitute a dangerous distraction from their ultimate purpose, and so must be carefully ignored.

Just as photography and then cinema made it possible for the first time for human beings to preserve and revisit their own personal and public histories, so sporting records, in both senses, both created temporal continuity and brought time under tension, in the challenge to go faster, higher, for longer. Sporting achievement seemed to demonstrate incontrovertibly the necessity of progress. Human history was divided into two great epochs: a long prehistory consisting of fragmentary, sporadic and convulsive effervescence, in which sporting effort was expended purposelessly and gratuitously; and the period of sport-time, 'since records began' which constituted sporting history proper. Despite a vague and sometimes uncomfortable awareness that there may well have been sporting achievements of the past of which we have no inkling, the assumption grew that any holder of a record was probably by definition the greatest performer of all time, 'all time' here meaning the time since sport began to be subjected to micro-measurement. A champion used to be one who commanded a particular *champs*, or field of contention; since the late nineteenth century the champion has been the one who has ascendancy during, and over, over a particular era.

Keeping Watch

Perhaps the most important distinguishing feature of modern sport is the importance of the spectator. Highly organized spectator sports were a feature of sporting competition in the ancient world – the Circus Maximus in Rome held up to 200,000 spectators for its displays of horse and chariot racing. But spectatorship became much less important during the medieval period, in which, for the most part, the only involvement one would be likely to have with sports and pastimes would be as a participant. As we have had occasion to note already, the primary meaning of 'sport' up until the beginning of the twentieth century was still hunting, but the fortunes of the hunt indicate clearly the new importance of the spectator and spectatorship. Hunting undoubtedly provided a spectacle and a performance as well as a vigorous activity but, with a few exceptions, one needed to be able to follow the hunt, on horseback or on foot, often over very great distances, in order to be able to appreciate it. The many stories in which the king is led by his quarry deep into the forest and away from the eyes of his companions is a sign of the hunt's capacity to escape spectatorship. During the eighteenth century, horse racing gradually became rationalized and as a result the open course was bent round into an enclosed and self-repeating circle. The word 'lap', which derives from a word which originally meant a loosely hanging flap, but then started to incorporate the idea of folding over, started only in the 1860s to be used to mean a single circuit of such a track. The point of a circuit of this kind is not just to make it possible to traverse long distances without the need to enclose or invade large amounts of territory; it is also to make it possible for the race to be kept continuously and intermittently in view. The excursive time of the hunt becomes the recursive time of the race, with the spectator's position being an actualization of the possibility of simultaneously following and surveying it. In the case of running, the growing standardization of the shape and composition of running tracks also allowed for more precise establishment and comparison of times and records. The athletics track became a kind of time-form, an imitation of the clock-face itself, in which what mattered above all was not the particularity of the space and place, but the amount of time into which it could be translated. This introversion of racing spectacles is another example of the general move from diffuseness and pervasiveness to concentration and limitation that has characterized sport over the last two centuries. Even where the sport in question was delimited in a small or clearly defined space, as with the soccer match or the prize fight, a further reason emerged during the nineteenth century for enclosing that space, namely the increasing possibility of charging for entrance. When Thomas Lord opened his cricket ground in St John's Wood in 1787, it had a high fence to prevent spectators looking on for free. The spectator's experience of the match or race meeting was at once 'free time' and measured, commoditized time.

In one sense, this brought about a new separation of the persons or roles of player and spectator. From now on, sports, overwhelmingly, would mean spectator sports. Where, without a spectator, the game may be broken and discontinuous, for the spectator, time-in and time-out form a taut continuity. The spectator increasingly became the unifying focus of the game, under whose eyes and from whose perspective the game is played out. It is the spectator who binds the accidental time of elapsing and occurrence into a powerful, intensive, mobile continuity. But the spectator does not merely look on. Sport spectatorship quickly became simply a different way of participating in the game – through cheering, jeering, chanting and even more direct kinds of intervention, such as throwing missiles, or pitch invasion. Soccer fans and baseball fans have perhaps been the most liable to breach the boundary between pitch and seats.[29] Modern sport is characterized by the importance to players of the interchange between the rhythms of play on the pitch and the rhythms of audible response in the crowd, each side being able to incite and inhibit the other (soccer players who have scored a goal will often put their finger to their lips to indicate that their goal has silenced the taunts of rival supporters). These rhythms and resonances move fast, but not instantaneously, and the phasing or miniature delays in the modulation of the visible (but largely inaudible) events on the pitch into the palpably audible (yet largely invisible) responses of the crowd, and in the other direction, accounts for much of the excitement of being present at a large sporting match. Players on the pitch in the South African World Cup of 2010 reported that it was hard to focus on the game amid the wailing wall of sound of vuvuzelas, disclosing the importance of the auditory feedback provided by the crowd. Sound is very largely temporal, and the drowning out of the variation of the crowd sound seemed to deprive players and spectators alike of the sense of temporal location, scale and orientation, leaving them feeling as though they were playing in some undersea dream.

Increasingly, however, there are also visual dimensions to the ways in which player and spectator share time. The use of action replays in sports stadia allow both to participate in the time-shifting that has become a standard part of the transmission of sports events via television. This is not restricted to pauses in play, or to the aftermath of the race. Nowadays, it is customary for runners in the final stages of races wanting to assess their lead to glance up at the stadium screen rather than taking the risk of turning to look behind them. The spectator's point of view is thereby if only momentarily integrated into the experience of the athlete's during the real time of the running of the race. With the use of technology for the confirmation and revocation of decisions, the division between player and spectator is closed even more, though as yet players are usually not permitted to see the video evidence that is increasingly being used to make these judgements.

As in other respects, the use of time-shift technology allows both for concentration and diffusion. The action replay or decision review suspends the playing time of the match, thereby breaking its continuity. These moments tend to be the ones that are abstracted from the broadcast of the match and replayed repeatedly in other contexts. At the same time, the action replay might be said to thicken the time of play, making it possible to hold it back from, or fold it into itself. At times, this can have very undesirable effects, as for example when the live action replay in Johannesburg's Soccer City stadium of a goal scored by Argentina against Mexico in the 2010 World Cup showed all too clearly that its scorer, Carlos Tevez, had been offside, leading to resentment on the pitch and a half-time melee between players and officials. It seems unlikely that soccer will be able to resist for long the extension of such technology for analysis and the resolution of dispute, and, as the number of devices multiplies on which such replays can be viewed, it will be less and less easy to keep the singular, uniform time of live play separate from the slowed down, spread out, doubled-over time of the replay.

The enclosure of the sports stadium had tended to create an autonomous chronotope, a temporality set apart from the competing rhythms of work and social life. As Murray Ross's remarks about baseball quoted earlier suggest, the width and inclusiveness of the synoptic prospect spread out for the viewers of certain sports, such as baseball and cricket, encourages this sense of a leisurely, spread out, yet contained time. But the real-time transmission of sports, first through radio commentary, and then through television broadcasting, has broken into that enchanted circle. In fact, radio and sport were mutually constitutive in the early twentieth century. Just one year after Marconi patented his radio invention, he used it to relay news of the Kingstown Regatta to the *Dublin Daily Express*, and was soon after hired by the *New York Herald* to broadcast reports of the America's Cup race off the New Jersey coast. Just as radio sold sports, so the broadcasting of notable events like the Dempsey–Tunney boxing match in 1927 encouraged a remarkable expansion in sales of radios.[30]

Radio and TV broadcasting enable the rhythms of sport's temporality to enter into composition and conversation with other rhythms, especially with sports like cricket, where there are plenty of gaps which can accommodate extended reflections by the commentary team, as well as the alternative activities of the listeners, who may be anywhere in the world. Cricket and baseball are characterized, not so much by the fact of their slowness, as by their sharp alternation between leisurely stretches where little is happening, and spikes of intense speed, making the commentary an endless alternation of sudden, saltatory lunges forward and pondering doldrums of recapitulation. These backward-looking gaps in the texture of the play had always from the beginning encouraged a more general retrospectiveness in both sports, in which there is plenty of time to knit together the present with the geologically accreting chronicle of records and achievements in the sport's history. This structure may also account in part for the fact that baseball and cricket are the most densely and obsessively statistical of all sports.

We may say that the rhythms of cricket and baseball made possible from the beginning that doubling of time that is found in the commentary. For the first couple of centuries of organized sport, reporting of sporting events occupied of necessity a different time and place from the event itself. Reports on big races, fights and cricket matches sometimes appeared in the sporting press up to a week later and their florid and circumstantial style highlighted the gap between action and discourse.[31] The twentieth century saw a move towards real-time commentary. Such commentary is the most important and transformative of the ways in which events are turned into descriptions and analyses. We like to think of such commentaries as instantaneous, and it is true that their aim is to operate in real time. But in fact the commentary always inhabits a small margin of delay, a temporal penumbra that actually serves to give to the commentated game a kind of depth, a capacity to capture or catch up with itself as it elapses, that the mere watching of it does not afford.

No other form of discourse is so temporally exposed as the commentary. The commentator must be, like the philosophical sportsman, prepared for anything, entirely open to the contingency of what happens to happen. But the commentator's job is to create continuity from a discontinuous series of events. An article from 1937 by Seymour Joly de Lotbinière, the BBC's Director of Outside Broadcasts, explained that '[a] commentator must be able to describe one impression in neat smooth-running sentences, and at the same time he must be registering his next impression. He must be watching the broadcast as a whole to see that it is not losing shape, and he must be noticing what effects are likely to be reaching listeners so that he can explain them and yet not talk through them'.[32] Like the simultaneous translator, the commentator must be at once alertly attentive to what is happening while also turning it into a completely different form. Commentary must also be synchronized with the characteristic tempi and rhythms of different sports.

In the early days of radio commentary, the emphasis was on providing an aural picture for the remote listener, which would give him or her the impression of occupying a ring-side seat. Indeed, the mixing together of different sounds in different locations still gives the listener an auditory vantage point that it would not be possible for anybody to occupy in physical fact. Commentators would practise with blind listeners, and in the early years, the *Radio Times* would publish a grid of squares corresponding to the field, allowing listeners to plot the movement of the play in actual visual space. This became awkward, and it anyway started to become clear that commentary had other jobs to do than simply providing the listener with a means of constructing a picture of the action. One might have thought that the coming of live TV coverage would have diminished the role of the commentator. It certainly changed the pace and style of some kinds of commentary – a twenty-stroke rally at Wimbledon could sometimes be played out in stony silence from the TV commentators, in stark contrast to the rather comic efforts of radio commentary to keep up with play, in which the most sedate baseline exchanges always seems to build up a desperate temporal deficit in the commentator if prolonged beyond a few strokes.

But the commentator has another role beyond the conveying of information, which is to transmit energy and fluctuation of feeling and to embody the temporal tone of the match. This means that it is important that his or her discourse does not remain at a constant, appraising distance from the events unfolding, but is able suddenly to be overtaken by waves of excitement, which stretch and pulverize discourse, breaking into the steady pulse of sentences with animal howls and cries. So the commentator must be in charge of the game, anticipating and integrating its every move, and yet also capable of being entirely swept away by it. Some of the most effective moments in commentary come when some unexpected action is performed on the pitch – a sweetly struck goal, an unexpected drive for six, a passing stroke pulled out of nothing – that leaves the commentator unable to do more than gasp 'Ooooh!' or, in the case of the veteran BBC tennis commentator Dan Maskell, 'My word!' At these moments, the very failure of words, the capacity of the action both to streak away from speech and yet also to rend its fabric, create a heightened, ecstatic presence.

Children who have grown up over the last three or four generations, some of them becoming sportsmen and women in their own right, have experienced sport interlaced at all times with commentary. When I was seven, I would play out entire soccer tournaments on my own with a ball on our front lawn, every move being accompanied by its (my) awed or knowing voiceover. My sons have both developed the same skill of synchronized autocommentary. It is as though, without the commentary that doubles and in a sense transports the game to some other time and circumstance, the game would have no here-and-now presence. Commentary has become the confirming echo that ensures the game is really happening, that, by departing from the game, gives it back to itself.

It can sometimes appear that sport has become both continuous and ubiquitous in social life. The temporal tyranny of soccer in Britain and elsewhere is a deep concern to those with an interest in summer sports, this being an ironic reversal of the fact that soccer first became established as an occupation for cricketers during the winter months.[33] But cricket too has become an all-year game, with players following the summer around the globe, in the topography of the Empire on which the sporting sun never set. In fact, though, it would be more accurate to say that sport and its various environments have mutually penetrated each other. Only occasionally, as with truly global sporting events like the soccer World Cup final, does something like true synchronicity seem to occur. Most of the time sport and its contexts are involved in an almost inconceivably complex series of shared, overlapping temporalities, involving both dissonance and entrainment. Sometimes, the rhythms of a game can penetrate deep into social schedules. I once sat in an airport car park, listening on the radio to the final overs of a particularly tense one-day international cricket match. The sense of acceleration, constriction and time ticking away conveyed by the game was painfully echoed and amplified by the sense of the steady diminishment of the time available to me to catch my plane. As the final ball was bowled, and the outcome of the game was at last determined, I seized my suitcase and made for the terminal building, and was amazed to hear car doors slamming and to see similar sprints being undertaken from all quarters of the car park. But the many different ways in which sporting action can be transmitted through various media also means that their rhythms can be absorbed into social life in more subtle ways. Nowadays, when I work in the British Library, I will have web pages open that will be giving me updates on tennis, cricket and soccer matches in which I may have an interest. Global communications have made our world not contemporary, but rather densely contemporal, which is to say, sharing, exchanging, alternating and transmitting different times, speeds and durations. Nobody is precisely on the beat of the present moment, because temporal experience itself, especially the temporal experience of sport, has become thickly polyrhythmic.

There are some compelling reasons for seeing the temporal dispensation within which modern sport operates as profoundly different from that of the medieval world. The time of sport is intensely regulated and rationalized, and sport operates within an economy of strict demarcations, of work and leisure, participant and spectator. Time has given way very largely to various forms of timing. This all seems very different from the expansive, excursive, open-ended sports of the medieval world, in which such distinctions were much fuzzier and sport was much more diffused through social life. Indeed, for this reason, we may see sport as an important part of the forming of the modern secular time-world.

And yet, following the period in which sport was subject to its most intense time-rationalization, along with the expansion of sport into every area of social life, albeit in many more mediated forms than ever before, it might just as well be said that sport has regained something of the expansiveness and propagating ubiquity that it had in the medieval world of the chase and the festival.

Sport is nothing without striving and competition. But perhaps the most significant and formative antagonist for the sportsman is the oldest antagonist of all, namely the passing moment. In many ways, sport is an attempt to transform and redeem time. But it differs from other arts and rituals in that it is never tempted simply to suspend or deny the deep pull of time. Sport aims, not to pass the time, but to intensify and diversify its passage. In this, sport is always up against time, which is its intimate adversary. Sport is, for this reason, the most intimate form of time's adversity. It is for this reason that players and spectators of sports may say, with the speaker of Marvell's 'To His Coy Mistress', 'though we cannot make our sun / Stand still, yet we will make him run'.

four

Movement

Ecstasis

Let's call a body something which introduces a stable discontinuity in its spatial environment. A body takes up space, and thereby establishes a difference between that part of space that it includes and that which is excluded. What it means to say something is a body with extension in space is that it takes up the space it occupies exclusively. No other body can occupy the space it is in, nor can it be in any other place than that it occupies. A space and time that contains bodies is variegated and interrupted, made up of relatively stable and predictable discontinuities.

Much of the time, we live our own human bodies in this mode. We assume a position, make a stand, or take a seat, and by so doing affirm our unique occupation and command of a particular portion of space. Living bodies not only have extension and volume, they have the capacity to move themselves from place to place. Nevertheless, being able to move both within space and from place to place does not alter the fact that to be an embodied creature means to be condemned to spatiality, to what Heidegger called Dasein, a being-*there*, where the there signals the necessity of having to be, at every moment, in some particular place or another.

Considerations of this kind led to the paradoxes of Zeno regarding motion. For, if one conceives a body as always being in one particular, determinate position, the process whereby one changes that position, moving from one position to another, becomes unexpectedly puzzling. The body moves from one discontinuous condition to another. How? Where is it when it is in movement? Zeno's paradox of the flying arrow states that, if an arrow is in flight, it can either move to the place where

98

it is in a particular instant of time, or it can move to another place. But it cannot move to where it is because it is already there, and it cannot move to where it is not, because at that instant it is at rest in the place where it is. Hence, for Zeno, motion is illusory, or impossible. The solution to the paradox offered by a number of philosophers is that it is not movement that does not exist, but these static, finite, self-contained instants of time. This is all very well, but all of our measurement of time seems to encourage adherence to this fiction of such fixed instants. Henri Bergson finds in Zeno's paradox the proof that 'we cannot make movement out of immobilities, nor time out of space', and a warning against trying to understand pure duration according to the homogenizing categories that we derive from spatial thinking.[1] Such philosophical moves solve the problem, proving that, after all, movement may indeed be possible. But it is at the cost of introducing a puzzling split between two modes of thinking on which we absolutely depend, but which seem nevertheless to be incommensurable.

We may need to say that bodies in motion inhabit two different worlds simultaneously: one a world of discontinuous and mutually exclusive states, and the other a world of continuous movements, which allow it to violate the conjoined laws that say that a body can only be in one place at one time and that only one body can occupy a given space at a given time.

All sports involve the body, not just in exercise – that is, being made use of – but in exertion. In exertion, the body stretches and strains, first to reach and then to exceed its own limits. This is not quite as simple a matter as the mind or will pushing the body to its physical limits. For sport also provides an opportunity (not the only one, by any means, but an important one nevertheless) for the mind or will to learn from the body possibilities of reach, speed and extension that it might not have allowed itself to conceive. The idea of limit is not itself limited to the physical. What we call 'the body', is not simply at one end of the tug-of-war between the mental and the physical, but is the rope itself, the taut relation between the contrary pulls of limit and reach.

While this reaching beyond is constitutive of sport, it is a contingent part of other activities too. To have an embodied existence of the kind that human beings do is to experience the body, not just as a series of changing positions, but as a series of reachings, or projects and protentions, in which the body both is and is not in the place that it is. To claim that exertion is a feature of all sport is not to restrict it only to its most competitive forms or its most expert and highly trained exponents. For even the most casual kickabout or game of pat-ball involves a putting of one's physical self into some kind of play, some enlargement or variation of the body's postures, positions and possibilities.

If, considered as an object in the world, the human body always fills out and is itself saturated by the particular position it occupies, then, considered as a lived organism, it is always in motion, always newly arrived from some other position and about to set off for another. According to the logic of discontinuous space, the body is always where it is and nowhere else. But according to the logic of continuous movement that mysteriously intersects this space, the body is always in part elsewhere, already in part occupying a space that it does not yet occupy. The body is constitutively out of place, a kind of willing blur, always behind, beside, before or beyond itself.

If it is true in one sense that there is no getting away from the conditions of embodiedness, it is also true that there is no getting away either from the body's own capacity to go beyond itself, its tendency, so to speak, to *tend towards*. One of the things that one is stuck with in being an embodied subject is the fact that one's body is always in fact projective or ecstatic, in as much as it is always characterized by needs, tensions, leanings, predilections. It is never, that is, simply or neutrally in a given environment: it is always orientated, always inserted at a particular, interested angle to that environment. The space you are in in a body, that space that, with and as your body, you actually are, is a space that is, in Gerard Manley Hopkins's beautiful phrase, 'mined with a motion'.[2]

Jean-Paul Sartre takes the anticipatory movement of the tennis player as a metaphor for the way in which all human action can be thought of as projective, always pulled out of self-identity by a movement towards a future:

> The position which I quickly assume on a tennis court has meaning only through the movement which I shall make

immediately afterward with my racket in order to return the ball over the net . . . At one throw, as I am there on the court and returning the ball, I exist first as a lack to myself, and the intermediary positions which I adopt are only means of uniting myself with that future state so as to merge with it; each position has meaning only through that future state. There is in my consciousness no moment which is not similarly defined by an internal relation to a future.[3]

But this is a future that can never be arrived at, for, once it has become present, it has lost the projective pull of futurity; it is precisely no longer the future:

[M]y final position on the tennis court has determined on the ground of the future all my intermediary positions, and finally it has been reunited with an ultimate position identical with what it was in the future as the meaning of my movements. But, precisely, this 'reuniting' is purely ideal; it is not really operative. The future does not allow itself to be rejoined; it slides into the Past as a bygone future, and the Present For-itself in all its facticity is revealed as the foundation of its own nothingness and once again as the lack of a new future.[4]

The body is both the principle of the subjection to space, and the possibility of escaping it. It is at one and the same time the impossibility of being elsewhere than where one is and, if Sartre is to be believed, the impossibility of ever being simply in one position, precisely because the body is the means of changing position. Only in and through the body does one surpass it. The condition of being in a body means having in some sense to keep surpassing one's body, in reaching for a doorknob as much as for a drop-shot. Those who report so-called 'out-of-body' experiences always report experiences of a singular body, which continues to obey the conditions of the discontinuous occupation of space: typically, for example, the allegedly disembodied one floats or hovers. Nobody to my knowledge has ever reported the experience of being diffused throughout a space or being simultaneously in several places at once, which is what would presumably characterize an experience of being genuinely out of the body. Thus the allegedly out-of-body experience is the experience of being removed from one body to another, albeit an imaginary one, not an exit from the spatial condition of embodiedness as such.

These paradoxical conditions apply to all bodies at all times, but have a particular salience in sports, in which the body strives to exceed itself, and in which the tension between the discontinuous and the continuous, between inert space and space under tension, is always at issue. Sport involves, as I have said, *exertion*, a word that is formed from *ex-* out and *serere*, to bind or entwine. The actuation of potential, extruding, projection or putting forth does not merely imply a spilling or propagation. One does not leave oneself entirely behind in going forth. To exert is put yourself from yourself in such a way as to bind together the two moments of before and after, cleaving and cleaving to yourself. I become different but remain the same: I reach into my remaining. John Dryden captures these two aspects of exertion, the root and the branch, in his translation of Virgil's *Georgics*: 'apple trees, whose Trunks are strong to bear / Their spreading Boughs, exert themselves in air.'[5] Sport might be said to be an attempt to work through performatively the following self-implicating problem: is the relation between the discontinuous and the continuous itself a relation between discontinuous or continuous things?

Consider the situation in which the soccer player is about to take a direct free kick from just outside the penalty area. In front of him are ranged four or five opposing players who have formed themselves into a defensive wall. The player aiming to strike the ball has a number of options. He can blast the ball at the wall with such force that it is breached. He can try to make the ball swerve round the left or right of the wall, or fly over it and then dip abruptly into the goal, or some combination of the two. He can slip the ball to another player who has a better line of sight. This situation is repeated with variations in many games in which an attacking force is met by a defensive form – in rugby, American football, cricket, volleyball. In all such cases, one player or team attempts to affirm and enact the order of continuity, by magnifying their potential occupation of space by movement, or speed, tending towards ubiquity. The other ranges against that maximized continuity the principle of discontinuity, which declares to it *no passeren*. The defensive wall aims to minimize all potential, the attacking team to maximize it. Granite opposes gas; space plays time.

But equally, each side of the opposition provokes the other to mutate. That is, the one taking the free kick is constrained to try to find the tiny, almost unique loophole that will allow him to insinuate a way through the congested space of the defence. This scoring trajectory will contract and particularize space rather than expanding and generalizing it. Similarly, the wall must be ready to respond to every tactic of the attacking team, to reconfigure itself in a moment. The gas must be ready to thin and condense into a needle, the wall must be ready to diffuse into a gas. In the playing of a sport, the body moves abruptly, but also without pause, between these two conditions of the dense and the tenuous, sometimes aiming to be nothing but immovability and impenetrability, sometimes aiming at ubiquity and diffusion, sometimes shrinking down into the absolutely self-identical here-and-now, sometimes striving to be unidentically everywhere.

There are two forms of movement in sport, which rhyme with this contrast between the body hardened into a spatial form and the body softened into infinite potential. What we may call *absolute motion* aims to proceed directly from one point to another in space. It is seen in its purest form in the race, in which what matters is the subordination of all local contingencies to the pure imperative of maximum speed, or the absolution – the entire dissolution – of mass into pure motion. The race is in this respect the abstracted form of a kind of movement that is a constituent of all games – the charge to the goal-line, the shot driven into the corner, the slam-dunk, the all-out 100-metre sprint. In one sense, this may be thought of as the enraptured attempt to escape the capturing drag of mass, or position, to empty oneself into pure trajectory. But the ideal of the race, the absolute limit toward which it strains, is in fact not the abolition of space, but the abolition of time. The sprint to end all sprinting would take the runner from the starting to the finishing line in literally no time. Ultimately, then, in this ideal physics of the sprint, there would be no elapsing of time at all, but only space, only now crunched in upon itself, since every space would be immediately accessible to every other (there would be space, and positions within it, but no distance between them). We may therefore say that absolute movement tends towards its own reduction.

But sport also involves what we may call *accented motion*, multiplying varieties of oblique or modulated movement, of curve, swerve, spin, deflection, diagonal, dummy, break, slice, sidestep, shimmy and feint, which inflect and texture absolute motion, and in various ways take the long way round to their goal. Absolute motion aims to compress time into space, accented motion suffuses space with time, taking its time with space, warping and complicating space by threading it with intervals and elapsings.

Angles

In his mathematical children's fable *Flatterland*, Ian Stewart suggests an easy way to overcome the problem of how to conceive more dimensions of space than the three we perceive. A bicycle is a solid object existing in three dimensions, or spatial axes – left–right, front–back, and up–down. Move the handlebars of a bicycle, and the movement may be accounted for as a complex amalgam of different movements in the usual three dimensions – up a bit, along a bit, a bit closer. But it may also be conceived of as movement in a new direction, which is not perpendicular to the other directions, but cuts slantwise across them. Vikki, the Alice-like enquirer in Stewart's dimensional fable, wants more convincing by her instructor, the Space Hopper:

> 'But if it moved through a new Dimension, in what direction does the Dimension point?'
> 'In the Turn-The-Handlebars direction,' said the Space Hopper, 'which is different from the Turn-The-Front-Circle direction, which is different from the Turn-The-Back-Circle direction, which is different from the Turn-The-Pedals direction. That's four new dimensions, in addition to the original three.'[6]

The shifted position of the handlebars does not move outside three-dimensional space, but it seems nevertheless to open up a new bearing within it. Descartes's grid will suffice to determine the position of any point in space, through the combination of verticals and diagonals, but if we are to model the movement from one position to another we will have to have recourse to diagonals, to mediate the x, y and z axes. The power of the diagonal to open up some new quarter of space within space is suggested by the fact that, in a drawing on a flat surface, depth is indicated by the convention of slanting lines. For similar reasons, the diagonal suggests the anamorphism of the individual human perspective, that is always both firmly and inescapably in its place, but also oblique to, or aside from things in themselves. For Jean-Paul Sartre, being can only ever be being-there, and being-there always means being at a particular angle to the world, such that '[f]or me this glass is to the left of the decanter and a little behind it; for Pierre, it is to the right and a little in front. It is not even conceivable that a consciousness could survey the world in such a way that the glass should be simultaneously given to it at the right and at the left of the decanter, in front of and behind it'.[7] The fact that being means orientation creates a kind of mixture of necessity and contingency: 'while it is necessary that I be engaged in this or that point of view, it is contingent that it should be precisely in this view to the exclusion of all others.'[8] My obliquity to things is not just a contingent fact of my being: it is the absolute necessity of that contingency.

The myth of beginning given in the *De rerum natura* of Lucretius suggests the necessity of some inaugurating swerve or deviation in things. Explicating the atomist philosophy of Democritus and Epicurus, Lucretius asks us to imagine a world in which atoms simply rained down through empty space. In such a condition of what we now call laminar flow, in which separate streams of atoms flow in non-interfering parallel lines, there would be no collisions, nor yet collusions, no alterations of any kind. There would be no time, but simply a relation of static equality: A=A=A=A. Introducing the use of the equals sign in his *Whetstone of Witte* in 1557, Robert Recorde explained that he had chosen two parallel lines 'bicause noe .2. thynges, can be moare equalle'.[9] In order for there to have been anything at all, there would have to be at least one atom that swerved from its course, '*tantum quod momen mutatum dicere possis*' 'just so much that you can call it a change of direction': the clinamen.[10] Without this swerve, there is only necessity, endlessly repeating itself. This absolutely non-necessary waver, this minimal departure from self-identity, is necessary for everything in our universe to be. Everything would have to come from this inaugurating fissure, this chink of incipience, this 'atom of angle'.[11] But by now, in our world, that is the arborescent integral of millions of deviations, it is the laminar that is the unheard of exotic, not the deviant.

For Michel Serres, the body itself is not a vertical, but a diagonal:

> if the body plays the part of a statue, with its weight, toward the bottom, it sculpts a second one, through its lateralization, to the right or the left. It rests on its feet, but drawn to one side. It would be necessary to trace a composing oblique line that would give the true vertical line of the living being who is unceasingly attracted by this diagonal, and which would form the angle of its own fall with the normal line. Everything leans and is exposed on the side where it will fall.[12]

The diagonal is a vector, for it is never in place. It is approximate, which means that we can only ever approach it. Equilibrium convokes a shimmering of diagonals, as they approach and depart from the true north of verticality:

> We do not find the center, and we are inclined to abandon it. We lean to the right, to the left, to get away from it. Are we afraid of it? We neither know how to nor can we inhabit this fault line, this axis or this vortex: who would build his house in the middle of a current? No institution, no system, no science, no language, no gesture or thought is founded on this mobile place – which is the ultimate foundation and founds nothing.
>
> We can only head toward it, but at the very moment of reaching it, we abandon it, compelled by the arrows that depart from it. We spend only an infinitesimal moment there. Time and site of extreme attentiveness.[13]

One sees nothing at noon, in its bleak incandescence. There is only blinding glare. If God's eye were to pulse back to itself without residue, without loss, it must surely consume itself. There must be delay, phasing, diagonality. To inhabit a further dimension of space would mean that it would be possible to look in on us unobserved, just as a creature of three dimensions can overlook and look in on the roofless enclosures of the inhabitants of two-dimensional space. But to look directly down on something is to reduce its three dimensions to two, scouring away every hint and intimation about its height and volume. It is to reduce things to their diagrams, their outlines. It is to make oneself monocular, blind. The view from directly above, favoured by bombs, smart and dumb, is already a devastation, a razing. At the imaginary centre of things, I too vanish from view, my profile shaved down into pure, vertical equivalence – the gnomon *I*. As I lean sideways, or the sun tilts away from me, I start to cast a shadow, and come back into view. Two eyes are necessary for parallax. You can be where you are or you can see where you are, but not both, for if you can see where you are, then you are no longer quite in place, you have minimally departed from yourself, in the way you always must to know exactly where you are. Diagonals fix us in our place by slightly unseating us. We see that we are where we are not, that we are not in what we see, even if we are in the end nothing more than this finitude, this always particular angle of divergence from being able to see everything.

If there is *agôn* – striving, straining – in this diagonality, there is also the beauty of rhythm. For the diagonal invokes time and speed and desire ('inclination'). There is an excitement and incitement in a slope that there is not in a wall or a floor, precisely because we can be carried away with a slope, which can get us ahead of ourselves (the problem with slippery slope arguments, I once heard somebody innocently remark in a radio interview, is that you never know where they are going to lead).

When I was at school, we used to play rugby against a school whose pitch slanted dramatically from end to end. Lose the toss, and you would spend the first half with every step a clogged toil against your own dragging inertia. Trying to sprint meant extra, flailing uplift of the knees, to escape the pull of the rising ground, that seemed nevertheless to rise up like a clinging mist into your limbs, which slowly turned to pure, lugged heaviness. Every effort you made to overcome the slope magnified it, making the angle of subtension seem to grow more and more acute, tugging your head to the ground, as though you might be reduced at the end to a crawl, a climber up a cliff-face rather than a runner. Even if you were not also kicking into the wind, which always did seem to blow longitudinally from end to end of the pitch rather than across it, it was as though the very air were leaning downhill against you; when you tried to kick for territory, the ball would seem to hover sickeningly as though in the teeth of a gale. The screw-kick imparted by our full back, which would normally be expected to drill through space like a turbine, seemed to be unravelled by gravity. The shallow diagonal of our back-line became saggy and ragged with our fatigue. The slogging struggle became allegorical, and never did rugby's purgatorial language of offence and penalty seem so apt.

And yet, after a while, you started to find your hill-legs, as a cyclist or a fell-runner does on a long ascent. The anticipation of the angle of the hill began to give your ankles and knees an extra, answering kind of coiled potential. The pitch of grief began to tune your muscles like a pitchfork. Slowly, the steep slope seeped into your posture, the tilt of your neck, the rake of your hands. For rugby is a game in which much depends upon diagonals; the ball must be passed backwards, and, even when it is kicked ahead, it is an advantage for it to land at an angle and bounce with obliging compliance into the hands of the full-back who has run through the moiling press of players. The grotesque camber of the pitch gave you back to yourself, it brought you to your senses, and your senses to you. Now the hill seemed to be tipping you a wink, gently, generously nudging everything in your direction.

What was expected was that you would elect to play with the slope during the first half, in the hope of racking up a mound of points that your opposing team would not have the heart or energy to surmount with their depleted energy reserves. But it was not always an advantage to play with the gradient, and so sometimes, after the change-round after an uphill first half, there was a new and unexpected punishment. Now the ball seemed to be being tugged maliciously away from you, kicks for touch bounding hysterically beyond the end of the pitch. Careering downhill, your legs seemed to have lost all their traction, your team's passing lost the bite it had gained, the taut elastic that sutured your three-quarter line like the twanging string of the mountaineer's rope seemed to have been severed, as passes were thrown haphazardly forward and men wildly overran. You had to fight against your own advantage, pulling backwards as you were dragged forward, braking and accelerating at once. Now the angle you made with the ground yawned sickeningly obtuse, so the risk was not that your feet would slither away behind you, driving your nose into the ground, but that they would go clownishly away in front of you, like those of the novice roller skater.

The diagonal has always been enigmatic and rather suspicious (the shifty look, the bend sinister of illegitimacy). It is the vehicle and dimension of the incalculable, the infinitesimal, the asymptotic. As such, it also has magical power. At the beginning of the *Meno*, Plato shows a slave that it is possible to solve the surprisingly difficult problem of how to construct a square *b* with precisely twice the area of a square *a* by drawing the second square on the diagonal of the first. The Pythagoran Hippasos of Metapontum is said to have been drowned for revealing the demoralizing truth that the ratio of a square's diagonal to its side is $\sqrt{2}$, which is neither a whole number nor a fraction. The episode is cheerfully evoked by Samuel Beckett, the great comedian of the geometrical, in this exchange from his novel *Murphy*:

'Betray me', said Neary, 'and you go the way of Hippasos.'

'The Akousmatic, I presume,' said Wylie. 'His retribution slips my mind.'

'Drowned in a puddle,' said Neary, 'for having divulged the incommensurability of side and diagonal.'

'So perish all babblers,' said Wylie.[14]

The death of Hippasos, as described by Iamblichus in the third century, was more generally given as expulsion or being drowned at sea. Though there has been some doubt about this myth of the Pythagoreans and their terror of the irrational,[15] versions of the story have often been used to explain the disinclination among the Greeks, so brilliant in their apprehension of geometric relations and proportions, and in the exercise of deduction, to measure and calculate. And yet, Michel Serres has suggested, the observation of the ecliptic, the fact that the path of the sun over the year is at an angle to the celestial equator, opens up a gap in the middle of this rational scheme:

At the very heart of the formal project of cleaving only to the efficacy of Ideas or mathematical Forms, in the very dream of universal deduction, the powerful and hollow dream which meant that the Greeks could never arrive at modern science, inclination returns, introducing noise into the redundancy of the Same, to open the story of the beginnings of the world.[16]

The incommensurability of the side and the diagonal may be taken to be the concentrated image of the incommensurability of abstract or theoretical mathematics and the behaviour of things in the physical world. The rational and the irrational are not, perhaps, opposed, since this is a perpendicular notion, but are rather slightly, and all the time ever so slightly less, yet still eternally divergent. However close they may approach to each other, in embodied time, this gap will never entirely close. 'Physics', according to Michel Serres, 'is indeed an affair of angles.'[17]

Sporting movement continually plays diagonality against directness, incidence against perpendicularity, obliquity against againstness. In the early days of rugby football, the game was built around the primal antagonism of the scrum, in which two teams were locked together head to head in grunting effort. Under these circumstances, it seems as though only brute strength and undiluted purpose can overcome the resistance, or keep out the attack. It was not until the 1870s that teams started to demonstrate there was another way round or through; introducing a slight disequilibrium on one side or other of the scrum will cause it to wheel, the energy required to deflect a force being much less than the energy required to reverse it, and will swing the oncoming team into unopposed space, making it possible for the flanker to break away. The diagonal here turns rapidly into a circle. A curve or swerve is an intensified diagonal (or may be analysed as such in terms of the order of discontinuity). It is a diagonal iteratively diagonalized: the tangential departure from straightness immediately gives way to another departure from that new direction, followed by another, and another. Swerving in particular seems to alter the space in which it moves, impossibly bringing to light extra spaces within space. This is why players are often, and rightly, said, not just to find, or move into space, but to 'make space' for themselves. The curve or the swerve can draw the mass of players aside like a curtain, making possible sudden incisive dashes into the gap.

This may account for some of the curious locutions employed in sport with regard to position and movement. Many of these terms make perfect sense in relation to the fixed dispositions of players and pitch – left, right, middle, wing, forwards, backwards. But sport also depends upon an elaborate topology of inside and outside. One understands how in general terms one moves inwards towards the centre of the pitch, and outwards towards the edges. But there are other, much more occult and mysterious kinds of enclosure and outering in sport, which take their bearings not from the pitch and its markings, but from the topologies of play. Games with scrums, like rugby and American football, literally create spaces of invisibility, black holes, in which the normal rules of the game have no force. Players are said to play 'inside' and 'outside' of each other. The space of the field of play is full of pockets, nooks and alcoves, as well as sudden gaps and clearings.

Eccentricities

There are, as I suggested in chapter Two, two orders of space involved in play: the invariant space of play defined by the court, pitch or field and the dynamic play of space formed from the movement of players, as they fluctuate between the conditions of the continuous and the discontinuous, the fluid and the solid, movement and mass. It is this second kind of movement-space that calls for and is itself subject to the effects of oblique movements. Just as the curve is an infinite series of movements away from movement, so the swerving movement is a movement away from the space formed by the players in motion, a deviation that seemingly creates the new, vacant space into which it moves.

Swerving used to have a bad reputation, and the value of directness and upright dealings survives in phrases such as 'unswerving devotion'. The guileful arts of spinning, curving and swinging seem to belong to recent eras of sport. John Nyren argued in 1833 against the advice given to young players by a bowler named Lambert, who seems to have been the first 'to give a *twist* to his balls', by introducing the 'deceitful and teazing style of delivering the ball' that would become known as the off-break, and skittled out large numbers of Kent and Surrey opponents of the Hambledon Club, 'who could not tell what to make of that cursed twist of his'.[18] The first bowler to get the ball to effect a curve through the air rather than off the pitch was Noah Mann Sr, who employed the technique for the Hambledon club during the 1780s. The first baseball pitcher to throw a 'curve-ball' is thought to have been Arthur Cummings, who pitched underarm, in a game between the Excelsiors of Brooklyn and the Harvards of Cambridge in 1867.[19] The term 'curve ball' spread during the 1870s, and was said to be 'in common use' by 1877.[20] W. F. Hopkinson, who offered an explanation of the phenomenon, speaks of seeing a cricket ball swing in the air as early as 1865, though he also suggests patriotically that the English cricketers who toured America in the 1880s rediscovered the arts of the curve ball among baseball pitchers.[21] For some time there was scepticism about whether such a thing as getting the ball to arc as it moved through a still atmosphere was even possible. Even now, there are many arcane mysteries attaching to the swing of the cricket ball; not all swing bowlers are sure of how they are doing it, or whether they are going to be able to do it at all in given conditions. There is still puzzlement about why heavy, low-lying cloud, or even the simple passage of the sun behind a cloud, should intensify the tendency of the ball to swing – along with some considerable doubt, particularly from Brian Wilkins, who has probably done more scientific investigation into the swinging cricket ball than anyone else, as to whether humidity has any regular effect on the swing of the ball at all.[22]

Spin bowling seems to have been developed into its most arcane forms only during the twentieth century. It was in the early years of the century, and particularly during a tour of Australia and New Zealand with Lord Hawke's team in 1902–3, that B.J.T. Bosanquet developed the delivery known as the 'googly' (or the 'Bosie' in Australia), which involves bowling a ball with an action that looks as though it will be an off-break – that is, deviating on landing from the leg side to the off, or, with a right-handed batsman, from right to left – but in fact breaks in the other direction.

It seems to be the particular merit and fascination of the ball to be able to have spin and swerve imparted to it. Different kinds of ball exhibit different forms and degrees of responsiveness, and perhaps none so impishly as the table-tennis ball, the lightness of which makes it easy to impart extreme spin and swerve to it. The fact that table-tennis is played in such a restricted space, at least as far as the table is concerned, means that spin is used both to control the flight of the ball – allowing it, for example, to be hit from below the level of the table and yet still land in play because of the restraining effect of topspin – and to make its flight exceedingly unpredictable for one's opponent. The lightness of the table-tennis ball can make it feel as though one were playing with a pocket or concretion of air itself, and the game itself to be a mingling of constraint and freedom.

All the forms of obliquity and deviation involve complex and rapid interchanges between and readjustments of the relation between anticipated and actual movements. The deadliest form of the curve ball or swinging ball is the one that veers or dips late in its course. In this case, it is not that a movement that is expected to continue in one line unexpectedly changes; it is that there is a change in the rate of change of trajectory that is itself made up of nothing but an infinity of departures from the straight and narrow. It is therefore a change in the very conditions of changeability. The curving flight, we may say, constitutes a particular kind of amalgam of actual and predicted movement, a knitting together of the 'as if' and the actual that includes purposively within it the projected but non-actualized possibilities. In fact there seems reason to think that some of the early suggestions that the curve ball was an optical illusion are in fact well founded, since recent studies have found that a ball that moves from the central to the peripheral fields of the striker's vision may give the impression of suddenly veering away to the side.[23] This provides even stronger warrant for seeing the curve ball not simply as a physical effect but as a constellation of movements, actual and virtual, physical and mental.

It is often said that the most fluent and accomplished movements in sport are also the most economical. It is certainly true that certain kinds of inefficient movements, that are excessive to their purpose and may involve a great deal of accessory jerks and elaborations, may strike us as ugly. But closer inspection may reveal that grace does not always correspond to the strictest economy – indeed, that graceful movements may sometimes be those that involve forms of flourish or enlargement beyond what is strictly necessary. There seems here to be an unexpected logic of what may be called the essentially gratuitous, in which grace is conferred precisely by the sense of what is performed just a little in excess of the necessary, when economy can appear as a kind of *style*, the performing of an act that just minimally shadows or quotes itself as a performance. The curve and the swerve seem to embody in particular this gratuity, in the margin or fringe of possibility that it always includes.

Dive

The most familiar form of the curve is the parabola, the mathematics of which had been of interest to archers and artillerymen for centuries. It too seems like a blending of the necessary and the contingent. For all the majesty and elegance of Newton's apprehension of the universality of gravity in the universe, the most astonishing thing about this particular law of physics is that fact that the force of gravity is so extraordinarily weak and, in everyday experience, so easily resisted and warped. A fluke congeries of carbon and water such as I am is capable of preventing the fall of objects to the ground; indeed, if one of my names, human, seems to indicate my earthy provenance, another name I give myself, *Homo erectus*, makes the spurning of the surly bonds of earth my defining principle. In the end, or the long run, of course, things dip, decline and surrender to the force of gravity. But the way they do so, in arcs and curves of various kinds, loops out the compenetration of gravity and grace, at once the calculation and the calculated result of unimaginably complex and beautiful problems of adjustment of opposing and oblique forces. Few things give human beings more delight than the fantasy of dwelling a while in the semi-arrested interval of variegated fall. The invention of the human cannonball act by Guillermo Antonio Farini in 1877 allowed human beings for the first time to identify themselves entirely with the projectiles they had become used to despatching through the air.[24]

Diving is perhaps the purest form of this counterfactual willingness to sport and cavort with the possibilities opened up by what would otherwise be the most certainly fatal kind of precipitate descent. Garrett Soden suggests plausibly that the delight in controlled falling derives from the fact that human beings have two conflicting instincts, 'one designed to protect us from gravity, the other urging us to play with it', and suggests that this derives from our mixed inheritance as both tree-dwelling and land-dwelling animals.[25] Indeed, the human all-round ability with acrobatics in different environments is one of the few areas in which human beings outdo other creatures: 'when it comes to controlled falling, we have no peer.'[26] The movements of the diver, like those of the acrobat, are almost all gyratory, the closing of the curve on itself, in a defiance of the order of the direct and the perpendicular. The point of the dive is to use the conditions of necessity to incorporate as many unnecessary and literally pointless actions as possible within the necessarily limited space of time that the descent allows.

The fact that humans have gone to such lengths and heights to prolong and decorate this brief interval seems to indicate the desire to do as much as possible to set aside the fact of gravity. It is certainly the case that the supreme moments in many sports seem to involve the principle of joyous ascent, as though to break for good with gravity. In fact, though, the absolute removal of gravity seems also to remove the tension, beauty and joy of the parabolic descent, in which one must be determined to lose, but to lose in the most playful way possible. The designation 'gravity play',[27] invented by Chris Baker of the Dangerous Sports Club in 1979 to encompass modern sports like bungee-jumping, skydiving, skysurfing, BASE jumping (parachute jumping from tall objects such as buildings or cliffs) and BMX acrobatics, seems apt. There is no tension in an indefinite interval. The manoeuvres of a hang-glider are not a maximally accented version of the movements of a diver or parachutist; they are playing an entirely different game.

Some recent developments in sport, prompted by its increasing visibility, suggest that the disciplined fostering of *agôn* need not be entirely at the cost of the disorderly principle of *ilinx*. In soccer, in particular, the scoring of goals (comparatively rare events, compared with other sports, on which a great deal may turn) has for some decades been accompanied by extravagant displays of festivity, which often depend upon the principles of sudden disorientation and the world turned upside down, just at the point at which one might expect the values of coordination and concentrated purpose to be asserted. Scorers of goals routinely execute handsprings and backflips, or may fling themselves to the ground, in a reversal of the expected gesture of arms spread and raised to the sky. Most tellingly of all, the careful quartering and quarantining of territorial position which characterizes modern soccer, with each player responsible for patrolling a particular zone of play, gives way to a tangle of limbs as the scoring team fling themselves on the scorer, in a wriggling mass of limbs and extremities. Here, the sleek victory-machine of the scorer's body has become the clownish, metamorphic chimera-body of the trickster.

In a number of sports, the scoring of goals or points is achieved by a triumphant grounding or touching down of the ball. In soccer, in which the goal acts as a surrogate ground, the motion is often completed by the player's ritual celebrations of the fact of scoring, which may involve a dramatic slide, either on the knees, or face down, with arms wide in a kind of magnificent, skidding prostration. Far from achieving height, the climax of the game is a kind of exaltation of abasement. Whatever is achieved in the time and space of play is achieved against the drag of time, fatigue and gravity, to which the players must eventually succumb. Victory is achieved over this succumbing not by disavowing it, in feeble spasms of levitation, but through the grandeur of *cadenza*, or dying fall. Rugby players have developed a whole repertoire of different forms of diving over the line to score a try, aiming, it seems, to prolong indefinitely the rapturous moment of mid-air suspension. (Since the advent of high-speed cameras the ideal seems to have become the perfectly horizontal dive, producing an image resembling Superman in flight.) There is another kind of dive, resorted to not only by the goalkeeper or fielder in various sports, but also by players of racket sports such as badminton and tennis; this is the dive, not of triumph, but of a kind of exultant desperation, that forces one to abandon the safe haven of uprightness and turn one's own body into a projectile. Again, prostration is mixed with splendour, as the diver attempts to occupy the impossible interval of pure movement and, taking the catch or making the volley at full stretch, to find a point of stasis within it.

When coaches map out sporting tactics and movements, their tendency is to break them up into simultaneous but separate actions – as though the playing of a game involved the aggregation of a number of independent movement tracks, as the assembling of a piece of music may involve the mixing together of different, parallel sound sources.

This involves a very considerable simplification of the way in which sporting movement in fact takes place. It translates into the simplified diagrams of position that are employed so mystifyingly in discussions of soccer strategy, which give the impression that players are meant to do nothing but patrol a small zone, out of which they never move. In fact, though, these positions are relative, not to the static pitch, but to the dynamic landscape of the play. Thus a team that actually plays with its defensive line just in front of the goal is courting disaster, since it gives the attacking team almost the whole length of the pitch in which to play. In fact, the defensive line should strive to play as far up the field as they can, since the need to avoid being caught offside will squeeze the opposing side into a much smaller space of play than they would wish. The movement-space of the game is often drastically different from the given space of the pitch. The movement-space stretches, contracts, warps and compounds that given space.

What is more, this movement-space is itself constantly in motion. This is to say more than that it is changeable, as a result of the changing dispositions of players that are constantly forming and reforming during play. It is also constantly in communication, being transmitted in the form of anticipation and responses from player to player. The movement involved in a sporting contest is therefore not to be understood as the simple aggregation of the different movements effected by all the different players, along with the ball, complex though this is, but as the intensive interaction of the players and their movements. With every movement that I make, say as a tennis player, executing a return from the baseline, I not only reach forward into the new position I wish to occupy, I also reach into my opponent's internal mirroring of that movement and his projection of its outcome. That reaching into what I guess my opponent will make of my projected movement becomes part of it. In a sense, the server and the returner are not opponents at all, in the sense that neither one simply faces up to the other, but intimately knitted copartners.

The player who successfully feints, at delivering a punch, bowling a ball, or hitting the ball in a particular direction, manipulates the fact that sporting movement is powerfully contagious. Not only is each individual player in advance of or aside from themselves in their movement, but those movements, actual or implied, also induce corresponding or reciprocal movements, which the feinting player himself must anticipate. The art of the feint is to outstrip these anticipations, to mire one's opponents in their own movements, by tempting them to make a move that will be equivalent in its predictability to standing still. Hence, perhaps, 'selling a dummy': by accepting the changeling pass, taking seriously a possibility that never in fact comes to pass, the purchaser of the dummy is themselves dummied, that is, turned from somebody capable of initiating movement freely on their own account to an entity which is merely acted upon, or moved passively from place to place. The ludic exquisiteness of the reversal comes from the fact that the player is dummied or 'wrong-footed', not by their slowness, but by their own effort to anticipate, to reach beyond the present moment. All movements in sport are mimetic compounds of this kind, in which movements are in the process of being transmitted back and forth by contagion and expectation. Every pace is a *pas-de-deux*.

five

Equipment

We have seen that the particular kinds of competitive physical exertion we know as sports require a specific place and a delimited time in which to play. This chapter begins from the recognition that many, if not most sports also require some kind of accessory equipment, or something to play with.

What does it mean when we say, of things like bats, clubs, balls and shuttlecocks, that we play *with* them? Roland Barthes sees this relationship to playthings as entirely antagonistic, seeing the struggle against things in sport as part of a new competition between humans and things, rather than between humans and other humans, or other species:

> in sport, man does not confront man directly. There enters between them an intermediary, a stake, a machine, a puck, or a ball. And this thing is the very symbol of things: it is in order to possess it, to master it, that one is strong, adroit, courageous ... to this question of the ancient duels, sport gives a new meaning: for man's excellence is sought here only in relation to things. Who is the best man to overcome the resistance to things, the immobility of nature? Who is the best to work the world, to give it to men ... to all men?[1]

Certainly, the things of sport may sometimes seem to take on the role of the antagonist – for example in throwing sports, in which the hammer, the javelin, the discus or the caber provide a kind of resistance to be overcome. But these objects are never quite or entirely the things against which one strives. Strangely, if one exerts all one's force and skill on the object in question, in order to throw it as far as possible, one is also in a sense throwing with it. One does not merely throw the javelin, one uses it to make one's throw. In a sense one might be said to use it against itself. While remaining one object, the javelin is nevertheless divided into two sets of aspects. The one consists of the inertial properties that it shares with other physical objects, and which represent a barrier or resistance to throwing – weight, shape, texture and the other things that obtrude, obnubilate or otherwise seem to object to the actions of the thrower. The other consists of the properties which assist the thrower – the capacity of the javelin to cleave through the air, the affordance it offers to the hand and arm. Playing with a sports object opens up this kind of play of functions within it, separating them into those that assist and those that resist the aim of the sport. So one 'plays with' such an object in two senses – playing with it as what we call a plaything, asserting one's will and freedom of action over it, and playing with it as one plays with a playmate. The two senses are clearly distinguished in a sentence like this: 'He won the match he played with him so easily that he was just playing with him.' The meanings of the two kinds of 'playing with' may be clearly separable, but it is less easy to separate the instances to which they apply.

When we refer to the equipment that we play with in sports, we are not referring for the most part to clothing. Indeed, the idea that the playing of sports requires special kinds of clothing is itself relatively recent. Schoolboys regularly played sports in their ordinary day clothes well into the nineteenth century, and, though pugilists would strip to the waist, and the glowing blacksmith would doubtless roll up his sleeves before he ran up to bowl, for the most part the idea that the playing of sport requires special kinds of outfit or clothing equipment is a phenomenon of the late nineteenth century. Sports clothing has broadly three uses; to provide comfort, to enhance performance and to protect against injury. All of these may come in time to have a central importance, such that the playing of the sport seems unthinkable without them. But there is nevertheless a distinction to be made between the apparel and equipment of which we may make use in pursuing the sport (shorts, running spikes, gloves, face masks, gum shields), and those things through which we pursue the sport. The former are accessory, the latter essential. It may be both usual and advisable for me to wear a snow suit, gloves and goggles when skiing, but if I decide to ski naked or in a nurse's uniform, I am still recognizably, if somewhat perversely, *skiing*. But if I decide to dispense with any kind of equipment affixed to, and substantially longer than my two feet, designed to allow me to slide over snow and ice, I am simply no longer skiing at all, but skating, snowboarding or just skidding. Skis are not optional or dispensable extras in the practice we know as skiing. Similar conditions attach to the ball in soccer, the mallet in croquet and the racket in tennis. Playing with these things needs to be understood as playing the sport through or by means of them, rather than merely playing along with them.

Naturally, not all sports involve this kind of equipment. Racing sports such as running and swimming may require no more than the body and the measured extent of space or time in which and against which they occur. But for those sports in which equipment is essential to the very definition of the sport, there is a deep, purposive and complex relationship between the one who plays and what he or she uses to play with. These are sports in which certain kinds of equipment have passed across from an accessory to an essential condition. Pads and gloves evolved in cricket at the end of the nineteenth century in order to protect batsmen from injury, but they have subsequently become essential components of batting technique, their place and function being determined in the rules of the game. Thus, a batsman can employ the pad as a quasi-bat, both to keep the ball away from his stumps and to score runs.

Heidegger uses the word *Zeug* to refer to material objects that we use for particular purposes, a word that has often been translated with the sporting word *equipment*.[2] What sporting equipment like bats and balls has in common with hammers (Heidegger's canonical example) and screwdrivers is that the equipment in question is *material-for*. A hammer is a material object that is designed for or adapted to the purpose of driving, compressing or otherwise modifying other material objects by means of repeated blows. I can, assuredly, use a hammer for other things – for keeping my plans in place on windy day, for example – but then I am not using it as a hammer; that is, something to hammer with. The same is true of a cricket bat, which, in point of fact, is sometimes adapted for use as a kind of hammer, when the handle is employed to tamp the stumps back down into the ground after the wicket has been broken by the ball. The parallel seems clear: the hammer is used to hammer things with, the bat is used to hit things (cricket balls) with, and both can sometimes be used for other things.

There seems to me, however, to be an instructive difference between the equipmentality (would that there were another word) of hammers and cricket bats. If I use a hammer, I perform with it a function that might perfectly well be performed by some other implement. There is nothing in the definition of a hammer's use that absolutely prescribes its use in a given situation, if something better, easier, safer, more powerful or more subtle were to become available. It may be an essential part of the definition of a hammer that it be designed or regarded as being for the purposes of hammering, but our use of the hammer to hammer things with is contingent; that is, arising from and depending on variable sets of conditions. Indeed, it is part of the definition of a hammer that it might be possible or even advisable to replace it with something else in certain conditions. Now I think we should see in this a general condition of all definitions of instrumentality – namely that there could always be something else that might do the job as well, and could therefore be substituted without loss, and even with advantage. If the use of the thing called 'a hammer' in particular is specifically required, or of one kind of hammer in particular, then it is likely to be as a result of extra rules or conventions that apply in specific contexts and don't really have much to do with hammers or hammering at all – conventions that might govern the size and composition of the hammers used in conjunction with gavels by High Court judges and chairmen of meetings, for example. So, in general terms, a hammer is the thing to use when you want something (anything will do, but a hammer is best) to hammer with.

When I use a cricket bat, things seem very different. Where hammering does not absolutely require hammers, cricket depends upon the use of cricket bats. Where a hammer is merely the best, but not the only thing I can use for hammering, a cricket bat is specifically enjoined for the playing of cricket. If I come to the crease unprovided with anything that resembles a cricket bat, no matter how superbly it may perform a cricket bat's functions, then not only am I not playing cricket, nobody else is either. You can use a cricket bat for many other purposes than hitting cricket balls, but it is nevertheless part of the definition of a cricket bat that it is the thing that, if you wish what you do with it to count as batting in cricket, you must use. Not that the nature of a cricket bat itself is exhaustively specified. Certain aspects of the cricket bat are clearly defined, sometimes as a result of experimental challenges mounted by players, but others allow for variation. The laws of cricket require for example that the overall length of the bat shall not be more than 38 inches or 96.5 centimetres, that the length of the handle shall not exceed 52 per cent of the overall length of the bat and that the width of the bat shall not exceed 4.25 in/10.8 cm at its widest part. Until 1979, though it was usual for bats to be made of wood, and traditionally, since the nineteenth century, of willow (and even more specifically, *Salix alba caerulea*, the variety of white willow known as cricket bat willow), there was no rule specifying this until December 1979, when the Australian fast bowler Denis Lillee began his innings at a Test match against England in Perth with a bat made of aluminium. He was forced to change it for a wooden one after the English players complained that it was damaging the ball, and thereafter the rules were changed to specify that bats must be made of wood (though still with no specific requirement as to the kind of wood, or indeed woods). And there remains no specification at all as regards the weight of the bat.

Why can cricket only be played with a regulation cricket bat, and badminton with a regulation shuttlecock? I think the reason for this is that sports and games which are played with material things do indeed involve as part of their function a play with them, now in the sense of an exploration or actualization of their possibilities, a practical investigation of how much play – in the sense of tolerable variation, as in the play of a joint – they can afford. You play cricket with a cricket bat because part of the purpose of playing cricket is to see what can be done with a cricket bat in cricket-playing circumstances (namely, somebody bowling at you balls intended to knock over your stumps). This means that the objects used in sports are never merely ancillary to the purpose of playing the game, never merely the thing you happen to have lighted on with which to play it. The playing of the game is the playing of the game with that object, and the object of the game is therefore in part always to undertake a forensic trial of the object's possibilities. One plays with the object in order to put its properties and possibilities in play, to discover and determine what play there is in it.

Subject, Object, Project

This is a different kind of relationship from that which we usually feel we have with objects. Normally objects are thought of, in a simple-ish dichotomy, either as obstacles to human purposes, or as instruments through which to achieve them. Either the object is the absolute other or opposite to the subject who must overcome its resistance, or it is drawn into the sphere of the subject, becoming a prosthetic extension of the arm or foot. The point of the sporting object is precisely to complicate this simple alternative.

Is there a different kind of play with sporting objects than with playthings more generally? Once again, the important differentiation that makes something a sport rather than a game is the fact of physical exertion. To be sure, the sporting object often provides a kind of inertia against which the sportsman strives: a golf ball, tennis ball or soccer ball may all be driven at certain times with maximum force, in order to turn the static object into a projectile. But the aim of this is never to destroy the object, which must be conserved, even as it is subject to extreme, even deforming pressure. The point seems to to be to try to disclose the possibilities of the object, not by testing it to destruction but rather by, as it were, 'persisting' it to the limit. In this way, the principle of physical exertion is extended from the players to the instruments of their play, even as those instruments are the means by which the players exert themselves. We should remember that the word exert has a core meaning of thrusting or pushing out, emitting or exhibiting. The thing that exerts or is exerted is expressed, unbound from its merely in-itself condition in order to show what potentialities it has.

Many sports, and perhaps even the majority, involve a contrast between projectors and projectiles. Often the projector can be the human body, or some part of it specialized to a projective purpose – the hand in fives, the foot and head in soccer. But human beings have also delegated their projective functions to various projective or percussive instruments – clubs, sticks, rackets, mallets. The job of the projector is to convey projective force to a projectile – a shuttlecock, puck, ball. Both projector and projectile are objective, in that they do not themselves have will or intention like the player who employs them, but they do not seem to be the same kind of object. The projector is, so to speak, a subjectivized object, an object that has moved over to the side of the subject, and that therefore literally colludes with it. The projectile is an objectified object, if such an apparent nonsense may for a moment be entertained – an object the purpose of which is to be entirely done-to. It is a pleasing surmise that, given that the very word *object* preserves in it the idea of being thrown (*ob*-, against and *iacere*, to throw), there may be an implicitly sporting kind of contention embodied in our way of thinking about things in general.

It is usual to regard projective instruments as prostheses, auxiliary extensions of human powers and capacities. But this would be to forget the distinction I offered a little earlier between equipment, or objects-for, in the general sense and the particular kinds of object of which we make use, and the particular kinds of use we make of them, in sport. For the golf club is not really a way of improving on an action that we might conceivably perform in some other, more immediate or unaccommodated way. Although golf clubs have been subject to many changes and enhancements over the centuries, and continue to evolve in fascinating and unpredictable ways, the first golf club was not devised as a better way of propelling a ball round a course – after one had tried kicking it, for example, or nudging it along with one's nose. For there just was no game of golf until there was something that performed the office of a golf club. And that office was not just to extend or enhance powers, as is usually the case with a prosthesis (prostheses may be awkward sometimes, but nobody wears an artificial leg to reduce their mobility or a pair of spectacles to impair their vision, or, if they do, they are not using them as prostheses). The projective instruments employed in a sport are indeed extensions of human powers, allowing us to clout a tennis ball much harder and faster, and to propel a golf ball very much further than we could ever throw or kick it. But they are also restrictions, and play an important part in the apparatus of unnecessary restriction that is essential to every sport. The beauties and efficiencies of their design are there to minimize the fact of the impediment that they essentially and in themselves are.

It is for this reason too that that we should allow no simple identification between the projective instruments of sport and their users, or assimilation of the former to the latter, such as we find, for example, in remarks such as these:

> The experience of the appropriation of sports implements into the phenomenal self . . . 'tells' me that my being extends beyond my skin and out into and with the objects of the world. It 'tells' me that my personal identity as free results partially from a kind of special relationship with the objects of the world which makes them a positively enhancing part of me rather than apart from me.[3]

But I do not merely appropriate a sports implement, or simply and wholly implement myself through it. For we have seen that an important part of the function of a projective object is to restrict the possibilities of its projector, to limit and discipline their freedom, even encouraging them towards the condition of an object themselves, through training routines and repetitive drills that channel and constrain the repertoire of their movements. Left to my own hapless devices, I would simply swipe across the line of the ball's flight with my tennis racket, flipping the racket with my wrist, in a quick, convulsive, inefficient movement, and therefore miss the ball most of the time. I must learn to stand side-on rather than face-on to the ball, to draw the racket back much further, and much earlier than feels necessary, to transfer my body-weight from my back foot to my right foot as I hit through the line of the ball. I must learn not to tighten my grasp on the handle at the point of impact, as every so-called instinct tells me to, but slightly to loosen it: only then will the ugly twang of the strings become the deep, satisfying, dry *pock* of the well-struck ball. If my racket eventually becomes an extension of my arm, it is only after my whole body has been remodelled and rebalanced, in a series of subtle adjustments that take account of the predilections of my racket in the first place. If I wish the racket to become me, I must first become it, or become the kind of me that it requires and will most readily respond to. *Wo es war, soll ich werden*, said Freud: where it was, there shall I be.[4] This applies well to the situation in which an object stands in for, or stands out in front of some organ or function of the body – the club, the bat and the racket that, according to one etymology, derives from *rachette*, the palm of the hand, or the *rascette*, the carpus or wrist-bone. But there is another replacement given in Freud's formula: where there was I, let it instruct and permeate me. In fact, as Michel Serres has suggested, there is a continual cycle of transformations and exchanges, as human beings objectify themselves in tools and apparatus of all kinds, and then, in an answering movement, assume or assimilate those externalized objects back into their bodies.[5] Serres's leading example is the wheel, which he suggests derives from the rotary movements of the body in walking and running, is externalized in the form of wheels and tyres, and is then reinternalized when we learn to ride bicycles. To learn to ride a bicycle means

> to rediscover in the lower body those wheels which it has thrown out into the world, and whose fortunes have improved and whose evolution has developed at a distance from the one who no longer recognises them as its own. Learning to ride a bicycle consists in sensing these, assimilated into the bike, through the rim and the pedal, and, in the same way, sensing that we have never walked or run otherwise than through them, for we had invented upright-ness, straightness and carriage, arising from the circular torques of the legs, well before we ever met them in objects, in mobile equilibrium.[6]

One of the strangest things in sport, though it is not unique to it, is the effect of the follow-through. If you think merely of hitting the ball, whether with stick, club or racket, its flight will be hard to pre-dict and control. Instead, you must concentrate, not on the point at which motion is imparted, but on the line of flight you wish to impart to the ball. If you watch a golf player following the drive, they always follow the guidance offered by Harry Vardon, six times winner of the US Open, in his *The Complete Golfer* of 1908:

> I do not approve of keeping the eye fixed upon the place where the ball lay, so that the grass is seen after the ball has departed. Keep your eye on the ball until you have hit it, but no longer. You cannot follow through properly with a long shot if your

eye remains fastened on the ground. Hit the ball, and then let your eye pick it up in its flight as quickly as possible.[7]

Similarly, with a rugby player following the drop-kick at goal, you can see clearly their efforts to will the ball to stay aloft just a little longer, to tuck in just a little to the left. David Beckham, gifted in his youth with the extraordinary ability to loop a football thirty or forty yards and land it with perfect pace, spin and bounce at the feet of an oncoming striker, seemed to let his right foot hang in the air for a second or so after he had despatched the pass, as though the ball were still attached to it by a long piece of elastic, and his foot were a rudder making a few final adjustments.

I used to think this behaviour was purely magical, and it does indeed obey the 'law of participation' operative, according to Lucien Lévy-Bruhl, among tribal peoples, according to which 'objects, or articles manufactured by man, always present themselves charged with mystic properties' and 'objects, beings, phenomena can be . . . both themselves and something other than themselves'.[8] Willing the ball to move towards its target seems to testify to a belief that I have not merely kicked the ball, but forced some small portion of myself into its substance, that can continue, until its power is dissipated, to steer the ball. I was, and still am, somewhat, rather scornful of this sort of magic. If I have taken an exam, or have had an interview, and am waiting for the outcome, nothing that I do in the interim can affect the result which is now, as we say, out of my hands, though most of us under those circumstances feel under pressure to wait for the outcome in particular ways, lest thoughts or actions jinx it. We all know that the piano player who lightly lifts the finger from the key it has just struck, like a father gently pulling away from the child who has fallen asleep on him, cannot really make any difference to the sound of the note that has just been played, since the hammer has already struck, and recoiled from, the wire, and the sound of the contact has already begin to dissipate. This view is articulated by P. A. Vaile, who criticized golfers 'for thinking that the follow-through has an influence on the flight of the ball, although obviously nothing that the club does after impact can affect the carry', and provided the following, impeccably reasonable proof: 'Supposing now for the sake of argument that a stray bullet had caught the head of his club, at say six inches after the ball had left it and had smashed it to pieces, the result of his stroke would have been just as good.'[9]

And yet we continue to believe in the exchange of qualities between objects and persons and in the persistence of a relation between projector and projectile, in something like the principle that quantum physics calls 'entanglement'. I noticed myself when I was young that the awkward, ineffective players (I was usually one) would stab, lunge and flail at the ball, through a mistaken belief in the principles of physics: namely, that everything is concentrated in the point of impact. The good players seemed naturally not to be economical (as one is so often told to be), in their stroke-making, or in their kicking of the ball, but extravagantly exaggerated. Where the poor players fixated with fiendish intensity on the point of impact, these others seemed to feel, as James Braid articulated it in 1914, that 'the despatching of the ball from the tee by the driver in the downward swing is merely an incident of the whole business . . . for . . . the success of the drive is not only made by what has gone before, but it is also due largely to the course taken by the club after the ball has been hit'.[10]

It is perhaps not so much, or not only, that the player and the ball get entangled in the process of imparting the impact, as that time gets convoluted. It is not really the case that what matters most is what happens after the impact, but it does seem to be plausible that, with the golfer, footballer or pianist, the execution of the stroke in the first place is affected by the anticipation of the follow-through. So the anticipated future of the stroke in part loops back to determine its past. The shape of this loop in time matches exactly the shape of the loop of logic that applies to magic. Magic doesn't actually work in practice, which is governed entirely by actual (practical) considerations, but the belief that magic does work, and the practical enactment of that belief, can in fact be highly effective. Perhaps there is no absolute differentiation between magic and material, since magic is always, to some degree, part of the fact of the matter.

A similar complexity attaches to the projectile objects of sport, even though I just now said that their role is to act as objectified objects. The point of a golf ball or tennis ball is assuredly in large part to be available to be hit towards a target. But all projectiles, even balls, have certain properties which prevent them from ever being purely passive. They have uneven properties, which will themselves be activated differentially by differing circumstances – soccer players must expect balls to fly further when they are playing at altitude, for example. These properties solicit and answer to the particular and different kinds of force that may be applied to them.

Sporting objects can also exhibit striking reversibility. When released from the hand of a Jeff Thomson or Wasim Akram, a cricket ball is unmistakeably and terrifyingly a projectile, but one that preserves in it the subjective intent of the projector, since its purpose is itself to act as a projector, by hitting the stumps, or the legs of the batsman defending them. The aim of the batsman, if or when, around half a second later, he succeeds in laying a bat on the ball that has been bowled at him, is to change this projective object into a projectile one.

The point of projectiles is, of course, that they be projected – thrown, kicked or hit. In some sports, the primary aim is just to project the object as far as possible. However, the direction of this projection is never indifferent, even if there is an obvious difference between sports like golf, in which accuracy is as important as distance, and the discus, where it is really only the safety of spectators or bystanders that determines that the direction of the throw be restricted. Nevertheless, the very word 'project' suggests that all such launchings or propulsions are really in some general sense forwards or in front of us, insofar as these are the directions in which we feel we strive to transcend ourselves into what is not yet; if a new sport were to arise of throwing a javelin or caber as far as you could behind you, the fact that records in the event would be set and striven against would put them figuratively in front of the participants as standards to be matched or transcended. This is to say that the trajectory of a projectile is always forwards, into the future.

However, the point of most projectiles is precisely that, that they are aimed at a particular point: a soccer ball must be kicked between the posts, a basketball dropped through the hoop, a tennis ball hit into and then out of the court. Projectiles are rarely, therefore, simply thrown, kicked, or hit *away*: they are also aimed *towards* and *at*. This helps to answer the difficult, larger question of what the aim of sports in general might be. It is often said that games do not have any other aim than the playing of the game itself, but the fact that most modern sports are competitive exercises, in which playing means playing with the intention of winning, means that all sports in fact have aims. These aims are very specific and seemingly very various. Wittgenstein thought that trying to establish the essence of a game was misguided, since although there are family resemblances between games, there is no one form that they all share.[11] I am not sure that we should give up so readily on deriving some parsimonious definition of the aim of sports.

To begin with, perhaps we may plausibly distinguish three forms of sport, in terms of the different ways of winning they exemplify. First of all, there are races and competitions of distance and weight, in which the aim is to be the fastest or strongest, as measured by a length of ground, a bar set at a certain height, or a certain known weight. Then there are goal-based sports, like soccer, in which the aim of the game is to penetrate the territory of the opposing team, the goal being, as it were, their citadel or innermost heart. Finally, there are keep-up games, of which the best example is probably volleyball. Here the aim of the game is to prevent the opposing side from playing, where 'playing' may often mean keeping the ball away from the ground, or in motion in the allowable area of play. A good spike in volleyball or slam in tennis will rightly and expressively be called 'unplayable'; for indeed, in these games, to lose means to be rendered repeatedly unable to play and finally to be put out of the game altogether. You play with somebody, or something, by trying to prevent them playing with you.

On the face of it, it would be hard to assimilate these three kinds of game to each other, or to reduce them to some more essential underlying shared end. Unless, perhaps, we follow the hint contained in that last word, and think of all games as in a sense aimed at the ending of the play. There are, of course, many ways in which play can be discontinued or abolished, the easiest being for one of the parties simply to refuse to take any further part. But it is rarely enough for a game simply to be aborted or brought to an end. For the purpose of games is to bring play to an end in the allowable terms of the game.

We may borrow the terms of *Beyond the Pleasure Principle*, in which Freud speculates richly and riskily on the operations of the death drive, a concept that he introduces for the first time in this essay. Freud assumes, with magnificent gloominess, that the aim of all organisms must fundamentally be to die, since this is the only way to ensure the reduction of tension to an absolute minimum, or the attainment of the state of absolute equilibrium that, for Freud, is the source and aim of all pleasure. But the fact that organisms have become so complex, congregating together so many different time-scales, phasings and periodicities, means that it is not an easy matter for them simply to switch themselves off. Like a modern computer that needs to undertake a complex series of epilogue operations before it can be shut down, the complex organism finds itself having to go through various enforced detours in its effort to achieve death, or unbirth (the condition signalled by the 'denatus', died, of some Latin epitaphs). This, Freud suggests, is the explanation of 'the organism's puzzling determination (so hard to fit into any context) to maintain its own existence in the face of every obstacle'. The instinct to preserve life and to assert oneself in the face of death, which one might well see symbolized and purified in the struggles of competitive sports, are therefore no more than

> component instincts whose function it is to assure that the organism shall follow its own path to death, and to ward off any possible ways of returning to inorganic existence other than those which are immanent in the organism itself . . . What we are left with is the fact that the organism wishes to die only in its own fashion . . . Hence arises the paradoxical situation that the living organism struggles most energetically against events (dangers, in fact) which might help it to attain its life's aim rapidly – by a kind of short-circuit.[12]

Perhaps we may suppose that games and sports similarly strain for cessation, not by breaking off play, but by going on and through with it. The aim of sports is therefore the death of the game in the game's own terms. The mediators of this paradoxical duality are sports objects, and preeminently balls. The ball in sports has attracted some symbolic interpretations, most notably that of Robert W. Henderson, who maintains that, whether standing for the head of Osiris, or for the sun, the source of all life, 'in ancient Egypt and throughout the adjacent lands, the ball represented the idea of fertility, the life-giving principle'.[13] I think this can be accepted only if the fertility and life in question are the open possibilities of the game, which would be to say that the ball symbolizes the kind of life the game itself has and sustains.

This is not a straightforward matter. For objects such as balls are in fact both dead and alive, inanimate objects that are infused with will and life, principles of intention that have been frozen into physical form. Michel Serres has taken the ball in sports as the emblem of what he calls the 'quasi-object'. In one sense, he means by this an object that is not quite, or not just, an object, since it oscillates between objectivity and subjectivity, depending on whether it is sitting motionless on the penalty spot, or is being propelled at the feet of an attacking forward. But, more than this, the ball itself brings about a flaring and flickering, on and off, in and out, of subjectivity among the players. When I have possession, I am lit up as a subject – though I am just the temporary carrier of the collective subjectivity of the team. When I pass the ball, I transfer that light to another. When the ball comes to rest, it illuminates an 'I'; when it is in motion, it constitutes the 'we' of the team, or of the game. No simple partition of the 'I', the 'we' and the 'it' is possible, for these three phases are themselves always emerging out of movement and passage:

> This quasi-object that is a marker of the subject is an astonishing constructor of intersubjectivity. We know, through it, how and when we are subjects and when and how we are no longer subjects. 'We': what does that mean? We are precisely the fluctuating moving back and forth of 'I.' The 'I' in the game is a token exchanged. And this passing, this network of passes, these vicariances of subjects, weave the collection . . . The 'we' is made by the bursts and occultations of the 'I.' The 'we' is made by the passing of the 'I.' By exchanging the 'I.' And by substitution and vicariance of the 'I.'[14]

Serres's point is dramatized very well by the Spot the Ball competitions that were popular in British newspapers in the 1970s. Readers were asked to study a photograph of a soccer match, from which the ball had been removed, and to guess from the positions, expressions and attitudes of the players where the ball was. The entrant who put a cross in the correct position won a prize. Here, we might seem to have the opposite of the situation just described by Serres, in which it is the ball which differentially illuminates the players, for now it is the players who reveal (or, in many cases) conceal the presence of the ball. There may be a distant reminiscence here of the practice of concealing the ball that was evidently sometimes employed as a diversion in medieval games of football, and survives as a tactic in both rugby and American football. But the Spot the Ball competition confirms the fluid interrelationship of players and objects; the ball is an indexical sign of possession and control; remove the ball, and the players become indexical signs of the ball. An interesting confirmation of this fluidity is the fact that, although the position of the ball could have been verified precisely by simply restoring it to the photograph from which it has been removed, the competition was always judged by a panel of experts who decided where it ought to have been (this because it is not legally possible to gamble on an event that has already happened).

Goals

Regarded as Serres's quasi-object, the ball is a mediator between the animate and inanimate, the life instincts and the death instincts. And there is a more direct sense in which this may be so. For in most games balls exist to be hit, sometimes with maximum force, as though absolutely to have done with it and put paid to the possibility of play with it. Sports writers sometimes speak of tennis players hitting the ball so hard that they seemed never to want to see it again; in baseball and cricket, the lofting of the ball out of the ground is the supreme achievement of the striker. The point of hitting the ball is to propel it out of the field, or court, to put it to the symbolic death of being put out of play. The ball that is not in play is often called a 'dead ball'. The golfer aims to sink the ball into its hole. Even in pacific games like pool or snooker, the aim of the game is to drop the balls out of sight into the pockets. And yet one can never really hit the ball out of play. In different ways, the ball comes back, like a boomerang, thereby preventing that premature cessation of the game that might otherwise result from the mere accident of having lost the ball.

Perhaps the most elementary game that depends upon the reversibility of throwing away and returning home is the ancient sport of

Irish road bowling, in which an 800 gram ball or 'bullet' is thrown around a course of several kilometres in length, with the player taking the fewest throws winning.[15] Here, the crucial role of the bullet is clear, in constituting the work of the play, in the sense of work derived from physics, of a mass that must be moved through a distance, and thereby constituting the relay of exertion that brings a player home to himself. John Newbery's *Little Pretty Pocket Book* offered in 1760 a brief characterization of the playing of baseball and a moral:

The *Ball* once struck off,
Away flies the *Boy*
To the next destin'd Post,
And then Home with Joy.
    MORAL.
Thus *Britons* for Lucre
Fly over the Main;
But, with Pleasure transported,
Return back again.[16]

The pleasure which transports the player is a pleasure in transport itself, the transport away from, and back to the self. Like Freud's complex organism, striving to die only in its own fashion, by going through the detour of a long life lived all the time towards the consummation of death, and in the service of a death drive that recruits for its devious purposes all the ruses and resources of the will-to-live, the ball aims to die or be put out of play only in its own fashion; that is, only in terms of the consummation that the game itself allows. So, no matter how hard or how far you hit the golf ball, it must be played from where it lies. No matter that your shot on goal is sliced up into row z of the stands – the game will continue when the ball comes back. In my youth, one would have to wait for the ball to bounced over the heads of the crowd back on to the pitch – now, a series of identical balls is available to ensure that play can be resumed straight away. Putting the ball out of play does not dispose of it, since putting the ball out of play is a tactical move within the play, or a contingency of which play takes account. That is, the only way to put the ball fully and irrevocably out of play is to sink it into the designated hole, or to bury it, as the expression goes, in the net for a goal. The only way out of the game is through the narrow aperture that lies, almost inaccessibly, at its core. The game itself is the necessary detour for the route of the game that is its goal. The fact that the scoring of goals has now itself been made reversible – though in the earliest games, the scoring of one goal was usually enough to bring the game to an end – is a sign of how complex and convoluted the relations are between playing and ceasing, living and dying in play. The goal that might once and for all have put paid to play is now just another, not entirely conclusive phase of it.

This is made more complex by the fact that many sports involve a false goal or anti-goal, in the form of the catch. If the ball that you have lofted is caught by a fielder in baseball or cricket, then you have not consummated your innings, but are out – that is, you are dismissed from the play rather than yourself transcending it. The fact that a lofted ball that represents an easy catch is sometimes said to drop 'straight down the fielder's throat' indicates the kind of symbolic jeopardy involved in being caught. Instead of completing your trajectory and bringing you home to yourself (it is a compelling piece of logic that hitting the ball irretrievably out of the stadium is what enables the batting side in baseball to score what is called a 'home' run), joining with the parabola of its flight your effort and your aim, the catch turns you into the relay that loops together the opposing side's aim and outcome.

Going out and coming home are related in such complex ways that direction becomes uncertain. The quickest and most effective route to goal may often in fact be the seemingly longest way round, and Polonius's advice holds good: 'thus do we of wisdom and of reach, / With windlasses and with assays of bias, / By indirections find directions out' (*Hamlet*, II.i). The sporting object is designed to follow this devious path in two opposite directions at once, in which out is in and away is a way of getting home. The rules of cricket as explained to an uncomprehending spectator embody this reversibility of inside and outside very well:

> There are two sides, one out in the field, the other side in. Each player goes out to bat and stays out until he's out, at which point he comes back in. When they are all out, the side that

has been out goes in, and the side that has been in tries to get the other side that is now in out.

Freud noted this essential reversibility in the game he saw his grandson playing that has become known as the *fort-da* game. Freud writes that the child would repeatedly throw a cotton reel attached to a piece of thread into his curtained cot with the cry 'o-o-o', approximating the German *fort*, away, then joyfully reel it back in with the cry '*da*' – there, or back again.[17] Freud points to the principle of mastery involved in the game – the mastery, he proposes, by the child of his mother's periodic absences, which could be mimicked and thus controlled by symbolization. This reversibility could itself be reversed, for Freud points to another, more aggressive version of the game in which the toy is not meant to come back, or even meant not to come back. The child would angrily throw a toy on to the floor, crying 'Go to the fwont', for which Freud offers an Oedipal explanation: 'He had heard at that time that his absent father was "at the front" and was far from regretting his absence; on the contrary he made it quite clear that he had no desire to be disturbed in his sole possession of his mother.'[18] One might say that there is a difference between the reality symbolized by the play and the play itself, namely that, in reality, nothing is truly reversible, and nothing ever quite comes back, while in symbolic play, things always can be reversed, because repeated. But the two games themselves represent, taken together, variants of each other and are therefore (and, this time, for Freud rather than for his grandson), a kind of play, or alternation, between two kinds of game, the reversible game of coming back and the irreversible game of staying away.

This in turn implies that there is a meta-game involved here, and perhaps in the playing of all games. For one plays, not just with the particular things that may be symbolized by the objects in the game, but also with the powers of playing itself, as it yo-yos between reversibility and irreversibility. Playing the game means trying to stop playing it, by making it impossible for your opponent to return the ball; but, if your opponent does succeed in blocking or parrying the shot, or even in returning it with redoubled force, they may begin a rally, from French *re-*, again and *ally*, from Latin *ligare*, to join together. The thing we call a rally is, like the alligator, whose name derives from the same root, a succession of joints, a series of joinings formed from partings, a suturing made of severances. Originally, the term *rally* as applied to sport was a borrowing from military usage, and signified a recovery or mustering of forces against a significant deficit. Gradually, following what seems to be the inexorable logic of games, that they tend to find ways to multiply forms of reversibility, the rally has come to mean, in tennis and other racket sports, an extended exchange of shots. The fact that, in the rally, it is the very effort to end the rally that extends it, repeats the logic of in and out, and home and away, that generates and is regenerated by the playing of the game.

Bouncing Back

There are many sporting objects, but we may say that the essential object, the object to which all sporting objects tend and approximate, is the ball. In a sense, one might say that the ball is not one object, but a kind of abstract or compound of many other kinds of sporting object. The ball has two essential features. The first is its perfectly spherical shape. The second is its elasticity, and associated indestructibility.

The spherical shape of the ball embodies at once the principles of uniformity and of unpredictability. A shape traced on any part of the surface of a perfect sphere can be lifted off and fitted exactly to any other part of its surface. The ball embodies and signifies the indifference of its differences, and even perhaps the indifference of the difference between signification and embodiment. This uniformity has taken a long time to achieve. There were at least five kinds of ball in use among the Greeks and Romans. There was a ball made of compressed wool or hair, known as a *pila*, which was often used for handball in courts, and so would have had some bounce. A *harpasta* was used for a game like rugby, and probably did not have much bounce. There were also balls made of glass and stone, presumably used for rolling games like skittles. In a game called *paganica* (the 'peasant game'), the ball was hit with a curved stick. A ball called a *trigonalis* was used in a triangular ball game. The Romans also had a ball made of an inflated bladder, known as a *follis*.[19]

One of the things that had to happen for the uniform ball to co-evolve was the invention of the lawn mower by Edwin Beard Budding in 1830, which made it possible to achieve a predictably even surface for the ball to travel across.[20] The absolute flatness of the pitch is a kind of topological twin to the uniformity of the sphere: the sphere, as it were, rolled out. But modern sport also depends upon the appearance in Europe of a substance unknown to it before its violent acquaintance with the cultures of the New World. Cortes reported on balls made of rubber that he had seen being used for sport at the court of Montezuma, and was impressed by their superior bounciness when compared with the inflated balls in use in Europe.[21] Oddly, almost three centuries were to elapse before the many possibilities of rubber, made from the dried sap from a number of different South American trees, became apparent. It was not until Thomas Hancock, building on the work of Charles Goodyear, patented the vulcanization process in 1844, which impregnated the rubber with sulphur to ensure that it retained its properties across a range of temperatures (early rubber products cracked in the cold and melted in the heat), that rubber entered decisively and definingly into modern life.

Many cultures have celebrated the principles of spring and resilience to be found in living tissue, but the nineteenth century saw the beginning of a world built increasingly around the possibilities of the artificial kinds of life embodied in manufactured elasticity. The nineteenth-century physicists P. G. Tait and W. J. Steele gave the name 'coefficient of restitution' to the bounciness of an object – that is, the ratio of the speed of approach of an object to a collision with another object to the speed of its recoil.[22] Coefficients of restitution come out in the range between 0 and 1, where 0 would be the absolute inelasticity of an object that came to a dead halt when it collided, and 1 would be the absolute elasticity of an object that recoiled with the same velocity as it approached, with no loss of energy at all. We can say that the coefficient of restitution of the modern world increased markedly after the wide diffusion of rubber.

Michel Serres has suggested that the human body is characterized by a certain capacity for stretching, and an innate predilection for stretching beyond what is native to it:

> Without this superductility, we could not grab, on the mountain face, those out of reach handholds, nor could we vary the ways of grasping them, direct or inverted; without this

margin, who could dance, what yogi could meditate? Manual dexterity, in work or art, draws upon it. Reaching up, or pretension to it, remains proper to man . . . Beyond the force that pulls, the effort of stretching plays on this supplement of length and angle, variable yet limited, limited yet variable: a little more, just a little . . . Thanks to this, we do what we can't do, attain the inaccessible, retrieve the ill-placed, extract and unblock the inaccessible, skirt obliqueness. The body teaches us this surplus, in which all excess is born, whether perverse or divine. It knows how to go beyond and elsewhere. It is a fine proof of our potential.[23]

Sport is one of the arenas in which this definitive exertion, this extension of habit and the inhabiting of extension, is enacted. Rubber and the other elastic substances that have extended the range and increased the variability of modern sports tune up our reach and responsiveness, while also seeming to imitate the actions of extension and recoil that they themselves stimulate. The ball that bounces extends out into the world the principle of muscular extension itself. Stretching can be torment as well as exhilaration, but rubber represents a kind of ideal and inexhaustible resilience. For balls to embody the principle of reversibility, they must be able to survive the most violent concussion. Rubber balls could absorb force without being terminally damaged by it, precisely because they could give back that force.

So the importance of rubber was that it actualized the essential reversibility of values and the sovereign value of reversibility that sports explore. The increased uniformity of balls, along with their increased resilience and more regular bounce, meant that they could approach to the condition of pure and absolute reversibility. This meant an increase simultaneously in the skill of players and the control they could exercise over the ball, and new forms of unpredictability, the most important of which were the many arts of spin and swerve. Balls of variable composition and unpredictable durability do not encourage the development of the intimate bodily knowledge of the ball's behaviour and possibilities that became possible once the balls became uniform and therefore abstract – once balls became local instantiations of 'the ball'. And yet, the elasticity of the rubber ball was only an actualization of the marvellously various potential that seemed to be contained in all balls, and that called forth from the physician Galen, for example, this praise for its capacity both to stretch and to relax all parts of the body:

> Something which keeps all parts of the body moving alike and admits either of the most violent strain or the greatest relaxation, this can be found in no exercise but the small ball. The game can be sharp or slow, soft or violent just according to your own inclination, as your body seems to need it. You can exercise all parts of the body at the same time, if that appears best, or if it should seem preferable, some parts rather than others.[24]

Writers on earlier games were impressed by how subject balls, and especially footballs, were to wildly unguessable movement and capricious influence. Richard Carew, describing a hurling match in his history of Cornwall in 1602, wrote that

> The ball in this play may bee compared to an infernall spirit: for whosoeuer catcheth it, fareth straightwayes like a madde man, strugling and fighting with those that goe about to holde him: and no sooner is the ball gone from him, but hee resigneth this fury to the next receyuer and himselfe becommeth peacable as before.[25]

The unruly and unpredictable motions of the ball and the movements of those in pursuit of it became proverbial for the unsteadiness of worldly fortunes, as the character of Morello explains in James Shirley's 1633 comedy *The Bird in a Cage*:

> Your Lordship may make one at Football,
> 'Tis all the sport now a dayes.
> What other is the world then a Ball,
> Which we run after with whoope and with hollow,
> He that doth catch it is sure of a fall,
> His heeles tript up by him that doth follow.[26]

But these kinds of ball still derived most of their energy and playful possibility from the impulsions of the players. The rubber ball, by contrast, seemed to be able to absorb, store and release energy. In doing this, it made the two dimensions of up and down, air and earth, life and death, persisting and desisting, destitution and restitution, reciprocally convertible. Its descent is harboured in its ascent, its resiling rise is garnered in its fall. The elasticated rubber ball not only oscillates between opposite conditions, it seems to blend them in its very being, which is a compound of density and rarefaction. Unlike an inflated bladder, which contains a pocket of air, with which the enclosing bladder does not mingle, a kind of airiness seems to be part of the fabric of rubber. Rather than simply being acted on by force, the ball stores it up and sprays it out, shifting about the motion it is shifted by, and thereby, in its delays, relays and releases, rowelling and texturing time.

To the degree that they embody and image reversibility, all balls are anomalous with respect to ongoing, irreversible time. But, in a reversal of this very tendency to irreversibility, some balls have been designed to store up the temporal accidents to which they are exposed, to embody a biography, a chronography of their life-time, in the changes they undergo during play. When one begins to play with a squash ball, it is sluggish and reluctant, expiring at ankle height when bounced. A dozen or more firm drives against the wall, and the ball starts to feel warm to the touch, and to bound with generous vigour. The rhythm of serve and return in tennis is coordinated with a larger rhythm of ageing and renewal with respect to the balls, which are replaced after every 7, 9 or 11 games, depending upon which federation's rules are being followed. Where baseball is played with an endless supply of new and presumably identical balls, which constantly reset or restitute time every time the ball is hit out of the stadium, the cricket ball is designed to soak up accidents of all kinds. The shock of being struck repeatedly, by bat and ground, will roughen its surface, and the seam will begin to get unpicked. In response, the bowler will try to maintain its shine on one side only, since this lunar asymmetry encourages it to swing in the air. A complex and utterly paradoxical code has evolved to regulate the process whereby these kinds of irregularities are imparted. A bowler is permitted to polish the ball using only his natural exudations, principally spit and sweat. A long debate was fought out over whether hair-oil constituted such a natural product and therefore a legitimate unguent for the ball, these discussions resembling Thomas Aquinas's agonized meditations on what parts, if any, of the body were to be regarded as excrements (hair, toenails, teeth?) and therefore ineligible for resurrection.[27] No material may be used in a bat that is likely to inflict undue damage to the ball. When precisely to introduce the new ball, after it becomes due (since the new ball will suit some bowlers and conditions better than others) is one of the most complex decisions that a captain of a bowling side has to take. But this is not the only circumstance in which the cricket ball may be replaced. In the most remarkable example of the reversibility of reversibility and irreversibility, cricket umpires will furnish themselves with a selection of balls of different ages and degrees of wear, in case the ball is lost, or knocked significantly out of shape, and the captain of (usually) the batting side requests a replacement.

Elasticity did not just make for a loosening of possibility in sports, in the form of new, puzzling and delightful unpredictability; it also ensured forms of corporeal tightening, for example in the new kinds of sporting garments that began to appear at the end of the nineteenth century and made it possible for more women to participate in sports.[28] The players of sports therefore took on some of the enhanced flexibility of the balls with which they played; because they were themselves more firmly constrained, their movements could be freer and more ductile.

Moreover, movement from the irregular to the regular, and from the rough to the uniform is not itself uniform. Some games have evolved a kind of regulated irregularity, or formalized deformation of the sphere. Probably the oldest of these is the bias that had become standard in the balls used in the game of bowls by the middle of the sixteenth century. One story suggests that the advantages of the bias were discovered during a game of bowls in 1522. Charles Brandon, Duke of Suffolk, was risking forfeiting the game after his ball split in half following a vigorous throw. When he replaced it with the ball from the head of a banister post, with the square stump on the amputated face crudely lopped into shape with his sword, he discovered after a couple of throws that he was able to use the uneven course of the ball to curl it round others that stood in his path to the jack and win the game.[29]

The origins of other kinds of irregular projectiles are similarly odd or eccentric. Badminton evolved from the game of Battledore, which involved simply trying to keep an object in the air with two rackets. *Shuttlecock* is probably a modification of *shuttlecork*, since the object itself was often made of this substance. The addition of feathers to the cork, in a kind of ruff, was perhaps suggested by the fact that pieces of cork were used to park quill pens, and feathers helped keep the object in the air, and also suggested the move from *cork* to *cock* (this possibly being the reason that the shuttlecock is known as the *birdie* in the USA).[30] But feathers were used in many different kinds of ball, and indeed there was a version of the game played in other Northern European countries that was known as 'featherball'.[31] The utility of the shuttlecock is precisely that it helps prevent the object from flying too rapidly, which made it easier to keep it aloft. When, some time in the 1850s, the game evolved into a competitive form, in which the aim was to prevent one's opponent from keeping the shuttlecock up, this slowness was turned to offensive uses, as in the drop shot, and the sudden alteration of speed in the smash. If the uniformity of the ball offers a neutral or indifferent background against which differentiating forces can be predictably applied, the versatile asymmetry of the shuttlecock complicates that formula, compounding regularity and irregularity in the aleatory machine of its physical form, which will, according to the play, alternate between the condition of a regular irregular, and an irregular regular.

The origins of the distinctively flattened and pointed ball used in rugby and American football are equally unclear. The game of football played at Rugby school in the early nineteenth century allowed both for kicking and handling, but the hands could not be used while moving forward. It was ignoring this restriction that constituted William Webb Ellis's fabled 'fine disregard' of the rules, rather than handling the ball as such. The balls used in this game were manufactured by the firm of Gilbert and employed pig's bladders, which has been said to account for their characteristic plum shape. But the same kinds of bladders were used for the balls used in football games in which kicking predominated, so we should assume that the oval shape performed in certain ways that fitted it for the handling and running game that rugby became. The elongated ball probably both emerged from and assisted the development of handling skills: a ball that was thinner in one dimension allowed it to be grasped more easily while running, even in one hand, and perhaps passed more easily as well. At the same time, the oval shape discourages kicking the ball along the ground for any considerable distance, thereby accentuating the difference between rugby football and what would become known as association football. So one might even see the lengthening of the ball as part of the tendency of sports to incorporate the aerial dimension, as a way of giving the play another dimension of variability.

Like the shuttlecock, the rugby ball is not just a quasi-object, which moves in and out of the condition of objectivity, but also a quasi-regular object, which fluctuates between predictability and unpredictability. A completely round or regular shape approaches to thecondition of an abstract form or idea, as it has infinite symmetry. The quasi-regular object is midway between form and body, insofar as these alternatives may be regarded as a mixture of the ethereal and the earthly. Aristides Quintilianus offers an allegory of the human form as the effect of gravity tugging at the Platonic circle as it descends from the empyrean, the region of pure forms, into the damp and clinging conditions of the earth.[32] One may perhaps see the oval of the rugby ball as an equivalent image of pure form being deformed into mortal existence. It is thereby an image of the mixed body that is formed every time a human being, the creature whose name attests to its earthly vocation, rounds itself out in play, which is to say, reaches beyond and comes back to itself via the relay of a sporting object. There is probably no play possible without the intercession of some object, even as the objects of play are shaped by the forms of play they potentiate.

six

Rules

Games and sports are rule-bound endeavours. To play a game or a sport is not simply to play, to divert or disport oneself freely, but to play by the rules. And these rules are not mere conveniences, designed to make the play safer or more entertaining, though this may sometimes be the motivation for the generation or alteration of rules. The status of rules in sports is very singular. A rule, as Jean Baudrillard has observed, 'is much more unbreakable than the "law," which can be transgressed. You can do anything with the law. With the rule, on the other hand, either you play or you don't play. If you play, the rule is implacable. You can't get round it. It would be idiotic to transgress it.'[1] Playing is the willing but unnecessary subjection to necessity. You can live without obeying the law without ceasing to be alive; but if you do not play by the rules, you are not playing in a special, more flexible or creative way: you are not playing at all.

What do the rules of a game determine? They determine the purpose of the game, what it means to win, and the way it is to be played. One wins a match or a battle, one wins a tournament or a trophy, but one wins *at* a sport. One of the meanings of winning is gaining, French *gagner*, and these locutions seem to intimate that, by winning a match or a battle, one appropriates it. But the cautionary little preposition *at* indicates that, in sport, the form of one's winning is always defined by a structure of rules which precede and survive any instance of their application. Sport holds out the prospect of a sovereignty that is greater and more unconditional than in any other area, but only because it defines and establishes the conditions of that sovereignty, to which the winner must accede in order for it to be possible for them to win at all. This marks a difference between sport and, say, conceptual art. In sport, the player never gets to choose the ways in which they can win, which makes it always possible for them to lose, and, usually, to lose in a way that is impossible for them to conceal from themselves or spectators. In many forms of conceptual art (except, one is tempted to say, those which voluntarily and genuinely subject themselves to some form of game-structure), it is not possible for the artist or originator of the artwork or practice to lose or fail, since such art practice typically makes rules for itself. Sport in this respect is exposed and conceptual art is insulated. In sport, in other words, winner can never take all, precisely because sport is the name for an activity in which winning can be precisely determined and decisively established. There will be a great deal more to be said in the next chapter about the nature of winning. The remainder of this chapter will be concerned with the ways in which winning is defined and measured.

In large part rules govern the kinds of bodily movement that will be permitted and required in a sport (in fact, even in non-sporting games, the game is made up of what are called 'moves' or 'goes'). There can be no sport without bodily motion, and that motion must be both purposive, aimed at a goal (one of the things which distinguishes the movement of sport from that of dance), and regulated. Regulation is essential to sport because regulation defines the particular form of arbitrarily impeded action that is necessary for any kind of sport. Rules exist to allow and disallow certain kinds of movement, defining particular kinds of freedom by means of specific restrictions.

Rules also exist to make the play purposive, allowing the game in question to have an outcome, in terms of victory and loss. Hence the nice chiming of meanings when one speaks of the 'object' of a sport; the object of a sport (to score goals, perhaps, or traverse a given body of water as fast as possible) is usually defined by the particular kinds of object one comes up against in the pursuit of it; the aiming-towards and the coming-up-against are the same thing. A diversion or physical amusement can only be a sport once there is a way to win, and therefore also to lose, at it. The procedure involved in the practice of keepy-uppy, and similar diversions, is clear: keep the ball bouncing repeatedly off the foot and other parts of the body for as long as possible. In this sense, keepy-uppy is a version of the play with gravity involved in diving and acrobatics. Keepy-uppy starts to look like a sport only from the moment at which players compete against each other. The game of battledore had been played on just such a keep-it-up principle for some centuries, with players working together to keep the shuttlecock in the air between them. The game of badminton emerged out of the serene and sociable pursuit of battledore and shuttlecock only when – probably in a British officers' mess in Poona, or, rather less likely, in the Duke of Beaufort's Badminton House – it was codified in such a way that it became possible to win at it. The point of rules is to allow the game to have, and therefore to be played towards an end, in both usual senses of that word – a conclusion and a purpose. This means that, rather than merely passing or occupying the time, games and sports are orientated towards an outcome, which will lift them out of continuous, ongoing time.

It is not for nothing that the final games of long sequences are called deciders. It is one of the constitutive anomalies of sport that, although nothing is ever in fact conclusively decided, since a rematch is always in principle possible, sport functions as a way of making decisions. Sports are a way of coming to know, and rules are necessary to ensure that they do indeed deliver knowledge – or at least the sensation of knowledge that comes from decision. It seems to be a necessary condition of a sport that it should be impossible for it to end without either a clear winner or a defined state of equilibrium (the draw) being declared. An encounter in which it might be impossible to say who had won (and this perhaps accounts for the majority of competitive encounters, including many wars) could not easily count as a sport. The tight relationship of sports and rules comes from the fact that sports can themselves be thought of as ways of determining or getting to know who is better or best. The determining and decisive function of rules does not supervene on sports from the outside; it arises to make it possible for sports to be what they definitionally are, namely ways of reaching decisions.

What does sport decide? In a sense, nothing but who wins. This is much and little. Although winning at sports can easily, and usually quite idly, be overlaid with claims that sporting prowess is a measure and consequence of other kinds of quality – endurance, courage, leadership, cooperativeness – it would not usually be wise to assume that these qualities are indeed what have determined victory or are transferable outside the sport. Sports decide who wins, but only at that sport. Perhaps the function of sports is to give us the reassurance that such decisions are possible; more than this, that there are ways of getting human actions to be decisive on their own accounts. Sports are at once an act of knowing and an act of showing, a showing that we can come to know.

Rules may often come into being in order to prevent particular kinds of play, restricting the range of choices that players may have. Sporting rules and scores always in a sense limit or finitize the infinite possibilities of play. But rules are not only or always to be seen as restricting the freedom of movement. Often, rather than reducing the possibilities of play, rules actually produce them. Rules may often arise from the desire to enlarge the possibilities of a particular game, or to prevent it from subsiding into dreary stalemate. The various tweaks applied to the rules of cricket and rugby, in order to discourage defensively playing safe, are good examples of this. The offside rule in soccer has been adjusted at intervals for a century or more, to encourage more entertaining and adventurous play. In the codification produced by the newly formed Football Association in 1863, a player was offside whenever he was closer to the opponent's goal line than the ball. With forward passing proscribed at this point, the one method of attack was for an individual player to dribble forward, at the head of a phalanx of players, all hoping for a back pass. In 1867, the rule was changed to allow a player to be onside as long as there were three players, including the goalkeeper, between them and the goal line. This worked well for a time, but also encouraged among defenders the tactic of pushing forward in a line to force attackers into an offside position. The offside-trap was countered in 1925 with another rule-change that made it necessary for there to be only two defenders (usually one outfield player and the goalkeeper) between the attacker and the goal line.[2] Rules in this case are not opposed to the openness of play, but rather designed to foster it. Without these kinds of rule, the sports in question risk degenerating into dour, featureless and utterly predictable struggles.

Sport has also seen a steady movement from immanent to external rules, overseen and applied by some kind of neutral arbiter, such as an umpire or referee. It is ironic that cricket, which depends so much upon elaborate external accounting measures for the keeping of scores, should also be one of the last games to function largely through the method of appeal. For most of the time, cricket seems to run itself, not requiring the intervention of the umpires except at times of dispute or uncertainty, such as the taking of a low catch or a claim that a batsman has been out leg before wicket. Cricket even features what might be called inverted appeals, from umpire to players, quaintest of all surely the practice of the umpires 'offering the light' to the batsmen, that is, giving the batting side the opportunity to suspend play in poor light conditions. Sports were run very largely by these principles of internal regulation until surprisingly recently. Soccer is perhaps the most striking example: referees would be stationed along the touchline, and their judgement called upon only when teams appealed for fouls or goals.[3] The nineteenth century was the most decisive era in the formalization of rules, which is to say, the development of explicit codes, standing abstractly apart from the play, and obtaining in all circumstances. Gradually, that is, implicit codes were subject to the process that the philosopher Peter Sloterdijk has called 'explicitation' (*Explizierung*).[4] As the rules became more abstracted from the playing of the game, the regulative role of the official, as the mediator between rule and play, became more important. Soccer referees came off the touchline and entered the field of play. This interfolding of inside and outside is intensified in modern mediated sports in which the role of the referee may be supplemented by technological assistance, sometimes using sensing devices planted in the heart of the play, which are nevertheless interpreted at a distance from it.

The ordering of sporting motion by rules goes beyond the establishment of the conditions whereby scores can be made, and the game played to a decisive outcome. Increasingly, with complex national and international organization and interchange, sport develops an architecture of metarules, which govern, not the way in which games are played, but the conditions under which different kinds of sporting competition can take place. These rules concern, not what happens on the pitch, or the court, or in the swimming-pool, but the behaviour of players and officials outside the time and place of the sporting event.

Numbers Game

It is possible to win a game in many of the same ways as one wins other contests – one can pummel one's opponent until they pass out or give in, for example. But such outcomes are often harder to ensure and demonstrate than might be thought. Rules seem to be necessary in large part to make it possible to decide and agree who has won. In nearly all games, the way in which this outcome is decided is through the keeping of score, a word which has as its primary signification, from Old Teutonic *sker-*, the act of cutting, a similar idea, as we saw in chapter Three, to that embedded in the etymology of the word 'decision', from Latin *caedere*, to cut. The unfolding, open time-in-process of the game as played is translated by the act of scoring into a fixed, finite and final result. The score has a kind of primary signification in marking the beginning of the game off from ordinary time – the runners at the Greek Olympics would start the race from a line scratched in the ground, and the batsman's denting of the crease in cricket as he takes guard is the first mark that he records on the way to making his score. Such marks form an incision into unremarked quotidian time, marking the moment from which one begins making marks, counting, keeping score.

All sports involve numbers. Winning and losing, the calculation of odds and possibilities, fairness, timekeeping, measurement, all involve ways of keeping score, and almost all sports depend upon the keeping of some kind of score as a way of determining victories and outcomes. Remembering Zeno's paradoxes of motion, we can say that scoring involves a conflict and convergence between two entirely incommensurable orders, the qualitative syntax of bodily motions and actions (*kinesis*), and the quantitative calculus of number (*ratio*). The order of bodily motions is continuous, in that there is no way of absolutely distinguishing the beginning and ending of particular actions, motions and passages of play. The order of scoring is discontinuous, in that it breaks up these movements into clearly defined and discrete entities: there is no sense in which the first half of a match can be said to shade into the second, or the second goal to move gradually towards the third. It is not possible to score fractions of runs in cricket – you either make it to the other end, or you are run out. You can almost score a touchdown or a goal, but you cannot score an almost-touchdown, or almost-goal. There are many other kinds of rules to which sports are subject, but all of them involve this translation of continuously changeable processes into discontinuous quantities, and of temporal actions into spatial forms.

And yet, even though number seems in some sense alien to pure play, sporting play of any kind always seems to require number, that is, the violently artificial slicing up of the world into fixed quantities, precisely in order that they can be played with. We have seen in chapter Five that, although play may be the expression of subjective freedom, it always requires the accessory of objects – play needs playthings, bats, balls, sticks. Subjects need objects both to take leave of and bring them back to themselves. Numbers are a kind of object, or objectification. This reduces the plenitude of the world, of course, making it calculable and tractable to human purposes – but it also, and in the very same gesture, opens it up to be played with, weighed, conjured, speculated upon and, most importantly, surpassed. How many times can I kick this ball up in the air without it touching the ground? How far can I jump? How fast can I traverse this length of ground?

Often the translation of play into score can appear crude, reductive or bizarre. This is nowhere more apparent than at the end of a contest in which one player or team seems clearly to have been dominant throughout, but ends up losing because of squandering their chances or because of a flukey, dying-seconds score by their undeserving opponents. One may in such circumstances feel passionately that an injustice has been done, and that the side that deserved to win has been robbed of their rightful victory. And yet it would be absurd and even a little deranged to claim that the better side had in fact, and despite the score, won, in any other than a moral sense (and moral victories only count in ethical philosophy, not in sporting competition). There is only one way to win in a sport, and that is to meet the conditions for obtaining a winning score. Those conditions having been met, there is no way for the winning team not to win, unless as the result of an infraction of some other rule.

Scoring always involves a gap between the quality of the game as it is played, and the quantitative register into which it is translated by the score. This gap is a feature of all sports. The two orders, of quality and quantity, are in essence incommensurable, meaning that there is no common measure available to translate one into another. This is ironic, since scoring is precisely the action of forcing measure on the immeasurable, of turning complex, approximate and contestable actions into mathematics. So, if all sports are competitive, perhaps the most general and abstract kind of *agôn*, which characterizes all sports, is that between number and motion, score and play. In sport, as in science, there has been a long, slow, yet still impressively successful struggle to overcome this struggle, to bring together the ideal order of mathematics and the complex, chaotic reality of movements of objects in the real world. Nonlinear and stochastic forms of mathematics are allowing us to advance some way into understanding and predicting the complex motions of dripping taps, turbid rivers and milling crowds. Ancient sports like folk football, or pre-Columbian ball-games, may have been very long drawn out, but were very often decided 1–0, since the scoring of a goal brought the game to an end. More recent sports like tennis and basketball (both of them formalized very recently), register scores at frequent intervals through the playing of the game, and so allow for a more sensitively textured record of the fluctuations of the game, as well as a way of aggregating it into an agreed outcome that seems to take account of more of what has transpired during the play.

So in sport, as in mathematics, we attempt to make the real converge with the rational. Without the rational, there would be no way of apprehending the real, except as a vague and indefinite sense of forms and forces. But in both areas it seems likely that the real will also always, in however small a degree (since the determining of degrees is precisely what is at stake here), exceed or deviate from the rational. There will be something, some unquantifiable but undeletable surd or remainder, which cannot be fully accounted for, though only accounting can disclose this with any reliability or precision.

However, although there will always be a gap between the game and the score, one that is parallel and equivalent to the gap between the rules of a game and the particular ways in which the game is played out, it is also the case that keeping the score emerges directly from the playing of the game and impacts powerfully and immediately upon it. Indeed, though the playing of the game is different from the tally that is kept in the form of the score, in many sports the entire point of the play is precisely to score, meaning that games and sports may be regarded as mechanisms for reckoning or taking account of themselves. In most games, it is not only the one who is keeping the score who is said to 'score' – it is also the players themselves. The score is not entirely on the side of the spatial and the quantitative, since scoring is itself cumulative, changeable and dynamic. In this sense, the performance and the accountancy of the game are not opposed, but aspects of each other; the game is the process of rendering account.

Over the years, many sports have developed a form of quantitative measurement that comes halfway between the playing and the scoring of the game, in the form of sporting statistics. These have no effective force, in that they do not contribute in any direct way to the process that allows us to count some as winners and some as losers – you don't get any credit for having kept possession for longer or made more completed passes than your opponents in rugby. But statistics are like scores in that they nevertheless translate discontinuous actions in time into temporarily stable states of affairs, rendering temporal actions as spatial representations. They can also become significant influences on the playing of the game. A tennis player may find it useful to know the percentage of first serves they are managing to get into the court, even though this statistic cannot directly affect the outcome of the match – only the number of games and sets won can do that. In games which have particularly fine-grained scoring systems, capable of capturing and scoring more of the action of the game in terms of numbers, it is almost possible for the real-time record of the match constituted by the changing score to act as a substitute for it. I can sit at a computer and gain a nuanced sense of the ebb and flow of a cricket match without even having to listen on headphones to the commentary, by watching the numbers change with respect to overs bowled, changing bowling and batting averages, and so on. In the period before it was possible to relay live action from the Wimbledon show courts to those unable to gain entrance outside, crowds used to follow the progress of a match by excitedly watching the scoreboard flipping over as points and games were won and lost.

Most children have played some version of an outdoor sport adapted for the rolling of dice or other chance procedure, such as the game of *Howzat!* Perhaps its attraction comes from the fact that the scoring conventions of cricket seem so flickeringly mimetic of the playing of the game itself. These require and permit one to register the fortunes of every single ball bowled, and therefore to take continuous accounts of things like scoring and bowling rates, and are traditionally set out in a beautiful ledger format that allows one both to see the completed curve of the game and to reconstitute the narrative of its unfolding. The six balls of each over in cricket are logged in a sequence of little cells, and anyone who has spent any time scoring a cricket match will remember the exquisite miniature pleasure of constellating the six dots that mark the bowling of a maiden over, from which no runs have been scored, into an M – or, even rarer and more relishable, a Cassiopeia-like W, to mark a wicket maiden, a maiden over in which a wicket has also been taken. Robert Coover's 1968 novel *The Universal Baseball Association, Inc, J. Henry Waugh Prop.* expands this idea into a full novel, which tells us of an accountant who has spent most of his spare time over many years playing a dice-game of his own devising that brings into being an entire baseball league, complete with its own archives recording the achievements of generations of players. Henry lives and breathes his version of the game of baseball, which is threaded, as a continuous activity of invention and fantasy, through his real life, though he is rather bored by the real game of baseball:

> Nothing like it really. Not the actual game so much – to tell the truth, real baseball bored him – but rather the records, the statistics, the peculiar balances between individual and team, offense and defense, strategy and luck, accident and pattern, power and intelligence. And no other activity in the world had so precise and comprehensive a history, so specific an ethic, and at the same time, strange as it seemed, so much ultimate mystery.[5]

In the past, it was usually only quite slow-moving games, or games characterized by alternation between bursts of action and long pauses for reflection and tactical adjustment, like cricket and baseball, that allowed the time for statistics to fill the gaps. Nowadays, statistics can be electronically generated quickly enough to provide a real-time accompaniment of the game as it unfolds, and games are subject to more and more fine-grained forms of what, on the analogy of music and dance, is called notational analysis.[6] This makes statistics something like a continuous autocommentary, an ever-more subtle and sinuous mathematical shadow to the playing of the game, now perhaps rather more on the model of the film score than the tally. If the rules of a game stand before it, defining its conditions and possibilities, and the score of a game stands as its summation after it is completed, real-time statistics increasingly emerge from and intertwine with the game. They are a simulacrum of the game, the way in which the game may be made to stand apart from itself (especially since it is usually commentators and spectators who have the readiest access to these statistics). And yet this simulacrum is also a component of the game (as we have already seen, players are also spectators and may themselves have access to statistics as they play). This is particularly the case since statistics need not always lag behind the game, but, as in the predicted scores and run-rate statistics provided in limited-overs cricket, allow for the projection of different possible future outcomes even as the game is being played, and for them to be taken into account as part of the game. Statistics therefore begin to double and diversify the body of the game, just as sport puts the individual body ahead and aside of itself. We are seeing the statistical ecstasis of sport.

Taking Your Chances

Just as, for most of its history, 'sport' meant something very different (the hunting of animals) from what it has meant for the last century, so the word 'game' has also significantly shifted its meaning (they are intriguingly connected, of course, in the use of the word 'game' to signify the kind of animals one hunted for sport). Until well into the nineteenth century, games and gaming remained almost indistinguishable from gambling, the competitive betting on chance. Although the idea of a game has loosened itself somewhat from these associations, chance remains an active participant in every sport. Rules in sport are tied up in a particularly complex way with the operations of chance, even though chance has appeared to be irreducible to rule and reason for much of human history, which has moved, with apparently excruciating slowness, from a belief in destiny and a fatalistic incuriousness about chance to a recognition of the unnullable yet partly tractable chanciness of things. Whimsical and capricious though their deities were, the Greeks seem to have felt that there was something impious in enquiring into the workings of chance and fortune; so although they were avid dice players, they developed no theory of probabilities. For the Greeks, the world was divided between fate – absolute determination – and fortune – or absolute, unknowable indetermination – and there was no connection between the two. In fact, there are few signs before the middle of the seventeenth century of anyone anywhere suspecting that chance might not be entirely lawless, and therefore not entirely inaccessible to human understanding and management.

From that point on, magical warding-off has given way to reasoned estimation and maximization of chances, not least in sport. The gradual development of a scientific understanding of physical laws opened up the prospect that the advance towards perfect knowledge might eventually be able to shrink the reach of chance to almost nothing – even if the discoveries of quantum physics have begun to suggest that, after all, chance may be intrinsic to things, that God, in Einstein's phrase, might indeed play dice.

But if human beings have taken a very long time to begin enquiring into the operations of probability, they have also taken every opportunity to stage and perform the exposure to the operations of chance. The history of probability theory is tightly bound to the history of gaming, and the concept of game is indissociable from gambling. The first book on probability was written by Gerolamo Cardano in the 1520s (though it remained unpublished until 1663) and takes gaming with dice as its central focus.[7] The advances in understanding which followed in the ensuing century, as a result of the work of mathematicians such as Galileo, Pascal and Fermat, were almost all stimulated by problems to do with dice games. Responding to a request from the Duke of Tuscany in 1610, Galileo was able to show why you had slightly more chance (in a ratio of 1:1.08), of throwing a 10 or 11 than a 9 or 12 with three dice,[8] while Pascal and Fermat were prompted to their reflections by the problem of how to distribute the stakes in an interrupted game of dice, the so-called 'problem of points'. This has an analogy in contemporary sport in the Duckworth-Lewis method, devised by statisticians Frank Duckworth and Tony Lewis, to determine what the target should be for a team batting second in a limited-overs cricket match that is subject to interruption, through rain or some other cause.

Chance seems to apply in two ways to sport and games. On the one hand, games are efforts at formalizing or methodizing chance. On the other hand, they are ways of subjecting oneself to it. Games are therefore simultaneously strategies for minimizing and for magnifying chance. The provisions of a game establish fair conditions, the kind of fair conditions that never exist in nature, precisely because of the skewing effects of random fluctuation that always exist, in order precisely to provide a field in which the operations of chance can be isolated and amplified. Of course, sport can be thought of as an attempt to draw everything into the sphere of will and intention. The tennis player who gets a lucky net cord or a drop shot from the frame of the racket will apologize to his or her opponent, acknowledging that they have benefited from something unintended. Luck or chance are the signs of the world's refusal to come inside the charmed circle of human rule, or to be aligned with the patternings of human value. But in order to effect that neutralization of every contingency that is the horizon of every sport, it is necessary for the players of sport, and for the sport itself, deliberately to expose themselves to contingency, in order to negate the negation of human will that contingency represents, to deflect the deflection of human purpose back into rectitude.

The coaction of law and chance in sport may seem odd, since we are accustomed to thinking of them as opposites. Laws are framed precisely to limit the operations of chance or randomness. But in fact they deeply interpenetrate each other, though without ever being able to coincide. For laws must always be applied to particular circumstances, to that which just happens to happen, which will always nevertheless stand round and outside law (standing round is literally what the word *circumstance* means). Were law ever simply to coincide with circumstance, there would at that point no longer be any law or any circumstance. A circumstance is only so in relation to the law from which it, be it ever so minimally, diverges; and a law is only a law because it can reach beyond the place, time and form of its enunciation, because it has application to the circumstances on which it can be brought to bear.

There are few systems of thought that attempt to bring together law and circumstance more systematically than the Jewish Talmud. Technically, the Talmud is a composite, consisting of the Mishna, the set of written laws derived from the Torah, the books of Moses, plus the Gemara (which perhaps comes from the Hebrew *gamar*, to complete), namely the commentaries on those laws. The Talmud does indeed have a number of prescriptions relating to games. But, more than this, it might be said to be game-like in its very structure. For the Talmud is not a set of bare prescriptions, but a set of examples of how to apply rules in different circumstances. It should be no surprise that there should be such a close affinity between laws and games. To be sure, games have laws. But laws also require something like the structure of a game – that is, a field of application, in which to be played out – to have any reach or effect. There can be no law without a field of the lawless or alegal in which to operate. The Talmud expands the sphere of law in an attempt to encompass the whole of the sphere of circumstance, but in so doing endlessly exposes itself to more circumstances or possibilities of deviation.

We might see the long and mysteriously delayed beginnings of a theory of probability in the middle of the seventeenth century as an effort to bring together the sphere of rational law and the sphere of accident or circumstance. Greek thought was arguably unable to accede to the condition of science, because it was too dazzled by its discovery of the rational absolutes of geometry, which could never quite be brought together with the grainy contingencies of the real. It could only abstract from the real, and therefore could only come after the fact, giving it only limited predictive powers. Science comes into being with experiment, or rather in the encounter of reason with experience. The two can never be identified, which is to say, subjected to the law of the absolute; rather they must always exist in a mixture. Reason cannot simply subdue contingency; it must learn in some way to take account of it, to make what headway it can into contingency by partly yielding to it. Probability theory is one of the most important forms of this concession of law to circumstance.

Probability may be thought of as the rules which, rather than being imposed on contingent circumstances, emerge from them. Let us take one of the standard set-ups of probability theory, a coin-tossing or dice-rolling scenario. If I toss a coin twice, I will not be unduly surprised if it comes up heads three times in a row. Only after, say, fifty heads in a row, will I suspect that the coin is a double-header, or is unequally weighted. If it happens a hundred times in a row, my suspicions of something fishy will be tending towards certainty. Human beings did not need probability to tell them that the force of contingency tends to recede with large numbers of events, provided they are repeated events that are independent of each other. The ratio of heads to tails in a sequence of tosses of a perfectly weighted coin tossed in absolutely equal and invariant circumstances will, over time, gradually tend to the ratio of 1:1. Here, time, which opens up a fissure or wound in the identity of law and actuality, gradually, given time, heals it again. The deductive law will tend to emerge inductively over time.

But what is the status of that presumptive 'will' in the phrase 'will gradually tend to the ratio of 1:1'? Does this mean that it must always do so, in just the same way, and at just the same rate in any and every sequence of throws? Not at all. This is itself a matter of probability rather than an infallible necessity. It is not certain that a larger sequence of throws will always produce a ratio that is close to equality, though it is certainly highly probable. But this means that statements about probability, which seem to show that certainty emerges through the playing out of circumstance as well as through a prior doctrine of chances, are themselves probabilistic. Most sports fans will acknowledge that the best way to eliminate the effects of chance is to make sure that sporting encounters last long enough to ensure that each opponent will in the long run have their fair share of good or bad luck. But how long is long enough? In practice, though there may be a certain rough justice in the equilibrium of bad calls and dodgy bounces suffered by different players over the course of a five-set match, or injuries suffered by different teams over the course of a season, one party or other will always seem to get more than its fair share of lucky breaks or misfortunes. It will always be a matter of luck how close to equilibrium the lucky and unlucky breaks end up being.

Not only that, but the theory of probability tells us nothing about the order of the way in which the final result tends towards equality. There are 22 different ratios that might arise from the tossing of a coin twenty times, all the way from the most unlikely (all heads, or all tails), to the most likely (10 of each), and by way of 19 heads to 1 tail, 18 heads to 1 tail, and so on. (By 'most likely' and 'most unlikely' here is meant, not in any one sequence of twenty tosses, but over time, given a large number of sequences of twenty tosses.) But, even supposing that the ratio comes out at 10:10, there are many different sequences of heads and tails in which that ratio might be achieved, about which probability theory can tell us little. Probability theory can never close this gap between the aggregate and the individual instances that make up this aggregate. Actuality may draw close to what probability theory predicts, but there will always be some fluctuation around the actual or true value. There will always be some maladjustment, or 'play', between the rule and its application, between necessity and contingency. Sport occupies, indeed perhaps it simply *is*, this space of putting into play.

In the sphere of education we feel, rightly, that we should do what we can to reduce the effects of contingency in the submission and assessment of work, which is where, in the end, everything gets weighed on the scale (an essay is itself an assay, a trial or testing by weight). So we attempt to articulate the criteria for the marking of essays, specifying in advance and as clearly as we can the different qualities and their degrees that are being assessed – logical coherence, rigour, use of sources, clarity of expression, originality. There is nothing wrong with such an exercise, which does indeed turn what might otherwise be an open and undetermined field into a more determined one. Knowing the rules of the game – the position and width of the goalposts, as we often say – the student is supposed to be able to pay more efficient and productive attention to the development of the qualities that we wish to encourage and reward in them. But there is a problem, which arises regularly in cases of disagreement. Two examiners may be in perfect agreement as to the assessment criteria, but in absolute disagreement as to how they happen to apply to a particular, disputed case. 'I entirely agree that we should reward rigour', says examiner A, 'I just don't think this essay displays it.' 'That all depends on what you mean by rigour', rejoins examiner B. How to resolve such a dispute? The temptation is to try to generate a set of rules for how the rules are to be applied in different circumstances ('By rigour is meant the precise and strictly consistent application of rational method'). But what is there to ensure that such a metaprescription will itself seem to apply self-evidently and without the need for interpretation to every disputed case? And where in principle does such a procedure end? Law will always be applied imperfectly or incompletely precisely because it will always be law, which is to say that it will lack the law that would be necessary to govern its application to all conceivable circumstances, since that law would in its turn need but lack a law to govern its application, and so on.

In a similar way, it is impossible for the rules of play of any particular game or sport to legislate fully for everything that is likely to happen on the field of play. This is not just because law is finite and the possibilities of play much closer to infinite, so that unpredictable contingencies are almost certain to arise (none of the whiskered worthies who drew up the rules of cricket, rugby or soccer can have foreseen the need to deal with interruptions to play caused by streakers). It is also, more fundamentally, that no rule can ever be self-interpreting without ceasing to be a rule, or ceasing to have anything to interpret.

There is another reason why probability cannot apply simply and straightforwardly to a game or sport. Absolute and precise rules of probability apply only under conditions of randomness or absolute nondetermination. But there can be no guarantee that any game will be entirely fair, leaning neither to one side or another, or if it begins so, that it will remain so, and will not drift out of precise equilibrium – as the wind changes, because the referee exercises an unconscious bias to one side or another, as cheating goes undetected. Of course steps can be taken to try to ensure that neither team suffers disadvantage, each playing for one half up the slope or against the wind, for example, but there is only a probability and not a certainty that these circumstantial details will be able to be balanced in such a way as to ensure that equilibrium is maintained. This is to say that, in any game, there are two kinds of fluctuation. There are the fluctuations that come about by chance within the game, and there are the fluctuations of the game itself, in and out of the ideal condition of equilibrium required for a fair game, which is to say, a game as such.

'The harder I practise, the luckier I seem to get', goes the old sporting saw. But no sportsman or sportswoman really believes this, otherwise they would not manifest such dependence on rituals, super-stitions and ceremonies of propitiation and apotroposis, the kit laid out just so, the kissing of the pitch, the signations, the serving rituals, the muttering of magical formulae. The vast majority of sports super-stitions appear to be conservative rather than acquisitive; that is, they involve practices that aim to avoid bad luck rather than actively to promote good luck. Many of these practices derive from *post hoc propter hoc* associations, in which good fortune that has followed a particular practice or circumstance is held to be caused by it and there-after irreproducible without it. The Argentinian goalkeeper Sergio Goycochea found himself so desperate after a long match that he had to urinate on the pitch ahead of a penalty shoot-out against Yugoslavia in a 1990 World Cup quarter-final. After his team won, Goycochea felt compelled to repeat the turf-watering ritual before every subsequent shoot-out in which he was involved. No doubt players of sports, who probably have to be more strongly motivated to highly repetitive behaviour than most members of the population in order to be able to get through the routines of practice required for high performance, are in any case strongly predisposed to the establishment and main-tenance of such rituals.

In 1873, Francis Galton invented a device called the Quincunx, which modelled what Carl Gauss in 1809 had shown was the normal distribution of random events.[9] A succession of beads is dropped down the face of a board studded regularly with pins, like a pinball table. The beads will deviate either to the left or right as they en-counter each of the pins, and will end up in one of a series of boxes running from left to right across the bottom. Most of the beads will tend to cluster in the middle sections, because they will have been deflected left and right an equal or nearly equal amount of times, while only very few will be found at the far right or far left, which would require them improbably to have been deflected in the same direction several times in succession. The more beads are dropped, the more closely the beads stacked at the bottom will approximate the characteristic bell shape of what is known as the normal curve, bulging in the middle and flattening out at the edges.

A game provides a similar kind of visualization of the contours of chance. As play begins, the teams provide a table or tableau of equi-probability, mirroring each other in their dispositions. The very word 'disposition' in fact embodies a telling flicker of possibility. To dispose the pieces on a chess board, or the fielders in a game of baseball or cricket, means simply to set them out, or put them in their positions. But one's disposition has also come to mean something like the opposite of this. If am disposed to something, it means that I am leaning towards, or have a propensity to it. My disposition is not just the way I have been set out, but also my distinctive attitude or angle on things. My disposition is the differential orientation towards action that my way of being set out gives me.

As the game begins, the players form themselves into a moving diagram of chances and choices. The virtual and the actual, figures and shadows, now start to change places, move in and out of phase with each other. It is as though the passages of play were continually lighting up lines of force and fields of possibility, as iron filings reveal the whorls looping round a magnet.

At the beginning of the game, there is something like a static landscape of possibilities, weighted or concentrated by various probabilities. One team, say, comes into the fixture with all its players fit and in form, and on the back of a string of victories. The other team has had much more sporadic success, is missing some key players due to injury and suspension and is playing away from home. The bookies are offering odds of 2 to 1 against a victory for the depleted away team. But this is only the summation or bottom line of chances, the result of a calculation, rather than its working out. The landscape of likelihood consists of much more than a simple, even slope that assists one side and retards the other. For there are other features of the landscape that give little lifts and flarings of advantage and disadvantage – cracks, gashes, chasms, pockets, potholes, ridges, declivities, tussocks and tumuli, which distribute probabilities in much more variegated and unpredictable ways. There is, for example, the very fact that the home team is so strongly fancied, putting them on what is known as a hiding to nothing, meaning that, even if they win, they will not be seen to have succeeded in much apart from supplying the expected result, whereas, if they lose, the surprise and disgrace will be considerable. The stochastic landscape has complex chiaroscuro. All probabilities have shadows, the shadow of doubts. With a dead certainty, the sun is directly overhead, and the upright pointer, the gnomon, casts no shadow. A 95 per cent chance of winning means only a 5 per cent chance of losing, or drawing, the sun having moved only slightly to one side. As the odds lengthen, so does the shadow, so that a barely probable event is seen as though late in the day, with the sun low in the sky, and the shadow stretching out three or four times as long as its original.

Among the suggestions for why it should have taken so long for a theory of probability to arise are that it was regarded as impious to enquire into the workings of destiny, or that conditions made it difficult for people to grasp the notion of equiprobability, or even chances, that is necessary for a theory of probability to be developed. I have a slightly different suggestion to offer for why a theory of games emerged so late, namely that gaming itself functions as a kind of theory. I observed earlier on that, when Galileo was recruited by the Duke of Tuscany to enquire into the probabilities of different outcomes with three dice, he was not being asked to determine the probabilities, but to verify and explain *what was already suspected*, namely that 10 is thrown more often than 9. In what sense, might we ask, could this have been known? We should perhaps assume that inveterate dice-players had just developed a kind of instinct or feel for the slight advantage that 10 had over 9. This does not seem impossible to me, though Deborah J. Bennett finds it implausible that any individual gambler could have distinguished the slight difference between 0.11574074 and 0.125, feeling that a more likely explanation is that 'this knowledge was part of gamblers' lore, accumulated from experience and passed down over centuries'.[10]

This raises an interesting question about what it means to know something. Should knowing something without understanding it, without, that is, being able to articulate it, really count as knowing it? Counting up or counting out, enumeration of all the different possibilities, was a necessary first stage in probability theory. Even now, there are very few people who do not sometimes have to be shown how probability works by some version of counting out. The dangers of premature abstraction are indicated by the mistake made by the French mathematician Jean d'Alembert, who claimed that the probability of throwing one head with two tosses of a coin must be 1 in 3, since there are only three possible outcomes (1 head, two heads, or no heads), neglecting the fact that, while there is only way in which to throw two heads or no heads, there are two ways in which one head can be obtained (head followed by tail and tail followed by head).[11] The probability of throwing one head is therefore 2 in 4, or 1 in 2. And yet, necessary though it is, simple enumeration, or working through the possibilities, does not seem to us really to count as calculation, even though the first operations with stones, that actually give us the word calculation, from *calculus*, stone, involved precisely this kind of 'blind' manipulation, and even though the fact that we still say that things do or do not 'count' indicates our continuing trust in this mode of verifying action.

Indeed, the value of such blind working through can be considerable. For some calculations, such as calculating the area of a complex shape, the most efficient way of coming at the problem may be to use something like the Monte Carlo method. This consists of enclosing the shape within a rectangle, and then using some randomizing procedure to distribute points at random inside and outside the area to be calculated. If the points are truly random, and if there are enough of them, they will (very probably) be distributed in the same ratio as the ratio of the target area to that of the rectangle in which it is enclosed. Counting up the points will reveal this ratio. Brilliant though this is, it feels like a kind of cheat, since it does not involve any grasp of principle, or corresponding calculative short cut.

The striking thing here is that the knowledge is only obtainable if the numbers and positions of the points are truly random, which is to say unknowable. The Monte Carlo procedure is a way of exploiting our non-knowledge. Gaming may be regarded as a similar way of trying to get at knowledge without possession of it. The essence of a game is that one should knowingly construct circumstances of uncertainty, in order to expose oneself to them. The game is the effort to coincide with a knowledge that you cannot be said exactly to have.

Let us attempt to enumerate the *dramatis personae* in sport or game. There are, first of all, the antagonists. Classically, there are two of these, the two opponents. But there are also sports and games in which competitors compete against each other by competing against a third element – time in the case of a race, or height in the case of the high jump. We may call this third element necessity, and specifically the necessity of limit, for there will always be a limit to one's possible speed, strength, endurance or flexibility. In classical games of opposition, the necessity of limit triangulates the antagonism between the two parties. In races, the presence of multiple opponents triangulates the antagonism between the runner and his limits. This third element, of physical limit, is in play in all sports, mediating the relationship between opponents.

But there is another intercessor. Competitors do not just strive against necessity, they must also work with and against chance. We can therefore imagine a set-up something like the following:

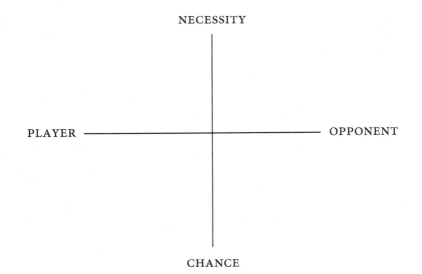

Participants in sport will often attempt to draw chance into conformity with human values and expectations, as we habitually do with the weather, turning chance into luck, good or bad. But in reality chance has no such orientation. This is why, although chance is symmetrical to necessity, in that it provides the conditions within which all human endeavour must operate, it is not precisely or necessarily opposed to it. If necessity represents the limits within the field of sport and game, then chance represents the pure openness of the game, the possibility of its being able to be played, the dimension of unpredictability which it must necessarily inhabit if it is to be a game. Although chance is distinguished from necessity, precisely because necessity is determined and determining, and chance is the indeterminable, it is also penetrated by it. The fact of contingency, of a certain degree of exposure to indeterminable or unnecessary things, is in fact a necessity. Sports and games are a dramatization of what Jean-Paul Sartre has characterized as the necessity of our contingency.[12] Like other kinds of striving, sport represents a willed exposure or opposition to necessity, finitude, limit. But sport is distinguished from other kinds of endeavour in the fact that, in it, the necessary and the contingent are so tightly, and paradoxically, bound together. In a sport or game, the exposure to necessity is itself arbitrary, that is to say unnecessary.

Sport is an actualization of chance, a playing out of the game. It is something like the opposite of probability theory, which attempts to calculate the odds of a particular outcome in advance. Although playing with or against probabilities may be a feature of many sports – playing the 'percentage game' in tennis, for example, by not taking any risks and waiting for one's opponent to make an error – sport itself is a kind of counting out or working through of chances.

Ordeal

Under circumstances of high uncertainty, when there was not enough evidence to reach a safe judgement, judges in many ancient and medieval systems of law might resort to various kinds of probative ordeal. Those suspected of adultery might be required to walk over hot ploughshares; accused thieves or heretics would have to plunge their hands into boiling water to retrieve a stone. This practice, and the predilection towards which it points, is preserved in the word *ordeal* itself, which is related to ordering and ordaining. An ordeal always seems to have the meaning of a test, in the interests of an apportionment, the doling out of guilt or innocence, bliss or bale. Sport inherits this ancient violence of agony as a form of decision-making. Sport is a way of seeming to put things to the test through the contrivance of an exposure to extremity and risk, to circumstances in which, we are oddly inclined to believe, the force of law will inevitably come to the surface. All sports are essentially forms of subjecting things to question, ways of making judgements, or rather surrendering the work of judgement to the play of things themselves. Chance in this process is given the force of necessity, given the task of scouring away error, delusion and dissimulation. This is precisely the opposite of the principle enunciated earlier on, that law will never coincide with circumstance, given that circumstances will always either outstrip or fall short of law. Here, by contrast, circumstance, the way in which things happen to happen, is given a juridical force. And, surprisingly, this juridical force comes from the intractability or unlawfulness of chance, from the very fact that, as sports commentators are wont to say, you cannot legislate for circumstance. The practice of sport is in fact the principle of the legislation of hazard.

Reflecting on the lucky goal that seemed to have been so decisive in AC Milan's victory over Liverpool in the Champions League final of 2007, Simon Barnes has suggested that the effects of luck are hugely and uniquely magnified in soccer, because of its preference for having everything come down to a single match – the final. Games such as snooker and even tennis tend to be played out over much longer periods, thus evening out the lucky breaks. But, as Barnes observes, 'Nothing in sport is so lucky as a lucky goal in football.'[13] Barnes thinks that it is no accident that soccer should nevertheless be the world's most popular game. It is, he says, the high importance of luck that makes soccer so intoxicating. I'm not sure that he is quite right in the detail of his claim. The effects of luck are not quite as easily smoothed out as he suggests: a net-cord that changes the course of a game deep in the middle set of a marathon five-set match may be only one out of a series of net-cords, but if that is the one net-cord that has changed the course of the game, then its importance will be huge. But he is right in essence, that in soccer, as well as in other sports, there is a certain drive to create situations – situations that, paradoxically, are tightly regulated – in which the role of chance or luck is made determining and irreversible.

Perhaps this in turn makes sport seem like a particularly elaborate form of divination, the descrying of meaning in the chance patternings of things, whether in the alphabet of entrails or the fluent cursives of the flight of birds. Divination involves the belief that the universe is bound together by resemblance, that things echo and foreshadow each other. But it is plain, even to those who hold such a belief, that most of the time these patterns of resemblance lie concealed. Divination involves the assumption that circumstance itself can be made to show forth certainty only under certain circumstances. There is always some kind of law, or prescribed form, for the making out of meanings and judgements. Maidens seeking to know the name or the face of their future husbands must perform various kinds of ritual, abstaining from food, buttoning themselves up backwards and so on. Divination must take place at certain times, or in certain places, must involve the utterance of certain words and the performing of certain actions. The invariant, the fixed, the necessary, forms a necessary approach to the putting of things to the test of chance, to the arbitrations of the arbitrary. In divination, as in sport, the determined and the undetermined must mingle and potentiate each other. Force must be applied in certain ways, perforce, in order that the unforced force of the necessary truth will emerge.

Ordeal involves decision, the reduction of possibilities. It mimics the process of time itself, which continuously reduces a wide spread of possibilities to a small number of actual outcomes. A game is a staging or setting-up of this percolation of more into less in the form of a determinate question or trial. A game, like a trial, aims at dealing out determinate judgements, setting truth aside from the error or irrelevance with which it may be indistinctly commingled. But a game also begins with a formal laying out or allocation of possibilities – with what, in cards for instance, is actually called the act of dealing (and the 'deal' is also an obsolete term for the first hit of the ball initiating the game in Cornish hurling). Following on from this preparatory dealing, the ordeal of the game will aim to deal out truth. Thus at the end of extra time, when the scores are still level, soccer resorts to the penalty shoot-out, which is regularly and rightly referred to as a kind of torment or agony for the participants and witnesses. In place of the haphazard, crazy-paved, candelabra branchings of the game, which has failed to yield a decision, there is now the careful delimitation of possibilities. The goal can either be scored or not scored (saved or missed). The hugely increased difficulty of scoring a penalty under these circumstances may well come from the way in which the deciding ordeal is set up, combined with the well-known human difficulty in grasping or accepting probabilities. The fact is that it is much more likely for a goal to be scored than for it to be saved, since there are only a few ways in which it can be saved and many ways in which it can be scored. But the set-up, which reduces the range of possible outcomes to only two (either score or fail to score), encourages a misrecognition of the outcomes as equiprobable.

Play has the same relation to number as probability. Probability and chance are the penumbra of number: probability can be assigned numerical value (indeed probability is never anything else than numerical), and yet probability never converges simply with number. Probability is not only the number we may assign to a likelihood; it is also the likelihood of a number. Just as probability can neither be distinguished from nor wholly identified with number, so number can neither be extricated from nor entirely exhaust play. Probability is the play of number that number itself makes possible.

Forcing chance to play its hand in this way, sporting events often seem to have the function of the disclosing of destiny, the making clear of what had to happen, even and especially if that destiny is actually fulfilled through chance events that did not in fact have to happen at all. Sport effects the agonistic passage from one condition to another – from the accidental to the necessary and from the impersonal condition of blind, indifferent chance to the personal embrace of the destined. Sport literally involves taking your chances, not in order to triumph over chance, but in order to take it into yourself, to make it your own.

To play a sport is to put oneself at stake, to wager yourself against the play of chance itself. There are always two contrasting intentions in this. One seeks to overcome chance, imposing purpose and direction upon the indefinite; but the other overcomes chance only by subjecting oneself to it, playing with and against it – playing it out.

Not Playing the Game

There is a rule that governs all sports, though it is never articulated within the codes of any one of them. It is perhaps distinguished from the laws and rules that provide the frameworks of individual sports, which essentially supply the impediments that are necessary for any sport, and so therefore are statements of prohibition rather than requirement. Even rules of positive specification, such as those relating to items of sporting equipment, or the lay-out of fields, have the function of prohibitions in that they make it impossible to play with a foot-wide bat, or on a circular football pitch. The specific rules that specify how sports are to be played are, we can say, rules that rule out. The unarticulated rule that governs the playing of every sport is not a prohibition but a positive imperative. It is the injunction that one must try to win. This unarticulated rule cannot be articulated as part of a particular ordering of conduct because it is the condition of acceptance of all of the rules of a game, the condition under which those rules become, in Baudrillard's formulation, implacable. One does not have to play at all, but if one does play, one must actually *play*, which means, not just that one might play within the rules of the game, but that one must accept the given of any game, which is that one will try to win it in the particular way that the rules of the game prescribe.

One must take the play seriously; that is, one must not *play at playing*. This is, in essence, what is meant by cheating. Marshall Swain and Myles Brand offer a more formal definition of cheating, as follows:

> A person, P, cheats with regard to a game if and only if:
> (1) P is a participant in that game as a player or coach; and
> (2) P intentionally breaks a formal rule of the game with the purpose of gaining an unfair advantage over P's opponents in the game.[14]

But this does not seem to me to capture very well what is usually meant by cheating, precisely because it restricts itself to the breaking of formal rules (although later in their essay, Swain and Brand revise their definition to encompass informal conventions as well). This is to identify cheating simply with foul play, or play that breaks the rules of the game. But one can break the rules of a game while also accepting them. Indeed, rule-breaking generally does involve an acceptance of the structure of rules, not least because some of these rules are bound to be broken involuntarily. Cheating, however, always involves a kind of dissimulation, the attempt to gain victory or some more local advantage through pretending to play a game that one is not playing, since one is relying on rules that one is not oneself observing. If one does not in fact try to win fairly, one may be practising a kind of deception on one's opponent, by taking away from them in turn the possibility of winning fairly and honestly. A player who feigns injury in order to gain sympathy, to impress onlookers with his courage, or to get himself removed from a situation which is boring or terrifying him, is not cheating, since, in a way, they are no longer even really playing. It is only if there is an attempt to gain some advantage in the game through the deception, by allowing one's opponents to play according the constitutive restrictions of the game while not accepting them oneself, that cheating can be said to occur. So cheating is not rule-breaking, which is a normal part of the game, but the pretence of rule-following. Cheating is therefore not 'not playing the game'. It is using not playing the game (trying to get the rules to apply asymmetrically) as a way of playing it.

Sports may have quite stringent penalties for simulation and deception, but there are no sports that have a specific rule that you must not cheat, that is that you must not merely pretend to play, since this is the very condition of entering freely into the contract to play. This is the sense in which all sports may be said to be governed by the metarule that, if you play the game at all, you must really play it; that is, you must try to win, or try to play well. Cheating always seems to involve some kind of dissimulation, and one can see that, insofar as it attacks sports at their very foundation, by denying the very possibility of entering into a free and reciprocal acceptance of the conditions of play, there should be such a deep revulsion among the players and spectators of sports regarding the act, or at any rate the idea, of cheating. The dissimulation of cheating involves an attack on what might be called the principle of seriousness in sport.

Nothing can prescribe this prescription, or force this force, since it must be accepted freely. You cannot require anybody to make the free choice that is involved in playing. If you are forced to play, the imperative to really play, that is really try to win, has no force, since, under these circumstances, one is not really playing at all. That imperative only has force if it is accepted without force, but then its force is absolute, because constitutive of the sport in question. Indeed, being forced to play involves a very similar dissimulation to that of cheating, since it violates the structural condition of freely chosen play that underlies all games. This free choice may not always, however, be identifiable with a conscious decision or simple state of mind. Those generations of sport-hating schoolchildren who were forced out on to muddy soccer or hockey pitches when they would much rather have been doing almost anything else may often, by withholding their consent, have succeeded in not playing at all. But if they ever found themselves, out of intimidation, doggedly defiant compliance or habit, actually playing the game with purpose, their actions will have constituted the consent their dispositions were withholding. Under such circumstances you may reasonably be taken to have freely and actively agreed to the requirements of the sport without meaning to.

This imperative to play in earnest can take us to the heart of the enigma of sport. Sport is often defined in terms of what it is not, in terms of the special rules and conditions that set it apart from ordinary life. In some senses, the kind of playing involved in sport resembles the playing that is found in theatre, cinema, dance and other kinds of performed reality. In all these cases, you will be able to make no sense at all of what is going on if you do not grasp the fact that the actor playing the part of Othello does not really feel homicidally jealous about the actress playing the part of Desdemona, or that the teams playing soccer are really, as they seem to be, struggling for possession of the ball (hence the befuddlement of the Martian who watches a soccer game for some minutes and then enquires why they don't just give each team a ball of its own to play with). The point of sport, namely the fact that it is set apart from ordinary relations of dominance and rivalry, that it is 'only a game', makes it seem equivalent to these kinds of performance. And yet there is something crucially different about sport. For one can never say of a game or sport that it is only a pretence. Even if it is 'only a game', by which we mean that it is not real, it is nevertheless really a game, that is to say, a game is really and incontestably going on.

For this reason, I am inclined to propose that one of the most important features of games, and sports in particular, is that they embody a principle of absolute positivity, or, put the other way round, repudiated absurdity. Unlike 'real life', which, despite its upright reputation, is plainly a treacherous fogbank of delusions and deceptions, vanities and velleities, sport is the forcing into being of a condition in which it is impossible to deny what is really happening. Despite all the claims that sport is a theatrical displacement of human desires, virtues and values, sport is in its essence zealously nonsymbolic and unillusory, despite the derivation of the latter from *ludere*, to play. Its aim is to provide a place and occasion from which all possibility of simulation has been scorched away, and in which one can be sure that whatever happens will reliably and irreversibly have happened. This is, of course, what encourages the practice of cheating, since the gains of victory under such conditions are so considerable.

In this sense, sport, which contributes so much to a contemporary culture of fantasy and distraction, can also be seen as pushing things into the condition of the manifest, aiming to show them in their being. Though it multiplies indeterminacy, the aim of sport is to raise (unless one had better say reduce) the potential to the actual. As I have just noted, sport often performs the juridical function of the trial, in that it is intended to deliver a judgement or decision. I said that a sporting context resembles a trial by ordeal more than a trial by evidence and judgement, since the sporting event aims to force evidence into manifestness. The link between sport and judicial ordeal may depend upon the principle of positivity: for, if sport cannot be one thing, how can it deliver its verdicts with one voice? Of course, the playing of sports involves a complex and contentious alternation between motivations, intentions and possible choices on the one hand, and choices, actions and actualizations on the other, but the aim and tendency of all sports is always towards the reduction of the virtual to the actual. Sports may have the reputation of encouraging aspiration and self-transformation, but their action is governed by the desire for the absolute coincidence of being and meaning.

Some forms of modern theatre has been impelled by the ideal articulated by Antonin Artaud of escaping from the condition of being the flimsy shadow or simulacrum of some other, more primary reality, by trying to present a kind of actuality that is in fact more actual than real life, with all its subterfuges, evasions and approximations.

Sport may be said to aim at a similar kind of absoluteness, a similar cauterizing of every if and but and maybe. This may be why some of the more demanding forms of theatrical or artistic performance actually seem to come close to the condition of a sport. The exhausted performers in Forced Entertainment's *Quizoola*, who are required by the rules of the performance to keep improvising questions and answers for many long hours, are not in any intelligible sense pretending to do what they do. This libido of absoluteness is exhilarating, sometimes ecstatic, but also often deeply unlovely, and callously toxic with respect to all the delicately subtle subjunctiveness to which sport also gives rise.

And yet, if sport is in its essence fiercely opposed to simulation, simulation is nevertheless an essential part of it. Outdoing one's opponent will often involve counterfeiting an intention, or doing one's best to disguise it altogether. Feinting is one of the most complex and compelling forms of sporting action. Such forms of guile have always had a shadowy status. The *reticularius*, the gladiator who aimed to entangle his opponent in his own movements by means of a net, was one of the lowest-status gladiators. There was something suspicious, sinister and underhand about the many ways of inducing swerve, in oneself or in one's projectile, perhaps because of the sense that it gives, not of succeeding within the rules but somehow subtly modifying them, in a way that is not entirely respectable. Walt Whitman complained in 1889: 'Is it the rule that the fellow who pitches the ball aims to pitch it in such a way the batter cannot hit it? Gives it a twist – what not – so it slides off, or won't be struck fairly? . . . The wolf, the snake, the cur, the sneak, all seem entered into the modern sportsman – though I ought not to say that, for the snake is snake because he is born so, and man the snake for other reasons, it may be said.'[15] The English batsman Arthur Shrewsbury similarly complained of Bosanquet's googly that it wasn't fair.[16]

Games often have zones of allowable but deprecated action, which are strictly permitted by the rules, but are regarded as in some way or other as being unsporting, or against the spirit of the game. One of the strangest was the discredit that used to be attached to hitting runs on the leg side in cricket. Though there has never been a rule that prohibits this, and runs scored on the leg side count just the same as runs scored on the off side, this style of batting was regarded until well into the 1920s as rather cheap and disreputable. It may be that this comes from the fact that these runs are scored in an area to the batsman's left, and are therefore regarded as in a sense not governed by the batsman's conscious intention in the same way as strokes to the off side. It may also be because such play encourages the batsman to take up a stance which obscures much more of the wicket from the bowler, depriving him of a fair target to bowl at. The fact that balls, especially those travelling at speed, are in general harder to hit on the leg side, and certainly harder to hit using the orthodox technique of getting the body and the bat in line with the flight of the ball, meaning that legside runs are often unorthodox and streaky, may also have contributed to the low esteem in which such play was held. Such forms of guile introduce strategic kinds of performance to the heart of sports. It is not always easy to distinguish absolutely the forms of lawful deception, or unserious play, from the kinds of playing at playing that we have distinguished as cheating.

There is an even tauter difficulty to be reckoned with. To be sure, the injunction to take sports seriously implies the requirement to abide by the rules. And yet, as we have said, a feature of sports is that the rules constitute constraints against which the players must contend. Implicit in this, if it is combined with the injunction to play the sport seriously – that is, to play it to win – is the tendency for players to push right up to the edge of what the rules will allow. Not to do this may open one to the charge of not in fact committing oneself fully to the struggle with and against the rules. You cannot tackle another player in soccer without at least running the risk of committing a foul. Often, too, the struggle with the rules will generate new forms of strategy, which have not been explicitly proscribed up to that point, but may seem to require to be curbed or forbidden thereafter. The tendency of honest play, then, which not only observes the explicit prohibitions but also keeps faith with the implicit imperative to play seriously, is paradoxically to push the player towards infringement. The very word 'infringement' suggests that the effect of the pressure to play seriously and to try one's best will be to encourage players to take risks with the rules – not flagrantly to ignore them, but to push them to their limits, to go to their edges. As the standard advice given to baseball rookies has it, according to Scott Ostler, 'If you ain't cheatin', you ain't tryin.'[17]

But this kind of prescribed pressurizing of the rules is different from cheating. For, whereas playing honestly resists and takes risks with the rules, and seeks advantage by finding ways to succeed within what the rules permit, or do not explicitly proscribe, cheating gains its advantage from the expectation of other players following the rules. Playing honestly challenges and purposefully contends against the rules; cheating dishonestly depends on and exploits them. Honest play is always at risk of rule-breaking; dishonest play depends upon the inhibiting force of rules on one's opponents. All play involves the occasional infringement of rules, but only cheating involves the simulation of play itself. The cheat is offensive because he is not serious, because he has deliberately misconstrued the nature of the activity in question.

Kant offers as a guide to moral rightness the test of universalizability: if I can will that every rational agent should act in the same way as I do, even if their actions directly affect my interests, then my actions can be regarded as justified. This is a powerful test for the determining of what is good, but, as has often been observed, it does not provide any way of arguing against the person who asks 'But why seek to be good at all?' (apart from the feeble and unsustainable suggestion that doing good is more rational, which will not survive long against somebody who finds more utility and advantage in doing wrong). A similar abyss divides the honest player from the cheat. As Graham McFee remarks, 'rule following cannot itself be a matter of rules.'[18] Cheating is despised (and the evidence is building that this is true of many social animals apart from human beings) not so much because it is reprehensible, but because it is absurd. Its extreme reprehensibility is due to this absurdity. As Baudrillard suggests, in the quotation with which I began this chapter, it is literally ridiculous to play games with the playing of games. Since the only way to play the game is to accept its rules, which are non-negotiable precisely because they are both arbitrary and freely accepted (which means that they are, in their own way, absurd), it is logically impossible to gain any advantage in the game by pretending to play it, since you are in fact no longer playing the game at all.

Cheating is therefore not an offence in the game, but an ontological affront to it. The animus against cheating comes from the desire to protect the possibility of play itself, which cheating throws into crisis. Wherever cheating is detected, it threatens to drain the reality of the game away, leaving it a frail and futile phantasm. For it is not just the cheat who is revealed to have been only playing at playing; insofar as the players depend upon the shared acceptance of the rules of the game to be able to engage in it, it turns out that they too will have only been playing at playing. Hence the bitterness and hot humiliation of players who discover after the fact that they have been taking part in a fixed or thrown match. Muhammad Ali never looked so genuinely enraged as when he looked down in helpless contempt at Sonny Liston, after he had crumpled to the canvas following the 'phantom punch', one minute and 40 seconds into the first round of their bout in May 1965. If sport is driven by the principle of absolute positivity, the principle that whatever happens should really and indubitably have taken place, cheating hollows out this positivity, rendering it an elaborate but absurd sham.

This is illustrated very well by the goal that France scored against Ireland in the qualifying rounds of the 2010 World Cup. As video replays showed clearly, Thierry Henry, finding the ball bouncing up unplayably at just below waist height, used his left hand to nudge it to William Gallas, who scored. There were outraged protests from the Ireland team, who would otherwise have taken France's place in the final tournament in South Africa, demanding that the goal be retrospectively disallowed, or the whole match declared void. But, in a sense, Henry had already himself voided the entire match of its reality.

This kind of dishonesty may often recoil with much more serious consequences on the dissimulator than on their aggrieved opponents. It seems to me to be much more common than it should be for a soccer team that has been awarded a penalty under dubious circumstances, especially as a result of a pretended reaction to an illegal challenge, to fail to score the goal. One might put this down to the extra, aggrieved alertness and determination given to the goalkeeper by the conviction that an injustice has been done, but it may also be that something of the derealizing effect of cheating may also deplete the capacity of the striker of the ball to be there in a sufficiently focused way. In the case of the French team in the 2010 World Cup, this derealizing effect seemed to be able, almost a year later, to paralyse the team, who played in a groping dream, as though they themselves felt that they had been reduced to flimsy stand-ins.

Handball is treated with odd seriousness in modern soccer. A player who deliberately handles the ball and thereby prevents a goal is very likely to be sent off. Even accidental handball, resulting for example from a purely reflex action of self-defence when a ball is driven directly at a defender, can sometimes earn the defender a booking. Given that such offences often occur in plain view, and with very little chance of going unobserved and unpunished, and that therefore the accusation of dissimulation would be difficult to sustain, it is hard to see at first why this is regarded as more serious than other kinds of foul play, which may be punished simply with a free kick. It is surely because the very suggestion of trying to gain some advantage by setting aside the principle of arbitrary exclusion that constitutes soccer as a game, namely that the ball may not be controlled or touched with the hand, introduces inanity and unmeaning into the heart of the game, evaporating the consensus that is the only thing that keeps the game in being. In the presence of the cheat, the whole game is thrown into crisis, and rendered ludicrous: it both is and is not a game, that both is and is not being played. Cheating is therefore as serious as it is because it is so unserious: it plays with the requirement that the game should at all times be taken seriously. The cheat's selective missing of the point of the game makes the entire point of the game go missing. This may be why we hear expressions like 'That's not cricket', or 'that's not playing the game': the cheat is elsewhere than in the game, and risks deporting the game from itself.

The difference I have proposed between breaking the rules and cheating is not one that is easy to sustain in practice. It would be easy to argue that nearly all rule-breaking involves an element of dissimulation, since the rule-breaker will rarely announce his own infraction and will commonly be prepared to benefit from the fact that it has gone undetected. It is rare for a player penalized for illegal play not to protest his innocence in some manner. But the distinction is not meant to act as a discriminator of different kinds of sporting action, but rather of different kinds of sporting attitude, even if they are embodied in action. My proposal therefore is that what gets called cheating is action that undermines the principle of absolute positivity by dissimulation. This is why different kinds of action can move in and out of the category of cheating. A soccer player who consistently fouls another player will probably not now be regarded as cheating unless the action is performed with a certain kind of extra surreptitiousness.

The tendency is for actions that begin by being seen as cheating to be drawn into the sport's repertoire of allowable deceits. A good example here would be 'diving', the simulation of injury or foul play, especially in contact sports such as soccer and ice hockey, in order to try to gain a penalty. In soccer, diving seems to have become much more common since the 1980s, probably in response to the toughening up of sanctions against the illegal and violent play that abounded up to that point, and seemed rapidly to be returning the 'beautiful game' to its uninhibitedly brutal origins. It seems to me that diving used to be regarded with much more disgust and outrage by players and spectators alike than it is now. Players who might at an earlier period have been deeply aggrieved at being penalized as a result of the flagrant and operatic playacting of their opponents now seem to shrug and accept it as part of the game. The rule that you must not kick the man rather than the ball is gradually evolving into the tactical principle that you should avoid any kind of contact with your opponent that he or she might be capable of amplifying through pretence into a punishable offence. On the whole, this seems to be helping to reduce physical contact in soccer, though oddly with no apparent reduction in the number and seriousness of injuries.

It does not seem to me to be very likely that players and athletes can be forced to resist all the forms of artificial enhancement that now abound, from the use of drugs, or 'banned substances', to different kinds of artificial supplementation. In the long run, it seems likely that sport will defend itself against these practices by absorbing them into the structure of its rules, rather than presenting them as a challenge to the sport as such.

The most cynical view of cheating is that the practices of cheating are now so widespread and so institutionalized among professional sportsmen and women that it seems scarcely possible to maintain the possibility of sport without pretence. Indeed, one might say that the biggest pretence of all is this very principle of positivity: the principle that in sport what happens should happen for real, which I have said is imperilled by cheating practices. Modern organized sport has only been in being for a very short time, and has altered vastly within that time. There is nothing to prevent it evolving away from the principles which have governed it up to now. After all, the view that one could not really be playing a sport if one were being paid for it, rather as a prostitute could not be credited with really enjoying the acts from which she earned her living, was still held to by many within living memory. Expansion of the kind that sport has experienced cannot take place without the pressure growing towards what has been called the de-differentiation of specialized practices. The larger and more influential something becomes, the harder it is for it to retain its identity and integrity.

And, if there is something admirable about the commitment to the principles of positivity and self-identity in sport, there is also something brutal about it. If cheating in sport is part of a general erosion of the principle that things should be exactly as they seem to be, it is also encouraged by the opposite tendency in sport: to dramatize the fact that we are never what we are, and therefore are always in part what we are not. Sport's absoluteness is a kind of violence practised upon every kind of uncertainty or unpredictability, and therefore, ultimately, on life itself. It will not be surprising for us to find, as we will in the final chapter, that it is often accompanied by actual violence, from which the sporting pursuit of victory is inseparable.

seven

Winning

Murthering Play

From its beginnings, sport has been hard to dissociate from violence. From classical times onwards, games and sports were thought of as training for actual combat. The most important and sustained mediator between battle and sport was hunting, one of several sports regularly designated the 'Sport of Kings'. Hunting is described in 1735 by William Somerville as 'the Chace, the Sport of Kings; / Image of War, without its Guilt'.[1] In another poem devoted to hunting, 'Field Sports', the sentiment reappears, following a description of the bloody climax of a hunt using falcons: 'Such are the Sports of Kings, and better far / Than Royal Robb'ry, and the bloody Jaws / Of all-devouring War.'[2] The most developed account we have of the early game of football, that of the Puritan Phillip Stubbes, makes quite clear how sustainedly violent a game it was, combining the intoxication of Caillois's principle of *ilinx* with the deadly earnestness of *agôn*:

> as concerning football playing: I protest vnto you, it may rather be called a fréendly kinde of fight, then a play or recreation. A bloody and murthering practise, then a felowly sporte or pastime. For: dooth not euery one lye in waight for his Aduersarie, séeking to ouerthrowe him & to picke him on his nose, though it be vppon hard stones, in ditch or dale, in valley or hil, or what place soeuer it be, hée careth not so he haue him down. And he that can serue ye most of this fashion, he is counted the only felow, and who but he? so that by this meanes, somtimes their necks are broken, sometimes their backs, sometime their

legs, sometime their armes, sometime one part thurst out of ioynt, sometime an other, sometime the noses gush out with blood, sometime their eyes start out: and sometimes hurt in one place, sometimes in another. But whosoeuer scapeth away the best goeth not scotfrée, but is either sore wounded, craised and bruseed, so as he dyeth of it, or els scapeth very hardly: and no meruaile, for they haue the sleights to méet one betwixt two, to dashe him against the hart with their elbowes, to hit him vnder the short ribber with their griped fists, and with their knées to catch him vpon the hip, and to pick him on his neck, with a hundered such murdering deuices: and hereof, groweth enuie, malice, rancour, cholor, hatred, displeasure, enmitie and what not els? and sometimes fighting, brawling, contention, quarrel picking, murther, homicide and great effusion of blood, as experience dayly teacheth.

Is this murthering play now an exercise for the Sabaoth day? is this a christian dealing for one brother to mayme and hurt another, and that vpon prepensed malice, or set purpose? is this to do to another, as we would wish another to doo to vs, *God make vs more careful ouer the bodyes of our Bretheren.*[3]

Stubbes's sardonic characterization of football as a 'fréendly kinde of fight' is paralleled in our time by the old witticism about somebody going to see a fight at which an ice-hockey game broke out. The particular place of football as embodying a sportive rather than sporting kind of violence is indicated by the repeated suggestion that the ball could be regarded as a human head. It was once believed that the game of football played at Kingston upon Thames in England every Shrove Tuesday commemorated a Saxon defeat of Danish invaders, in celebration of which the head of the defeated Danish leader was kicked around the streets.[4] To be tossed and tumbled unpredictably – to be made sport of, as the tempestuous winds and waves make sport of a ship – was to become a football. Our modern complaint that some issue or other is being used as 'a political football' is anticipated by the lament of the seventeenth-century nonconformist minister and theologian Richard Baxter that:

I must stand by and see the Church, and Cause of Christ, like a Footbal in the midst of a crowd of Boyes, tost about in contention from one to another; every one running, and sweating with foolish violence, and laboring the downfal of all that are in his way, and all to get it into his own power, that he may have the managing of the work himself, and may drive it before him, which way he pleaseth.[5]

In another text he reproached those who mocked religion, asking 'Hadst thou none to make the football of thy contemptuous sport, but the *sons of God*'.[6]

One of the most notable changes in sport is that, while it continues to be thought of as pleasurable, it has lost its associations with laughter. One of the last formalizations of an old regime of sportiveness as a simple, animal or infantile good humour is to be found in Milton's 'L'Allegro', which requests the spirit of 'Sport that wrinkled Care derides, / And Laughter holding both his sides / [to] Come and trip it as ye go / On the light fantastic toe'.[7] Sport may be intensely pleasurable, both to participant and spectator, but its associations and affects are no longer those of mirth and jollity. For the ancient and medieval worlds, sport was pre-eminently light, of mind as of toe. However bloody and murderous the play, the sport it provided was regarded as trivial and inconsequential. For the modern world, by contrast, sport has become deadly serious. Sport has become, as we say, professional. Indeed, it is more serious even than the business of earning a living, which most must do as a matter of necessity. The fact that sport is a freely chosen form of striving means that its demands are absolute and bottomless. Precisely because it is arbitrary and self-defining, and because it is not for anything but for itself, competitive sport requires terrifying, almost inhuman levels of sustained purpose and devotion to its arbitrary goals.

Or perhaps one might say that, rather than becoming detached from laughter, sport has taken a leading role in the formalization of laughter. The development of codified sports out of the more impulsive and diffusive notions of sportiveness in earlier periods is equivalent to the development of jokes, which slowly take the place of jests and jesting from the sixteenth century onwards. A joke is the concretion of law and freedom. According to Freud, the first great technician of the joke, the spurt of laughter that marks the climax of the joke is the result of an expected repression followed by its sudden lifting. In a joke, laughter is generated, not from the simple ebullition of good spirits, that simply cackles or farts in the face of earnestness and industry, but rather from an 'economy in psychical expenditure'.[8] This creates an intricate calculus of constraint and release, in which time is centrally involved; the energy which drives a joke is, for Freud, the anticipation of the need for repression, a sort of cathectic capital borrowed from the future, which, when it turns out that it will not be required, can be discharged in the purgation of laughter.

The joke therefore comes into being, not through sportive divagation but through a coordination of energies. A joke may well make use of elaboration and the proliferation of seeming irrelevance, as in the shaggy dog story, but the point is precisely that it makes purposive use of such time-wasting tactics, which are always held under the arc of tension provided by the expectation of the joke's culmination, a culmination which will reveal it to be not in fact a congeries of miscellaneous things, but a self-relating unity. This culmination has been known since the early years of the twentieth century as the 'punchline'. As in modern organized sports, jokes do not simply ramify or arboresce, seeming to unfold from within themselves the time they take; instead, subjected to time-discipline, they put the time they take into play, or, as we may as well say, they put it to work. Jokes are to jesting as sports are to sportiveness. The importance of sport in the modern world is the importance of being earnest, a word that, we might note in passing, appears to be related to the Old Teutonic *erre*, anger, which develops also into Old English words like *ornest*, meaning wager of battle, and Old Norse *orrosta*, and Old English *orrest*, meaning battle.

Opponency

We saw in chapter Two that the violence that is specific to modern sports is founded upon a single important principle, namely that sport requires what are called 'matches', or the pitting of like against like, which has required the slow disappearance from sport of the conspicuously unequal competition between humans and other animals.

Where animals furnished sport by allowing the spectator to pretend that they were antagonists, human antagonists can be 'sporting' – can participate in sport with each other as equals. The problem with the play-antagonism furnished by animals is that it is fundamentally autistic; given that, whatever the actual danger and extremity the hunter may subject himself to, he or she is playing with himself if the human cannot but win. But, if the human cannot but win, this makes it impossible for the human *really* to win, that is, to gain a victory that is not certain from the beginning. Only uncertainty makes it possible to have an absolute or definitive victory. This is an instance of the strong bond that Roger Caillois observes in European societies between the principles of *agôn* and *alea*, of competition and chance.[9] Sport between cospecific equals comes about in order that it be possible for there to be consent – especially consent to the violence and suffering which seem intrinsic to sport. But this in turn is not principally in order to increase fairness, or reduce cruelty, but in order to make it possible to *win*.

The most important aspect of the seriousness of modern sport is that one cannot play unless one plays to win; not to do so is, as we saw in chapter Six, fraudulence and dishonour. Winning, as opposed to succeeding, implies an antagonist, someone who is as prepared as you are to risk losing in order to win. Winning forms subjects; the one who wins automatically becomes a certain kind of enhanced subject. And winning also requires and creates losers, which is say, it depletes subjectivity. To be a loser is to lose one's distinctness. Emmanuel Levinas has proposed a theory of ethics which, for all its implausible austerity, has been highly influential. Levinasian ethics is based upon a kind of primal guilt, in which being or becoming a human subject means that 'I myself already ask myself if my being is justified, if the *Da* of my *Dasein* is not already the usurpation of someone's place.'[10] My being is thus the depletion or privation of another's. Much has been written about the ethics of sport, but it seems that sport could never satisfactorily be accounted for with an ethics of the Levinasian sort, for, in sporting activity, I have no choice but to strive to displace and to disadvantage another, who can occupy no other place than that which I myself aspire to occupy. I cannot win in sport without beating my opponent, without humbling them, diminishing the scope of their subjectivity and pride in themselves. Losing is not the performance of an action, but being deprived of the possibility of action: losing is something that is done to you, rather than something that you yourself do. Winning is privative; it cannot operate neutrally or indifferently. Winning is perhaps not always or necessarily sadistic, but the pleasure in winning, or the prospect of winning, must always in part be so, since it involves the pleasure of inducing suffering, the suffering of having to accept defeat, in others.

Even in games in which there is no opponent, and in which the aim is ostensibly to strive against different kinds of physical limit, there are always proxy losers, those who fall short of the unsurpassable achievement of the winner, and are therefore denied the winner's place. At the very least, there is an internal division within the competitor himself or herself: the self who clings to past limits and possibilities is sacrificed to the self who overcomes those limits.

As with many familiar concepts, it may be harder to settle precisely what it means to win than might be thought. Winning does not mean subordination, subjugation or supremacy; it is never sovereign, for the power and authority of the sovereign come from a primal asymmetry, in which the monarch has power purely from himself, or from divine right. This doubles the autistic formula of divinity: 'I am that I am' (Exodus 3.14). But victory in competitive sports is always conditioned victory, which cannot define the terms of its own preeminence. In competitive games, as Caillois makes clear, 'the goal is not victory at any price, but prowess exhibited under conditions of equality, against a competitor whom one esteems and assists when in need, and using only legitimate means agreed in advance at a fixed place and time.'[11] Paradoxically, it is only the strict conditions attaching to sporting victory that make it possible for victory to claim the specific kind of absoluteness that it does. The King is sovereign because of the contingent fact that he just is. The athlete gains the crown because he has submitted himself to the demands and disciplines that define what it is to win. He can prevail only because he is handicapped. Champions are those who command a field of action (the *champ*), but they are themselves commanded by the field of possibilities that are delimited by the game. Champions are said to be those who can focus intently on their goals, keeping their eyes on the prize. But this makes them subjects who consent to be absolutely determined, or subjected to this singular aim or arena of achievement.

Winning requires there to be what is called an opponent, and relations of opposition. The opponent is more than an enemy or an antagonist. An opponent is simultaneously wholly abstract and utterly personal. Anybody can gain enemies, or arouse the animosity of those whose interests may happen to be opposed to one's own. This is what Anthony Julius has called the 'rational enmity' of contingently opposed interests.[12] My hostility to my neighbour who is draining off water from the river that flows through my land may well be of such a contingent kind; it arises because of where we both happen to live and resources that we are forced to share. My relation to an opponent is completely different, since I have no grounds of personal dispute with them (or, if I do, they have no bearing on our sporting antagonism, since they cannot make my opponent any less or more of an opponent). There is nothing I wish to gain from victory over an opponent, apart from the possibility of winning itself. There are particular reasons for somebody to be or become my enemy, and they are not reasons that need to be apparent to me. It makes perfect sense for somebody to be said to be my enemy without my being aware of it. But, since I must enter freely and knowingly into a sporting competition, I must know my opponent, or at least know him to be my opponent and acknowledge him as such.

This is dramatized in an often-replayed scene in which two opponents are fighting, usually in a public setting. One grounds the other, and seems to have secured their submission. The winner turns to take the salutes of the crowd, at which point his fallen foe abruptly rises and resumes the contest with a violent assault from behind. The victor believes that the contest is over and that his opponent is therefore no longer his opponent, and need no longer be acknowledged face to face. The ruse of the supposed loser is to reveal that, despite appearances, the relations of what, reviving an obsolete word, we might call 'opponency', are still in force. Now, turning away from the opponent is revealed, not as the completion of the contest, but as an ill-judged tactical failure within it.

If I can only have enemies where there are rational causes for dispute, so that only certain persons can be enemies to me, an opponent can be anybody, since the relationship of opponency is abstract and self-defining. A rational enemy is one who has a grievance, or a particular (even if irrational or unintelligible) animosity towards me. An opponent is one who is prepared and required to stand to me in the relation of opponency.

This relation is one of abstract equivalence. An opponent is entitled by the rules of the game to all the conditions of privileges that attach to me. It becomes apparent to almost every human being at an early stage of life that there are creatures in the world who are neither me, nor absolutely not-me in the way that a material object is. These creatures can be assumed to have the same kind of interests and motivations as me, though they can never precisely coincide with mine. In this, they are therefore at various angles of obliquity to me. But an opponent, such as is abstractly constituted in a game, can be regarded as having precisely the same interests and motivations as me, namely, for the period of the game, the desire to win it, and win it by causing me the loss of the game.

Ironically, once one has the apparatus that defines and conditions equivalence, it then becomes possible once again to conceive of inter-species competition, such as the race that was staged between South African rugby winger Bryan Habana and a cheetah (with a top speed of around 30 mph Habana had to be given a very considerable start to have any chance of crossing the line around the same time as the released animal.)

One might compare, as many have, the participation in a game to the fighting of a battle, in which outcomes at the time and on the ground are rarely as clear and definitive than historical chronicle would seem to suggest. In sport, as in war, one cannot be said to have won until there has been a surrender; the simple statistics of slaughter or of ground gained or goals scored do not suffice. Indeed, it is part of the penalty of being a loser that it involves acknowledging the fact of one's loss. But this will always limit the achievement of the victor, whose victory will be in part dependent upon this acknowledgement. Even in the pursuit of war, it is necessary for a superior army to hold back from exercising absolute exterminating force on the enemy, in order to leave them with enough infrastructure intact – communications, decision-making structures – to be able to recognize their situation as hopeless, and consequently to surrender. Only an enemy or opponent who has enough residual dignity and self-possession to be able to acknowledge their defeat can permit one's victory to be definitive. Complete or definitive victory therefore depends upon one's opponent not having been utterly crushed. So the defeated party turns out not to be utterly powerless, as one cannot take the risk of annihilating them utterly. Indeed, one might almost define a sport as a circumstance which makes it possible for there to be a loser, who loses as absolutely and definitively as possible while remaining almost entirely unharmed. This is nevertheless fully compatible with the argument proposed in chapter Six that one function of sport is to provide opportunities, which are rarely provided in other areas of life, for the absolute and unconditional decisiveness represented by victory.

This may be why, although some sports allow for crushing defeats, by margins that are almost unlimited, most have the convention that the game stops at the point at which an unchallengeable lead or advantage has been established. To do otherwise would be to compromise the absoluteness of the victory. If a player has won a tennis match 6–3 in the final set, the players do not continue trading games; if they did, it would seem to mean that the loser had not in fact conceded defeat at the point at which they should and must ('best of 13?'). So, in order for victory to be entire and absolute, it is necessary for it to be something other than total.

This reveals another paradox in winning against an opponent. Although the opponent is simply whoever he may happen to be in reality (my sparring partner, perhaps, or, as in the case of the Williams sisters in tennis, my sibling), the one who stands to me in the relation of opponent, nevertheless, that opponency has for the duration of the match a distinct and particular relation to me. This is the real meaning of opponency, the relation in which I stand absolutely face to face and toe to toe with an antagonist, neither of us looking aside. There is no angle of subtension, no diagonality, no shadow or play of reserve in this absolute symmetry, in which each looks at the other and sees, not that other, but their look, that addresses me (literally stands up to me, stands me up) as opponent.

Though he does not relate it to sport, Hegel's dialectic of the master and the slave in section IVA of his *Phenomenology of Mind* has an application to the pursuit of victory in sports. The opponent is the one that I must overcome, in order to achieve and demonstrate my infinitude, the fact that I am not dependent on anything outside myself. But this involves a risk, a trial or pitting of oneself against the negativity of what is not me. Though Hegel does not address the question of sporting competition anywhere at any length, his work depends upon the opposition of struggle and what he tends to call 'play' (*spielen*). Hegel uses the idea of playing (*spielen*) almost always in its older senses, of a free, formless and ultimately timeless dissipation, and indeed J. S. Baillie, the most commonly cited translator of the *Phenomenology of Mind*, tends to call on the older meanings of sport to translate the words *Spiel* and *spielen*. The universal struggle to survive, that war of all against all 'in which every one for himself wrests what he can, executes even-handed justice upon the individual lives of others, and establishes his own individual existence, which in its turn vanishes at the hands of others' does not at all provide the conditions for the emergence of mind or spirit.[13] For this amorphous struggle has no direction, no orientation, no steady purpose, and so is 'the mere semblance of a constant regular trend, which is only a pretence of universality, and whose content is rather the meaningless insubstantial sport [*das wesenlose Spiel*] of setting up individual beings as fixed and stable, and then dissipating them'.[14] Even the life of God seems to require this competitive bracing with otherness: 'The life of God and divine intelligence, then, can, if we like, be spoken of as love disporting with itself [*ein Spielen der Liebe mit sich selbst*]; but this idea falls into edification, and even sinks into insipidity, if it lacks the seriousness, the suffering, the patience, and the labour of the negative.'[15]

For Hegel, the only way for me to achieve full and independent self-consciousness is through being recognized by another self-consciousness. But this means that I in fact become dependent for my independence upon the one whom I subdue:

[J]ust where the master has effectively achieved lordship, he really finds that something has come about quite different from an independent consciousness. It is not an independent, but rather a dependent consciousness that he has achieved. He is thus not assured of self-existence as his truth; he finds that his truth is rather the unessential consciousness, and the fortuitous inessential action of that consciousness.[16]

The relation of opponency expresses this relation of reciprocity in struggle in the tightest possible fashion. Because the only way in which I can be free of my opponent is to overcome him, even though I cannot fully overcome him without revealing my dependence on the fact of his acknowledgement of my victory over him, my opponent is simultaneously the avenue to and ambushing of my free selfhood. It is perhaps for this reason that my opponent, arbitrary and abstractly exchangeable though he may be with any other opponent, will come to seem intrinsically and essentially *mine*.

This may tend sometimes to reduce the abstractness of opponency, as it comes to be focused on just one of the opponents whom I regularly meet, who comes to fulfil the function of the one whose recognition of my victory I most require under all circumstances of opponency. This relation of rivalry and dependence may account for the intensity and longevity of traditional rivalries in sport, in which self and other get tangled together inextricably. When things are not going well for the Arsenal soccer team at the Emirates stadium, the crowd will reliably launch into a chant of 'Stand up, if you hate Tottenham', the idea being that every home supporter has at this point to show their irrefragable allegiance to the club by rising to their feet to join the chant. Those who, like your author, queasily keep their seats, in timorous protest at all the other mob assertions of undying ancestral hatred that this resembles ('Stand up, if you hate the Jews!' – indeed, since Tottenham Hotspur are known charmingly as 'the Yids' this is in effect exactly what the chant is saying) are made squirmingly conspicuous, as a treacherous fissure in the wall of antagonistic unanimity. As you look at the row of impassioned backs and hams in front of you and listen to the sounds of the now ignored match from the muffled gloom of your seat, it is obvious that, should the opposition break through your defences and score, it will be because of you, stubbornly sitting there, letting the solidary energy leak out from the rampart of resolution. You are a traitor, one who puts his petty pride and qualms before the serious business of securing and solidifying belief, and are as vile as the one who meanly withholds his life-giving applause in the pantomime when Tinkerbell's light is expiring. It will cut no ice with the puffy, redfaced goon who drags you to your feet for you to bleat 'But we're not *playing* Tottenham – we're currently losing to somebody else altogether.' Whoever one's opposition may locally and contingently be, it is regarded as an sovereign source of comfort and strength to invoke the defining, immemorial rivalry with Arsenal's North London neighbours.

It is for this reason that Freud writes, in his *Civilization and Its Discontents*, '[i]t is always possible to bind together a considerable number of people in love, so long as there are other people left over to receive the manifestations of their aggressiveness.'[17] As Peter Sloterdijk has put it more recently, there is no universalism that can include absolutely everybody.[18] And the recipients of this aggression are very likely to be, not individuals or groups whose interests are entirely different, but those who are almost exactly the same. Freud called this the 'narcissism of minor differences', indicating by this the idea that it was not the out-and-out strangeness of the other that provoked or permitted violence, but the tiny margin of differentiation that prevented them from being, as they would otherwise be, entirely the same – my match.[19] Thus individuals, teams and whole peoples find themselves locked in immemorial hatreds (hatreds, that is, that nobody quite knows why they feel or even how to feel) of those who are almost the same as they are. Etymologically, a rival is one who is lives on the opposite bank of the river (the *rive*, or *ripa*). The topography of the metaphor is apt and expressive, for, depending on your point of view, a rival is either going in parallel with you in the direction of the river, or stands directly across from you. Your rival is the one who ordinarily might be thought to stand at your shoulder, alongside you, and facing in the same direction; it is when this position is rotated through 180 degrees that con- becomes *contra-*, alongside becomes against, and they become an opponent, the loathéd betrayer, the heretic, the apostate. The devil plays mixed doubles.

Choking

And there is indeed something devilishly duplicitous about winning. Winning must be difficult in order for it to be credible, since modern sports are set up to provide competition against near-equals, and there is something shameful and unworthy about completely trouncing one's opponents – at such times, one is likely to hear that the team winning 8–0 is displaying their professionalism, as a kind of excuse for the dishonour of being a bully. Not that playing weak opposition makes it easy to win against them. As I noted in chapter Six, a draw will be a victory for such opposition, since, as Henry Kissinger once said of wars between guerillas and conventional armies, 'the guerrilla wins if he does not lose. The conventional army loses if it does not win.'[20] But there are more specific difficulties in winning, which take the form of what is known cruelly as 'choking', the inability to complete a victory that one seems on the point of attaining. There are many reasons that may be adduced for this strange but insistent phenomenon, in which winning seems easy as long as it is hard, but becomes almost impossibly hard just at the point at which it ought to be easy.

We should expect statistically that, in a certain proportion of games in which one player or team seem on course to win, they will make mistakes that allow their opponents to snatch the result. The journalistic cliché for this is that a team manages under such circumstances to 'snatch defeat from the jaws of victory'. But these occasions may in fact be much less common than we think, since expecting them to happen means that we notice them when they do and don't notice that they haven't when they don't. In fact, it may well partly be the uncommonness of examples of choking that draws attention to them, and suggests that they may form a syndrome. Nevertheless, the very awareness of this possibility, and the attention focused on the alleged difficulty of consolidating a win, may of itself be enough to produce anxious inhibition in players and athletes.

The effect may be intensified in sports in which the scoring system produces threshold or inversion points. An example of the first is the century of runs in cricket, which seems to produce the phenomenon of the 'nervous nineties', which sees batsmen who have been single-mindedly butchering the bowling to build their total to that point suddenly reduced to tentative prodding and puttering. Tennis provides the best example of the inversion point, in the form of the break point or the match point. The player who fails to win a match point actually gives momentum to their opponent, who remains in jeopardy and yet seems to have been given some mysterious advantage. A similar phenomenon is furnished by the example of a soccer team who have looked dominant all the way through the match right up to the point where the opposition have a man sent off. The difficulty of capitalizing on the advantage offered by playing against depleted opponents is well known, and it can on occasion seem as though the advantage has been handed to the weakened team, who, far from crumpling, seem often to be fired with purpose and, if they feel the sending-off has been unjustified, which they nearly always will, self-righteous rage.

Freud writes about the character of those he describes as 'wrecked by success' in his essay 'Some Character-Types Met with in Psycho-Analytic Work'.[21] It is possible that those who recoil as the prospect of victory draws near may be suffering from Oedipal inhibition, the fear of killing the father that is symbolized in a victory for a male, and, perhaps the female version of the Oedipus, the fear of resisting internalized norms of passivity and obedience in the case of women. This may be generalized, for both men and women, in an unconscious desire to inhibit the intense and possibly even murderous fantasies that the desire to win arouses, which may even extend ultimately to the desire not just to kill but also physically to devour one's opponent, the ultimate form of negation of their separate existence. Hence, perhaps, the metaphor of choking; what the player cannot quite stomach is the sudden confrontation with the fantasy of swallowing their defeated opponent.

But there are many other possibilities, that depend less upon the attribution of exotic or perverse unconscious impulses. One is that the player has become locked into striving, through the sheer exhilaration of the stress involved in struggling to win. The sudden approach of the finish line involves a significant shift of effort. Instead of pushing forward, to overcome a considerable and continuing resistance, you are about to break through from the playing of the game into some other state entirely. Ending is much more than simply stopping. Ending has a duration, with a beginning, middle and end of its own. When you are drilling through a piece of wood, you automatically reduce the pressure as you are about to penetrate to the other side of the material. Landing a plane is a very different thing from simply aiming it at the ground, or a building, though both of these will assuredly bring it to an abrupt stop.

Ironically, therefore, one of the ways of seeing through the end-game successfully consists in pretending that it has not in fact begun. Billie Jean King used to try to avoid the dangerous slackening of tension involved in serving out a 5–3 lead to take the set (and the accompanying tension at the danger) by pretending that she was 3–5 down. Winning is like death. Everything in life leads up to death, and may in a sense be given purpose and orientation by it. The player possesses a being-towards-winning as human beings have what Heidegger calls a 'being-towards-death'.[22] But, as Wittgenstein assures us, 'Death is not an event in life: we do not live to experience death.'[23] You cannot live your death, since it is the event of your ceasing to be alive. And yet you must live it, if only because you are the only person who can. Similarly, one must somehow learn to win without as it were performing a special action known as 'winning', even though, because it is in fact the winning goal, point or sprint, it is just such a special action. One needs a new tactic or special technique for winning, as opposed to simply playing to get into a winning position, in order to prevent oneself from the dangerous tendency to start employing new tactics or special techniques.

If winning is a little like dying, one may be said to win, when one does, a little as one dies, that is without quite meaning to, or entirely being on the scene when it happens. You continue to play until the point where the game comes to an end, at which point you will have won. If you stop playing and start winning, then you put your victory in jeopardy. In order to win, or to avoid the paradoxical inhibition on winning that awareness of its imminence seems to bring, you must try to avoid being split and scattered. You must try to stay in the moment, playing the balls on their merits. But, of course, staying in the moment is as difficult and paradoxical a thing to pull off consistently as the other bits of nonsense that are routinely recommended to us, like 'be yourself' or 'act naturally'. You can only 'keep it real', or 'be in the moment' by an act of intense derealization and self-distantiation – pretending that you are not playing for the match after all, but just sinking a routine putt, or putting away a run-of-the-mill forehand – that in other circumstances would be regarded as pathological.

The difficulty involved in winning is interestingly redoubled in the difficulty that players and athletes have in discussing the difficulty itself. There is no insult quite so wounding as the suggestion that a sportsman has choked. Even in the violently candid sport of baseball, where there are very few inhibitions on what opposing players and coaches feel authorized to say to each other, to make the gesture of choking (a gesture which, by not using the word itself, and resorting to mime, mimes its speech-deleting effect, and thereby protests against the superstitious suppression of references to choking) is regarded as deeply disrespectful, and the occasion for apology and even censure. A large part of the offence is probably that the acknowledgement of the open possibility of choking seems to the superstitious to be a magical solicitation of the phenomenon it names. So, though the awareness of and anxiety about choking is ubiquitous in sports, the topic itself is systematically throttled.

But perhaps the most striking thing that the inhibition on winning reveals is the fact that the player has another adversary, whose influence is just as powerful and decisive as that of the apparent opponent. This is sometimes described as a kind of second, supervising censorious self, the inner critic whose demands can never be satisfied. This figure, which Freud called the superego, is, of course, the internalized form of external authority figures. But one might have thought that there would be less need in sport than elsewhere for recourse to the idea of internalization, since the external form of this supervising, censorious agency is so palpable and audible. It is often noted that anxiety at the prospect of winning is due to an increasing sense of others' expectations.[24]

War Minus the Shooting

Sport involves many different kinds of violence – violent impacts, attempts to hurt, diminish and humiliate, violently immoderate desires and desires for violence. It is tempting to see an analogy between the kind of violence that one sees enacted in sports and the play-violence practised by young animals. In both cases, the combat can seem extremely intense and may indeed result in physical injury; and yet a kind of unspoken inhibition is in force preventing the competition from taking the course that it would outside the context of the game. Those who have seen sport as a preparation for war, from the Spartans through to the Nazis, see a perfect analogy with this kind of behaviour.

For many detractors, there is simply no difference between violence in sport and violence in general. The association was set out crisply by R. C. Sipes in 1973: 'Since warlike societies are widespread so are combative sports.'[25] There are few who would doubt, for example, that sport and militarism reflect, nourish and regenerate each other, even if there is some doubt about whether this is all they do. Most of the contributors to the volume edited by J. A. Mangan entitled *Militarism, Sport, Europe* accept that the two are closely involved with and may be aspects of each other.[26] The subtitle of the collection, *War Without Weapons*, echoes the characterization that George Orwell offered of sport, in the course of a decidedly unenthusiastic response to the tour of Britain by soccer team Dynamo Moskva in November 1945: 'Serious sport has nothing to do with fair play. It is bound up with hatred, jealousy, boastfulness, disregard of all rules and sadistic pleasure in witnessing violence: in other words it is war minus the shooting.'[27] Orwell was writing in a period immediately following the exhausted end of hostilities in the Second World War, in which the desire to find in sport a kind of relief from bloody contention and ideological confrontation was understandably strong. Orwell explicitly takes issue with this common idealism:

I am always amazed when I hear people saying that sport creates goodwill between the nations, and that if only the common peoples of the world could meet one another at football or cricket, they would have no inclination to meet on the battlefield. Even if one didn't know from concrete examples (the 1936 Olympic Games, for instance) that international sporting contests lead to orgies of hatred, one could deduce it from general principles.[28]

Orwell scorns 'blah-blahing about the clean, healthy rivalry of the football field and the great part played by the Olympic Games in bringing the nations together', offering instead the judgement that organized sport is bound up with the development of nationalism, 'the lunatic modern habit of identifying oneself with large power units and seeing everything in terms of competitive prestige'.[29] Acknowledging that the sadistic pleasure in violence and, more particularly, the spectacle of violence (Orwell finds this sadism nowhere more shameless and uninhibited than in female spectators of boxing) was a feature of games and spectacles in Rome, Byzantium and medieval Europe, Orwell nevertheless insists that the danger and vileness of modern competitive sports is that they are caught up in politics.

An emphatic alternative argument has been advanced by Norbert Elias, who sees sport, not as a training and preparation for violence, but as a subtle deterrent of it. Asserting that sport 'is always a controlled battle in an imaginary setting', Elias nevertheless sees sport as an important part of what he calls the 'civilizing process'.[30] Elias suggests that sport develops in England in parallel with the development of parliamentary democracy as a way of containing the murderous schisms of the Civil War, arguing that '[t]he "parliamentarization" of the landed classes of England had its counterpart in the "sportization" of their pastimes'.[31] The problem to which every form of organized sport is a solution 'is how to keep the risk of injuries to the players low, yet keep the enjoyable battle-excitement at a high level'.[32]

But neither of these perspectives, which seem to agree that ultimately sports limit violence – whether in order to make it more disciplined and therefore more effective in a war situation, or in order to offer substitutes for actual violence in imaginary forms – seem entirely to fit the case of sports, which, far from imposing limits on violent behaviour, actually seem to allow for violence that is not possible or acceptable in ordinary social life. Thus play-sparring in animals is deliberately less violent than real conflict will be, while sport in humans is deliberately more violent than is usual; I would certainly regard it as surprising and demoralizing if I were subject in my day-to-day life to the kinds of punching, kicking and barging that are routine in many sports. It seems that, where the play-frame in animals acts to inhibit violence, in humans it often serves to release, amplify and sustain it. For Elias, this is because sport also exists to serve what seems like a contrary purpose, namely, to provide the kinds of arousal and excitement that increasingly are felt to be missing from contemporary life, with its elaborate and extensive inhibitions of excited behaviour and emotional expression. Sport designedly arouses these violent impulses, in order to allow their release in contained and non-injurious form, providing 'an enjoyable and controlled de-controlling of emotions'.[33]

It does seem plausible to regard the violence of sport as being transformed as a result of forming part of a sport, or occurring during the playing of it. The laws that govern violent and abusive behaviour in ordinary social life also apply in sports. But, though there is nothing to stop a policeman taking a startled sportsman into custody as a result of particularly dangerous or violent behaviour, the field of play does seem to act as a zone of legal exception, where ordinary understandings of violent, aggressive and disorderly behaviour are suspended, or significantly reinterpreted. This appears particularly anomalous in the case of boxing in which, as its detractors regularly observe, injury (particularly brain injury, some degree of which will always be incurred when a boxer is punched into unconsciousness) is not an accidental risk, but the specific aim of the sport. For some, this is a disturbing enough anomaly to put in doubt boxing's right to be called a sport at all, an argument that indicates that the displacement or symbolic transformation of violence is in some sense bound up with the definition of what a sport is.

What prevents footballers and ice-hockey players for the most part from routinely spending their Saturday nights in the cells is the assumption of consent, as articulated in legal terms in the common-law principle of *volenti non fit injuria* – no injury can be done to one who is willing. The participants in a sport are held for the most part to have agreed to run the risk of the injuries that might be expected to occur in the playing of the sport. So, typically, legal action is taken, not against participants in a sport, but the authorities responsible for it, for example when inadequate safety measures have been adopted.[34] Prosecution of players has certainly taken place: in 2000 the rugby player Mark Moss was convicted of assault leading to grievous bodily harm and sentenced to eight months in prison after he punched a player in the face, fracturing his eye-socket.[35] However, it remains difficult in contact sports to determine the difference between the violence which a player should expect to encounter as part of the game, and therefore to have consented to in agreeing to play, and violence which goes beyond that level. Most successful prosecutions have centred on incidents that have taken place off the field, or while play is suspended, where the intention to cause injury is much easier to demonstrate. Although it is perfectly possible for a player to be successfully prosecuted for a particularly injurious tackle during the course of play, the fact that penalties exist within the scope of the game, and the difficulty of negotiating the issue of assumed consent, has meant that prosecutions of this kind are less common than they might otherwise be. The understanding within boxing that a fighter is expected to try, among other things, to inflict injury on his or her opponent to the degree that they are physically unable to continue, means that the onus of responsibility passes to referees, who may be held liable for injury if they fail to stop a fight early enough.

Play-fighting among animals is usually designed to prevent actual or serious injury occurring. In the case of human sport, things are more complicated. The argument I have just mentioned, that boxing differs from other sports in that injury is the aim and not just the accidental outcome of the sport, cannot really be sustained in the face of the fact that most sports, especially when played professionally, regularly and predictably result in injuries. Sport actually produces more injuries, and in what may be regarded as a more systematic way, than in real life. Since many, if not most of these injuries derive, not from foul play or accident, but from pushing the body to its limits, or continuing to play through an existing injury, they may be said to be necessary rather than accidental outcomes of sport.

It is violence, along with the spread of attitudes and behaviours characteristic of sporting *agôn*, that poses the most difficult questions about the relations between sport and ordinary social life. Historians and philosophers of sport remain divided on the question of whether sport perpetuates violence or holds it in abeyance. In particular, it is harder to maintain the definitional distinctness of games from everyday life in the case of competitive sports than in any other form of games. The second part of Roger Caillois's *Man, Play and Games* is devoted to the development of an historical typology of cultures according to their favoured play-values. Sports and games may be autonomous, may give themselves their own law, but the question of what kind of law this is may need to be regarded as heteronomous, that is conditioned or confirmed from elsewhere. The paradox of modern sport is that it is at once set apart from ordinary life and an integrally functional part of it. This paradox is nowhere more intense than in relation to the competitive nature of games. For, if it remains true, as

Caillois continues to insist, that 'the proper end of games is never to develop capacities. Play is an end in itself',[36] nevertheless, the analogies between the values developed in competitive sport and the values encouraged in rationalized European and American societies over the last two centuries – of strength, self-reliance, disciplined purpose and the libido of contest – seem so strong as to be unignorable. Indeed, Caillois himself suggests that 'the transition to civilization as such implies the gradual elimination of the primacy of *ilinx* and *mimicry* in combination and the substitution and predominance of the *agôn-alea* pairing of competition and chance'[37] and devotes the second half of his book to showing the ways in which the conjoined principles of competition and chance have replaced those of mimicry and vertigo, in societies in which 'taking your chances', as the sporting motto has it, is paramount.

During the 1980s, and in especially in soccer, concern grew that the particular kind of affective compromise-formation represented by sport – violent competitiveness hemmed in and made safe by rules – might be breaking down, as violence on the pitch began to be accompanied by violence among spectators, which often spilled beyond the stadium into the streets beyond. It is both fitting and unsettling that this apparent breakdown should have occurred particularly with soccer crowds, since in many ways the history of the tempering and rationalizing of medieval folk football provides a model for the development of sport as such. As soccer has continued to grow over the last few decades, this kind of violence represents more and more an economic risk for the game's authorities, and so, for the most part, the threat of violence has been met and perhaps largely contained by tighter and more effective crowd control as well as control of the behaviour of players on the pitch. The assumption here is that the violence of the crowd is a contagion effect – that unrestrained violence between competitors on the field will induce mirroring violence between opposed supporters.

But this ignores what is perhaps the most striking form of antagonism involved in contemporary sport, which, far from paralleling the antagonism on the pitch, may be regarded as, so to speak, perpendicular to it. In discussing the phenomenon of choking, or the inhibition on winning earlier I suggested that part of the pressure felt by players and athletes in the imminence of victory is the increased awareness of the expectations of their supporters. I now want to go further than this and say that, under these circumstances, supporters become a kind of opponent. Winning anxiety suggests that the player's real adversary is the spectating crowd, that swirling sink of will and craving that comes to a point of incandescent focus as the prospect of winning approaches. The player finds himself skewered on the desire he strives to drive to the sticking point. Just as he is about to wrest the recognition of his supremacy from his opponent in the game, that intimate antagonist who is supposed to give all the meaning to his victory, a third party suddenly cuts across this dyadic face-off, complicating its intimacy and efficiency. The one thing that the player knows for sure about this third party is that it is absolutely behind him – as long as he wins. But if he does not and, more particularly, if he perversely seems to throw away victory just when he ought to be able to secure it easily, his betrayal will incur a terrifying wrath and abandonment, which will in fact largely dissolve the mirroring opposition between rival fans, both of whom may be united in booing him off the field. Nowadays, a player or team who simply fails to perform at the level of the crowd's expectations are more likely than ever to incur this kind of condemnation.

This hostility between the crowd and the players discloses a fact about modern sport that has rarely been recognized, namely that it provides, not just a spectacle of violent antagonism, but a violent antagonism of spectacle. One of the few commentators to have considered this aspect of sport is Angela Patmore, who suggested in 1979 that sport could be regarded as a kind of renewed experiment in the production of and response to extreme stress. She defines what she calls the 'sport experiment' like this:

> [B]y artificial means, by the use of symbols, tools, props, boundaries and time limits, conditions shall be imposed on subject or subjects which will excite the maximum degree of stress, both in the area provided and at the time designated. Death, where it is not presented as a possible stimulus, shall be represented or symbolized. Under these conditions, ability to withstand stress in the subject or subjects shall be measured, and be seen to be measured, in the performance of a chosen visible skill,

in the area provided and at the time designated . . . The exhibition of energies so generated shall be signified collectively by the term 'sport'.[38]

This is the open secret of sport's violence. It is a way of assaying (hence the language of trials, tests and contests) the degree of resistance to stress. And, while it may seem to involve a minimizing of the risk of physical injury (and even this may be open to doubt, given the pressure it produces on players to put their bodies at risk), it seems to require a maximizing of the psychological stress on players of sports to the point where breakdown is produced. For Patmore, it is the array of 'breathtakingly clever techniques for dislodging competitors from their mental stability in front of observers' that constitutes '[s]port's cruelty'.[39] As Arnold Beisser puts it in *The Madness in Sports*, '[t]he sports stadium is a nearly ideal laboratory for psychological investigation'.[40] This is largely because, unlike many forms of experiment, in which the observer aims to minimize the distorting effects of his presence on the experimental subjects, in sport, the visible and audible presence of the observer, and the pressure induced in the subject by that presence, *is* the experiment. When we watch a sport, we are looking to see how far they (and therefore we) can go before they collapse. Here the salient point is not the violence that may occur in sport, nor even the violence that might be encouraged by it, but the violence practised upon and through it.

Whether they are held to glorify violence or to temper it, the organized sports that grew during the eighteenth and nineteenth centuries had, and continue to have, an essential relation to violence. Sport may well be said to solve or at least limit the problem of violence; and yet the very way it does this also concentrates sport around the question of violence, making sport and violence indissociable and ensuring that violence is always at issue wherever there is sport. Violence is what gives modern sport its meaning, purpose and necessity – not boredom, not curiosity, not diversion, not play, not even 'excitement', insofar as, on Elias's account, excitement is identified almost entirely with the particular kinds of arousal provided by the experience or spectacle of violence. The advantage is clear of being able to contain, purge or sublimate violence in the way in which sport is said to do. The disadvantage is that, definitionally twinned as it is with the question of violence, sport necessarily prolongs and even perhaps amplifies a violence that might otherwise be dissipated much more quickly, or not even arise.

Nikotics

The view one takes of the violence of sports depends largely upon whether one judges that there is, according to a measure that will itself always be uncertain, broadly more or less violence as a result of sport. This requires that one develop some model of the economy of violence. If we revert to the question of the emergence of sport out of disporting with which this book began, it may be possible to generate a slightly more complex understanding of this economy. The argument that organized sports involve a containment of violence often focuses upon the history of football, and we have seen that football as traditionally played in medieval Europe was certainly a bloody and bone-cracking pursuit. But it is not clear that this was the only or perhaps even the principal reason that authorities sought to constrain it. For sports of this kind were just as likely to be condemned for being wasteful. Indeed, one of the most frequent complaints about such diversions as football was that they deflected the time and energy of working people which could more profitably be employed in refining the skills of war, especially the skills of archery on which English armies placed considerable reliance. A royal order of 1365 decreed that every able-bodied man in the City of London 'when he has leisure shall in his sports use bows and arrows or pellets and bolts', and forbade them 'under pain of imprisonment to meddle in the hurling of stones, loggats and quots, handball, football . . . or other vain games of no value'.[41] It was not violence as such that seemed the problem, but 'unthrifty or idle games, wherby the realme is likely to be without archers'.[42] 'Murthering play' was defined as unproductive because undirected violence. The problem was therefore not how to limit violence, but how to concentrate and conserve it, how to prevent violent impulses dissipating themselves unproductively, and thereby maintain the State monopoly on violence (beheading those convicted of football-related affray was one effective method).

I think we can see an analogy here with what Peter Sloterdijk has recently characterized as the economics of anger in his *Rage and Time*.[43] Sloterdijk characterizes rage in terms of the principle that Plato calls *thymos*, which encompasses, along with anger, the principles of pride, indignation and the desire for self-aggrandisement and aggressive self-assertion. Indeed, we can say that the feelings associated with victory in sport and war – the nikotic affects, as they may be styled – are part of the empire of the thymotic. Sloterdijk's argument is that European societies have had to find ways of managing anger, which is not to say diminishing it, but rather of focusing it in such a way that its energy can be conserved and directed, rather than expended wastefully in glorious but unproductive effervescence. Sloterdijk reads the history of political institutions wittily and provocatively as a kind of capitalism of rage, with rage-banks able both to concentrate and distribute wrath-capital where and when it can best be put to work.

Sloterdijk sees the economy of anger as designed to concentrate resources that might otherwise be frittered away, since the tendency of anger is to produce sudden, tension-relieving explosions. The commonest form in which anger is stored is in the desire for revenge. Anger must be turned into resentment and the desire for revenge in order to be made both durable and exchangeable: an anger that can be held in common is more likely to be an anger that can be augmented and conserved over a long period. In a sense, the movement towards organized sport involves a similar kind of concentration, but it is achieved in a precisely opposite fashion. The aim of the saving up of religious or revolutionary violence was to persuade the angry or resentful to delegate their anger to a central agency, in Sloterdijk's terms, to deposit their savings in the National Bank of Rage. (The Lord God who says 'vengeance is mine' is like the State which makes it a punishable offence to take the law into your own hands.)

The aim of organized sports, by contrast, has been to diversify and radiate the desire for and pleasure in victory which had previously been concentrated in royal or aristocratic centres of privilege. The move from distractingly chaotic diversions like medieval football to organized sports may be seen as a movement from a restricted economy of victory, in which the experience of glorious supremacy was reserved for the sovereign, whether in his rampages after deer across the appropriated forests of Southern England, or in his military adventures, to a distributed economy of supremacy, in which nikotic affect could be spread, albeit in sometimes frustratingly small rations, much more generally through the population. Thus the problem which sport helps to solve is not so much that of containing violence as that of multiplying and distributing the opportunities to participate in it. This accounts for the odd paradox that sports seem actually to increase rather than to decrease the total amount of violence. In such an economy, nobody, outside war-time, achieves the complete and ultimately intoxicating consummation of pure victory. Spectator sports allow for the extension of nikotic affect even more broadly, since they make possible the vicarious participation in victory. In the end, the code of sportsmanship will require that one be a good loser, and thereby allow the loser to participate in the winner's modest and temperate pleasure, as when the defeated captain congratulates the winner on his victory, rather than skulking away like Malvolio intent on revenge.

It is common to see the commercialization of sport as part of the move from sacred or traditional actions to secular ones, and as such a betrayal of the autotelic or *sport-pour-le-sport* principle of sport. Seen in terms of the affective economy, it presents itself rather as the way to propagate the privative rapture of victory across large numbers of participants, without maintaining the population in a permanent state of war, which, apart from other disadvantages, such as its tendency to deplete the population rapidly, also requires an infinite series of reliably defeatable opponents. It is the process of generalizing both the desire for and the pay-out of winnings (here to be taken literally, since the proceeds are paid in the nikotic currency of winning itself) that bridges the increasing ethic of competition in sports and in other areas such as politics. As Roger Caillois observes, sporting norms have come to characterize political contests in democratic states, which tend 'to consider the struggle between political parties as a kind of sports rivalry, exhibiting most of the characteristics of combat in the arena, lists or ring – i.e., limited stakes, respect for one's opponent and the referee's decision, loyalty and genuine cooperation between the rivals, once a verdict has been reached'.[44] The nikotic economy of sports also matches the distribution of success under a political economy which, in eighteenth- and nineteenth-century

England pre-eminently, also strove to generalize access to the possibility of winning. In both cases, the cost of the generalized access to winning means that it cannot be guaranteed or permanent. Opposed political parties must be allowed to contest elections at regular intervals, and a team that has been trounced will reliably be given their chance to reverse the outcome in the next match in the series or the away fixture. The cost of a de-monopolized nikotic economy is that winning is never once and for all: league table positions, like share prices, can go down as well as up. But the huge advantage is that there are no out-and-out and utterly hopeless losers. Everybody can find some team to support who will occasionally fluke a win or scrape a draw against superior opponents.

Glissade

The 'total football' developed by the Dutch soccer team in the 1970s effected a mobilization of the very idea of position. Each player was able and prepared to play in any position on the field, depending on where they picked up the ball and the conditions obtaining in the game. Here, a position was understood as a set of movement-profiles, that themselves were passed, like the ball, from player to player. These transmissions and interchanges of energies, potentials and speeds are particularly complex in team games, but they also play a large part in the many forms of sports in which the aim is not to subdue a human opponent, but to achieve a kind of convergence with a natural form or force. Off the cuff, and brilliantly, Gilles Deleuze noted more than twenty years ago the move towards such sports:

> We got by for a long time with an energetic conception of motion, where there's a point of contact, or we are the source of movement. Running, putting the shot, and so on: effort, resistance, with a starting point, a lever. But nowadays we see movement defined less and less in relation to a point of leverage. All the new sports – surfing, windsurfing, hang-gliding – take the form of an entering into an existing wave. There's no longer an origin as starting point, but a sort of putting into orbit. The key thing is how to get taken up in the motion of a

big wave, a column of rising air, to 'get into something' instead of being the origin of an effort.[45]

Deleuze's remarks indicate a movement from one kind of movement to another – a movement induced in a static and discontinuous field of action, in which force is applied in a determinate fashion at a fixed point, and a movement within an interactive and contagious field of movements, transmitted between and itself constituting mixed bodies. An order of action and production moves towards an order of induction and resonance. In the former order, objects and movements come up against each other in the space in which they occur; in the latter, movements condense into objects and objects are infused with movement in a space that they themselves agitate and inform. The new sports of the kind gestured to by Deleuze emphasize the importance of sliding or equivalent motions – skating, soaring, gliding, floating, hovering – expressed in prepositions such as *along* or *across*, rather than *at* or *against*.

It may be that we are beginning to see a new syntax of competitive relations in the kind of sports towards which Deleuze so presciently points. There is no waning of the libido of striving on display in surfing, skateboarding, bodyboarding, free running, snowboarding, kite-surfing or bossaball (which mixes soccer and volleyball with trampolining). But the sports that seem to be prompting the most interesting philosophical reflection are no longer those that raise questions about human rules and ethics, but those that seem to dramatize the human relation to the nonhuman world of things and forces. Gunnar Breivik has recently offered, for example, a 'Heideggerian Analysis of Skydiving', which finds that, as a novice skydiver, 'one exposes oneself to a unique combination of a radical breakdown of world, being-in-a-void, the experience of anxiety, and being-towards-death, which, according to Heidegger, should facilitate a more authentic understanding of what life is about'.[46]

Sartre provides the first great analysis of the sporting relation between human and nonhuman in the 'Doing and Having' chapter of *Being and Nothingness*, in which his aim is to show that 'a principal aspect of sport – and in particular of open air sports – is the conquest of these enormous masses of water, of earth, and of air, which seem *a priori* indomitable and unutilizable'.[47] The ideal action and relation is not one in which the object is simply altered, assaulted or assimilated.

Rather it is instanced in the sliding of skis over the snow, which brings about a synthesis of support and speed (only the movement of the skis over the snow makes it possible for the snow to act as a support), in which 'matter reassembles itself and solidifies in order to hold me up, and it falls back exhausted and scattered behind me'.[48] What is most important for Sartre is that the snow should be transformed only at the moment of his passage over it, and reform itself behind him without leaving an adulterating trace, which is why snow-skiing is improved by water skiing which 'though recently invented, represent[s] from this point of view the ideal limit of aquatic sports'.[49]

Sartre insists that the rapture of this action comes from the fact that '[t]his synthesis of self and not-self which the sportsman's action here realizes is expressed, as in the case of speculative knowledge and the work of art, by the affirmation of the right of the skier over the snow. It is my field of snow.'[50] Sartre regards as equivalent the two consecutive statements he makes, that 'the sliding appears as identical with a continuous creation' and that '[t]he speed is comparable to consciousness and here symbolizes consciousness'.

Writers on surfing seem drawn to the Sartrean account of mastery over things. Andy Martin's *Walking on Water* (1992) goes so far as to interpret Genesis 1:2, 'And the spirit of God moved upon the face of the waters', as an indication that creation itself might be seen as a kind of surfing: 'He moves across the surface of the sea: upon the face, riding the waves even as He creates them, surfing the world into existence.'[51] Surfers aim to siphon some of that divine energy:

It seemed to me that all surfers aspired to the condition of divinity. They all wanted to be mightier than the mightiest waves. I knew that during those brief immortal moments when I was standing on the board, walking on water, I too felt like a supreme being, until the ocean cast me down again and turned me once more into a creeping thing that creepeth upon the face of the earth.[52]

There is indeed a great deal of pride, aggression, rivalry and desire for position in Martin's account of the world of surfing, both in *Walking on Water* and also in his more recent *Stealing the Wave: The*

Epic Struggle Between Ken Bradshaw and Mark Foo, which, as its subtitle suggests, makes the sea the arena for a human struggle.[53]

But we are, I think, by no means required to see this creation in
quite such a solipsistic fashion, as though it came simply from the will
and the action of the skier or surfer, magically and momentarily trans-
forming the inert in-itself of the snow or ocean into something that
is uniquely and entirely for the sportsman. One of the features of both
of these sporting actions is the transformation it effects between sliding along parallel to the plane of the sea or snow – the belly-slide that
is natural to children, or the posture of the bobsleigh – and standing
proudly perpendicular. Normally, slipping means losing one's traction
in the surface, feeling your feet suddenly abruptly and ludicrously
running away, both from and with you, following by abrupt and comic
abasement. The skier or surfer, like the cyclist, learns to keep their foot-
ing and uprightness during the slide, by keeping the gravitational
centre just in front of the movement, and, by using curves to slow and
control their career, thereby entering and acquiescing to the movement what would normally defeat or undo the will to uprightness.
Andy Martin evokes well the magical moment of transformation for
the surfer, when he or she is suddenly flipped from ignominious
doggy-paddle to uprightness:

> There is something magical about the take-off. The initiate
> invokes the mysterious open-sesame to the wave, locking on
> to the vanishing point –like a subatomic particle in an accel-
> erator that expires in an instant – between the breaking and
> the broken, the green and the white. As in a conjuring trick,
> the eye hardly has time to grasp what it sees. You need slow
> motion film to catch the arch of the back, the whipping of
> the trunk, the follow-through of the legs, all that sudden and
> radical rearrangement of the parts of the body. One second the
> surfer is prone on his board. The next, with a single, smooth,
> swift movement, he is on his feet, legs akimbo, arms carving
> the air, swooping down the face of the wave.[54]

Here, uprightness and parallelism are rotated into equivalence.
To read this as a simple, Sartrean appropriation, a making mine of the

wave, seems reductive, wilful and rather petty. The participant in these new sports stands up on the wave, or hangs upright in air, as a result of a homeorrhetic interchange of energies, directions and movements. He or she resembles Hopkins's 'Windhover', evoked in a participial sequence that hold together in the suspensive space of the poem the movements that give the hovering kestrel its stability in movement:

> dapple-dawn-drawn Falcon, in his riding
> Of the rolling level underneath him steady air, and striding
> High there, how he rung upon the rein of a wimpling wing
> In his ecstasy! then off, off forth on swing,
> As a skate's heel sweeps smooth on a bow-bend: the hurl and gliding
> Rebuffed the big wind.[55]

Indeed, read attentively, Sartre's evocation of the action of skiing seems already to suggest something more, or other than simple appropriation, for it involves a complex transfer of qualities:

> Possession is a magical relation; I am those objects which I possess, but outside, so to speak, facing myself; I create them as independent of me, outside all subjectivity, as an in-itself which escapes me at each instant and whose creation at each instant I perpetuate. But precisely because I am always somewhere outside of myself, as an incompleteness which makes its being known to itself by what it is not, now when I possess, I transfer myself to the object possessed. In the relation of possession the dominant term is the object possessed; without it I am nothing save a nothingness which possesses, nothing other than pure and simple possession, an incompleteness, an insufficiency, whose sufficiency and completion are there in that object.[56]

It is principally the movement of controlled *glissade*, in what have become known as 'sliding sports', that embodies this new relation to the things of the world, in which the sportsman and the world give and take movement to and from each other. Once one's striving is no longer simply against a human or a natural opponent, but is rather triangulated by the intermediary of wind, rock or wave, one seeks to bounce back from or slide across an adversary that one aims to make one's auxiliary.

Sport is very old, but also very young. It may be that, following the emergence of the abstracted, regulated systems of strictly intrahuman forms of physical competition that have become dominant across the world, a new, more oblique and convivial kind of ludic exertion is beginning to assert itself, in the many forms of sport where the aim is not to gain victory, according to abstract rules and measures of dominance, but rather to attain splendour. Up to now, sport has mimicked the form of war that has been practised in human history, in the struggle of one opponent against another. We have become hypnotized by the struggle of human against human, obsessed by the question 'Who will win?'[57] But, as Michel Serres memorably observes, the mesmerizing spectacle of human combatants struggling for dominion – Serres reminds us of Goya's extraordinary drawing of two giants battling against each other with sticks while they sink into mud – has blinded us to the setting, or theatre of their struggle:

> Quicksand is swallowing the duellists; the river is threatening the fighter: earth, waters, and climate, the mute world, the voiceless things once placed as a décor surrounding the usual spectacles, all those things that never interested anyone, from now on thrust themselves brutally and without warning into our schemes and maneuvers.[58]

We are involved in a world war that we cannot, dare not, dream of winning, a war against the world. We have traditionally lost against nature, and we know that this can mean to lose big. But, only a short time after we stopped losing so definitively to nature, we have also begun to discover that if we take the risk of winning, we stand to lose everything. It would be just as absurdly and perilously overblown as the efforts in the past to find a kind of human destiny in sport to expect sport to provide us with a new model of consciousness, embodiment and value, or with the patterns of a transformed economic, ethical and legal relation with nature. Still, these newer sports, which seem to have begun to be drawn, though with no diminishment at all in the intensity of their purpose, toward the principles of splendour and flourishing, rather than the principles of winner-takes-all victory and finalizing decision, may help to equip us for the adjustments we may need to make in our attitudes toward nature. It would be cheering, given that the unnecessary necessity of sport has had such a large part to play in the second nature that human beings have made for and of themselves, to think that one might be able to make out in these new sports the beginnings of a third nature, in which the given and the made, the necessary and the unnecessary, could draw from and transform each other.

References

Introduction

1 Mark Perryman, *Philosophy Football: Eleven Great Thinkers Play It Deep* (London, 1997); *Philosophical Football: The Team That Plays With Strength in Depth* (Edinburgh, 1999).
2 Aristotle, *On Rhetoric: A Theory of Civic Discourse*, trans. and ed. George A. Kennedy, 2nd edn (Oxford, 2007), 1.5, p. 59.
3 Plato, *Euthydemus*, trans. Robin Waterfield, in *Early Socratic Dialogues*, ed. Trevor J. Saunders (London, 2005), 271d–272a, p. 316.
4 Harold Tarrant, 'Athletics, Competition and the Intellectual', in David J. Phillips and David Pritchard, eds, *Sport and Festival in the Ancient Greek World* (Swansea, 2003), p. 351.
5 *Isocrates: With An English Translation by George Norlin*, 3 vols (London and New York, 1929), vol. II, pp. 289, 291.
6 Michel Serres, *Variations sur le corps* (Paris, 1999), p. 5 (my translation).
7 Heather L. Reid, 'Socrates at the Ballpark', in *Baseball and Philosophy: Thinking Outside the Batter's Box*, ed. Eric Bronson (Chicago, IL, and La Salle, IL, 2004), pp. 274, 283.
8 Geoff Bennington and Jacques Derrida, *Jacques Derrida* (Chicago, IL, 1993), pp. 327, 341.
9 Ben Rogers, *A. J. Ayer: A Life* (London, 1999), p. 20.
10 Ibid., p. 26.
11 Lincoln Allison, 'How Cool Is This: A. J. Ayer's *Language, Truth and Logic*' (2005). Online at www.socialaffairsunit.org.uk/blog/archives/000458.php, accessed 14 March 2011.
12 Rogers, *A. J. Ayer*, p. 344.
13 Paul Weiss, *Sport: A Philosophic Inquiry* (Carbondale, IL, 1969), p. 8.
14 Robert G. Osterhoudt, ed., *The Philosophy of Sport: A Collection of Original Essays* (Carbondale, IL, 1973); Hans Lenk, *Social Philosophy of Athletics: A Pluralistic and Practice-Oriented Philosophical Analysis of Top Level Amateur Sport* (Champaign, IL, 1979); B. C. Postow, ed., *Women, Philosophy, and Sport: A Collection of New Essays* (New York, 1983); C. E. Thomas, *Sport in a Philosophic Context* (Philadelphia, PA, 1983); H. J. Vander Zwaag, *Toward a Philosophy of*

Sport (Fort Worth, TX, 1985); Pasquale J. Galasso, ed., *Philosophy of Sport and Physical Activity: Issues and Concepts* (Toronto, 1988); Drew Hyland, *A Philosophy of Sport* (New York, 1990); Martin A. Bertman, *The Philosophy of Sport* (Penrith, 2007).

15 Eric Bronson, ed., *Baseball and Philosophy: Thinking Outside the Batter's Box* (Chicago, IL, 2004); Jerry L. Walls and Gregory Bassham, eds, *Basketball and Philosophy: Thinking Outside the Pain* (Lexington, KY, 2008); Michael W. Austin, *Football and Philosophy: Going Deep* (Lexington, KY, 2008).

16 Bernard Suits, *The Grasshopper: Games, Life, and Utopia* (Toronto and Buffalo, 1978); Graham McFee, *Sport, Rules and Values: Philosophical Investigations Into the Nature of Sport* (London, 2004); Bertman, *The Philosophy of Sport*.

17 William J. Morgan, *Why Sports Morally Matter* (London, 2006).

18 Randolph Feezell, *Sport, Play, and Ethical Reflection* (Urbana, IL, 2004).

19 Hans Ulrich Gumbrecht, *In Praise of Athletic Beauty* (Cambridge, MA and London, 2006).

20 David Best, 'Sport Is Not Art', *Journal of the Philosophy of Sport*, XII (1985), pp. 25–40; Andrew Edgar, 'What Is Art? James and Collingwood on Sport', in *Sporting Reflections: Some Philosophical Perspectives*, ed. Heather Sheridan, Leslie A. Howe and Keith Thompson (Aachen, 2007), pp. 20–31.

21 Roger Caillois, *Man, Play and Games*, trans. Meyer Barash (Urbana, IL, 2001), p. 12.

22 Gaston Bachelard, *La Terre et les rêveries de la volonté* (Paris, 1948), p. 78.

23 Jean-Paul Sartre, *Being and Nothingness: An Essay on Phenomenological Ontology*, trans. Hazel E. Barnes (London, 1984), p. 328.

24 Bernard Suits, 'The Grasshopper: A Thesis Concerning the Moral Idea of Man', in Robert G. Osterhoudt, *The Philosophy of Sport: A Collection of Original Essays* (Springfield, IL, 1973), p. 204.

25 *Ulama: Jeu de balle des Olmèques aux Aztèques/Ballgame from the Olmecs to the Aztecs* (Lausanne, 1997).

26 Sartre, *Being and Nothingness*, p. 328.

one: History

1 William Camden, *Britain, or A Chorographicall Description of the Most Flourishing Kingdomes, England, Scotland, and Ireland, and the Ilands Adioyning, Out of the Depth of Antiquitie* . . . (London, 1610), p. 203.

2 B.J., *Two Letters Written to a Gentleman of Note Guilty of Common Swearing* (London, 1691), p. 64.

3 Thomas Adams, *Fiue Sermons Preached Vpon Sundry Especiall Occasions* (London, 1626), p. 22.

4 Thomas Adams, *The Deuills Banket Described in Foure Sermons* (London, 1614), p. 11.

5 Thomas Adams, *The Happines of the Church, or, A Description of Those Spirituall Prerogatiues Wherewith Christ Hath Endowed Her* (London, 1619), p. 71.
6 Ibid., pp. 89–90.
7 Adams, *The Happines of the Church*, p. 318.
8 Thomas Adams, *The Souldiers Honour Wherein by Diuers Inferences and Gradations it is Euinced, That the Profession is Iust, Necessarie, and Honourable . . .* (London, 1617) sig. A3v.
9 Norbert Elias and Eric Dunning, eds, *Quest for Excitement: Sport and Leisure in the Civilizing Process* (Oxford, 1986), p. 127.
10 Roger Caillois, *Man, Play and Games*, trans. Meyer Barash (Urbana, IL, 2001), p. 27.
11 Ibid., p. 23.
12 Ibid., p. 14.
13 Giorgio Agamben, *The Open: Man and Animal*, trans. Kevin Attell (Stanford, CA, 2004), p. 37.
14 Jean-Paul Sartre, *Being and Nothingness: An Essay on Phenomenological Ontology*, trans. Hazel E. Barnes (London, 1984), p. 581.
15 Phillip Stubbes, *The Anatomie of Abuses Contayning a Discouerie, or Briefe Summarie of Such Notable Vices and Imperfections, as Now Raigne in Many Christian Countreyes of the Worlde . . .* (London, 1583), sig. P5r.
16 Ibid., sig. P4v.
17 Emma Griffin, *Blood Sport: Hunting in Britain Since 1066* (New Haven, CT, and London, 2007), p. 233.
18 Samuel Beckett, *More Pricks Than Kicks* (London, 1970), p. 21.
19 Karl Groos, *The Play of Animals: A Study of Animal Life and Instinct*, trans. Elizabeth L. Baldwin (London, 1898).
20 Michel de Montaigne, *The Complete Essays*, ed. and trans. M. A. Screech (London, 1991). p. 505; *Les Essais*, ed. Pierre Villey and Verdun-L. Saunier (Paris, 1965), p. 452.
21 Barnabe Rich, *The Aduentures of Brusanus Prince of Hungaria* (London, 1592), pp. 73–4.
22 Montaigne, *The Complete Essays*, p. 516; *Les Essais*, p. 462.
23 Matt Cartmill, *A View to a Death in the Morning: Hunting and Nature Through History* (Cambridge, MA and London, 1993), p. 30.
24 Edward Cummins, *The Hound and the Hawk: The Art of Medieval Hunting* (London, 1988), p. 31.
25 Edward, Duke of York, *The Master of Game*, ed. W. A. and F. Baillie-Grohmann (London, 1904), p. 153.
26 George Gascoigne, *The Noble Arte of Venerie or Hunting* (London, 1575), p. 96.
27 Richard Almond, *Medieval Hunting* (Stroud, 2003), pp. 75–82.
28 Ibid., p. 35.
29 Ted Hughes, *Collected Poems*, ed. Paul Keegan (London, 2003), p. 766.
30 Pliny the Elder, *The Historie of the World: Commonly Called, The Naturall Historie of C. Plinius Secundus*, vol. I, trans. Philémon Holland (London, 1634), p. 199.

31 Antonin Artaud, *The Theater and Its Double*, trans. Mary Caroline Richards (New York, 1958), pp. 89–100.

32 Anon, 'Recent Sporting Adventure in the Old World', *Edinburgh Review*, CLXXXIX (1899), p. 213.

33 Anon, 'Sport in the Snow; or, Bear-hunting in Russia', *Temple Bar*, XCVII (1893), pp. 107–22.

34 Donna Landry, *The Invention of the Countryside: Hunting, Walking, and Ecology in English Literature, 1671–1831* (Basingstoke, 2001), pp. 95–6.

35 José Ortega y Gasset, *Meditations on Hunting*, trans. Howard B. Wescott (New York, 1972).

36 José Ortega y Gasset, 'The Sportive Origin of the State', in *History as a System: And Other Essays Toward a Philosophy of History*, trans. Helene Weyl (New York, 1961), pp. 16, 31.

37 Ibid., p. 18.

38 Ibid., p. 29.

39 Ibid., p. 32.

40 G.W.F. Hegel, *The Philosophy of History*, trans. J. Sibree (Kitchener, Ontario, 2001), pp. 260–61.

41 John M. Hoberman, *Sport and Political Ideology* (Austin, TX, 1984), p. 123.

42 Heinz Risse, *Soziologie des Sports* (Münster, 1979), p. 77 (my translation).

43 Ibid., p. 78.

44 Karl Jaspers, *Man in the Modern Age*, trans. Eden and Cedar Paul (Garden City, NJ, 1957), p. 68.

45 Ibid., p. 70.

46 Johan Huizinga, *Homo Ludens: A Study of the Play-Element in Culture*, trans. R.F.C. Hull (Boston, MA, 1955), p. 3.

47 Lewis Mumford, *Technics and Civilization* (New York, 1963), p. 307.

48 Robert Musil, 'Als Papa Tennis lernte', *Tagebücher, Aphorismen, Essays und Reden*, ed. Adolf Frisé (Hamburg, 1955), p. 820 (my translation).

49 T. W. Adorno and Max Horkheimer, *Dialectic of Enlightenment*, trans. John Cumming (London, 1986), p. 88.

50 T. W. Adorno, *Introduction to the Sociology of Music*, trans. E. B. Ashton (New York, 1972), pp. 49–50.

51 T. W. Adorno, *Prisms*, trans. Samuel and Sherry Weber (Cambridge, MA, 1981), p. 81.

52 Ibid., p. 81.

53 Philip Larkin, *Collected Poems*, ed. Anthony Thwaite (London, 1990), p. 127.

54 H. Graves, 'A Philosophy of Sport', *Contemporary Review*, LXXVIII (1900), p. 877. References hereafter parenthetically in text.

55 Allen Guttmann, *The Olympics: A History of the Modern Games*, 2nd edn (Urbana and Chicago, IL, 2002), p. 18.

56 Charles Harrison and Paul Wood, eds, *Art in Theory 1900–1990: An Anthology of Changing Ideas* (Oxford and Cambridge, MA, 1992), p. 156.

57 Michel Leiris, 'The Bullfight as Mirror', trans. Ann Smock, *October*,

LXIII (1993), p. 24.

58 Ibid., p. 39.

59 Ibid., p. 34.

60 Harrison and Wood, *Art in Theory*, pp. 728, 729.

61 Alain Finkielkraut, *The Undoing of Thought*, trans. Dennis O'Keefe (London, 1988), p. 113.

62 Susan Sontag, *A Susan Sontag Reader* (London 1982), p. 314.

63 Ibid., p. 317.

64 Roland Barthes, *What Is Sport?* trans. Richard Howard (New Haven, CT, and London, 2007), p. 63.

65 Walter Benjamin, *Illuminations*, trans. Harry Zohn (New York, 1968), p. 251.

66 Jacques Lacan, *Ecrits: A Selection*, trans. Alan Sheridan (New York, 1977), p. 5; Alan Meek, 'Benjamin, the Televisual and the "Fascistic Subject"', in *Screening the Past*, IV (1998). Online at www.latrobe.edu.au/screeningthepast/firstrelease/fir998/AMfr4e.htm, accessed 3 January 2010.

67 Kevin Krein, 'Sport, Nature and Worldmaking', *Sport, Ethics and Philosophy*, II (2008), p. 267.

two: Space

1 Maurice Merleau-Ponty, *The Structure of Behavior*, trans. Alden L. Fisher (London, 1965), p. 168.

2 Ibid., pp. 167–8.

3 Knut Dietrich, 'New Demands for Sports Facilities: Principles for Future Planning', in *Sport and Space: New Challenges to Planning and Architecture*, ed. Søren Riiskjær (Copenhagen, 1992), p. 24.

4 John Bale, 'The Stadium as Theatre: A Metaphor for Our Times', in *The Stadium and the City*, ed. John Bale and Olof Moen (Keele, 1995), p. 316.

5 John Donne, *The Elegies and The Songs and Sonnets*, ed. Helen Gardner (Oxford, 1965), p. 70.

6 Peter Sloterdijk, *Im Weltinnenraum des Kapital: für eine philosophische Theorie der Globalisierung* (Frankfurt am Main, 2005).

7 John Bale, *Running Cultures: Racing in Time and Space* (London and New York, 2004), p. 38.

8 Ibid.

9 Ibid., p. 39.

10 Bale, 'The Stadium as Theatre', p. 318.

11 John Milton, *Paradise Lost*, ed. Barbara K. Lewalski (Oxford, 2007), Book 8, l. 132, p. 229.

12 Michel Serres, *Genesis*, trans. Geneviève James and James Nielson (Ann Arbor, MI, 1995), p. 19.

13 Simon Inglis, *Sightlines: A Stadium Odyssey* (London, 2001), pp. 254–7.

14 Serres, *Genesis*, p. 52.

15 David H. J. Larmour, *Stage and Stadium: Drama and Athletics in Ancient Greece* (Hildesheim, 1999), p. 134.

16 Peter Sloterdijk, *Schäume: Sphären, Vol. 3: Plurale Sphärologie* (Frankfurt am Main, 2004), pp. 63–4 (my translation).

17 Johann Wilhem von Archenholz, *England und Italien*, 2 vols (Leipzig, 1785), vol. II, p. 61 (my translation).

18 Michel Serres, *Hominescence* (Paris, 2001), pp. 179–80.

19 Ibid., p. 180 (my translation).

20 Michel Serres, *L'Incandescent* (Paris, 2003), pp. 216–27.

21 Gerulamo Cardano, *A Book on Games of Chance*, trans. Sydney Henry Gould, in Ostein One, *Cardano: The Gambling Scholar* (New York, 1953), p. 191.

22 Bradd Shore, 'Marginal Play: Sport at the Borderlands of Time and Space', *International Review for the Sociology of Sport*, XXIX (1994), p. 353.

23 Michel Serres, *The Parasite*, trans. Lawrence R. Schehr (Baltimore, MD, and London, 1982), p. 227.

24 Don DeLillo, *Underworld* (London, 1997), p. 51.

three: Time

1 Andrew Marvell, *Poems*, ed. Nigel Smith (London, 2007), p. 84.

2 Murray Ross, 'Football Red and Baseball Green: The Heroics and Bucolics of American Sport', *Chicago Review*, XXII (1971), pp. 33, 32.

3 Ibid., p. 35.

4 Ibid.

5 Michel Serres, *The Troubadour of Knowledge*, trans. Sheila Faria Glaser and William Paulson (Ann Arbor, MI, 1997), p. 9 (translation modified).

6 Ibid., p. 31.

7 Robert Perinbanayagam, *Games and Sport in Everyday Life: Dialogues and Narratives of the Self* (Boulder, CO and London, 2006), p. 38.

8 Ibid., p. 39.

9 Ibid., p. 38.

10 Samuel Beckett, *Complete Dramatic Works* (London, 1986), p. 46.

11 Jean-Paul Sartre, *Being and Nothingness: An Essay on Phenomenological Ontology*, trans. Hazel E. Barnes (London, 1984), p. 329.

12 Mircea Eliade, *The Sacred and the Profane: The Nature of Religion*, trans. Willard R. Trask (New York and London, 1959), p. 69.

13 Peter Reichel, *La Fascination du nazisme* (Paris, 1993), p. 241.

14 Dennis Brailsford, *Sport, Time and Society: The British at Play* (London and New York, 1991), pp. 12–13.

15 Eliade, *The Sacred and the Profane*, p. 104.

16 Ibid., p. 88.

17 Ibid., p. 87.

18 Allen Guttmann, *From Ritual to Record: The Nature of Modern Sports*, 2nd edn (New York, 2004), p. 26.

19 Brailsford, *Sport, Time and Society*, p. 27.

20 Ibid., p. 94.

21 Jean-Marie Brohm, *Sport – A Prison of Measured Time*, trans. Ian Fraser (London, 1978), p. 176.
22 Jean-Marie Brohm, *La Tyrannie sportive: Theorie critique d'un opium du peuple* (Paris, 2006), p. 152 (my translation).
23 Ibid., p. 153.
24 Brailsford, *Sport, Time and Society*, p. 113.
25 John Bale, *Running Cultures: Racing in Time and Space* (London and New York, 2004), p. 22.
26 Ibid., p. 23.
27 Ibid., p. 27.
28 Guttmann, *From Ritual to Record*, pp. 51–2.
29 Fred Stein, *A History of the Baseball Fan* (Jefferson, NC and London, 2005), pp. 180–91.
30 Kevin G. Quinn, *Sports and Their Fans: The History, Economics and Culture of the Relationship Between Spectator and Sport* (Jefferson, NC, and London, 2009), pp. 90–91.
31 Brailsford, *Sport, Time and Society*, p. 146.
32 Quoted in Richard Haynes, '"Lobby" and the Formative Years of Radio Sports Commentary, 1935–1952', *Sport in History*, XXIX (2009), p. 34.
33 Brailsford, *Sport, Time and Society*, p. 126.

four: Movement

1 Henri Bergson, *Time and Free Will: An Essay on the Immediate Data of Consciousness*, trans. F. L. Pogson (London, 1910), p. 115.
2 Gerard Manley Hopkins, *Poems*, 4th edn, ed. W. H. Gardner and N. H. Mackenzie (Oxford, 1970), p. 52.
3 Jean-Paul Sartre, *Being and Nothingness: An Essay on Phenomenological Ontology*, trans. Hazel E. Barnes (London, 1984), p. 125.
4 Ibid., p. 128.
5 John Dryden, *The Works of Virgil Containing his Pastorals, Georgics and Aeneis* (London, 1697), p. 89.
6 Ian Stewart, *Flatterland: Like Flatland Only More So* (London, 2001), p. 46.
7 Sartre, *Being and Nothingness*, p. 306.
8 Ibid., p. 308.
9 Robert Recorde, *The Whetstone of Witte Whiche is the Seconde Parte of Arithmetike* . . . (London, 1557), sig. Ff1r.
10 Lucretius (Titus Lucretius Carus), *On the Nature of the Universe*. trans. R. E. Latham, ed. John Godwin (London, 1994), 2.220, p. 43.
11 Michel Serres, *The Birth of Physics*, trans. Jack Hawkes (Manchester, 2000), p. 11.
12 Michel Serres, *The Troubadour of Knowledge*, trans. Sheila Faria Glaser and William Paulson (Ann Arbor, MI, 1997), p. 24.
13 Ibid., p. 27.
14 Samuel Beckett, *Murphy* (New York, 1957), pp. 47–8.

15 Luke Howard Hodgkin, *A History of Mathematics: From Mesopotamia to Modernity* (Oxford, 2005), pp. 45–6.
16 Michel Serres, *Récits d'humanisme* (Paris, 2006), p. 154 (my translation).
17 Serres, *The Birth of Physics*, p. 10.
18 John Nyren, *The Young Cricketer's Tutor*, ed. Charles Cowden Clarke (London, 1833), pp. 32, 68, 69.
19 Allison Danzig and Joe Reichler, *The History of Baseball: Its Great Players, Teams and Managers* (Englewood Cliffs, NJ, 1959), p. 39.
20 Paul Dickson, *The Dickson Baseball Dictionary* (New York, 2009), p. 233.
21 W. F. Hopkinson, 'The Theory of the Curve Ball', *Outing*, x (1887), pp. 102, 98.
22 Brian Wilkins, *The Bowler's Art: Understanding Spin, Swing, and Swerve* (London, 1991), pp. 46–8 .
23 'Revealed: Why Curve Balls Are So Hard to Hit', *New Scientist*, 2711 (7 June 2009), p. 7.
24 Garrett Soden, *Defying Gravity: Land Divers, Roller Coasters, Gravity Bums, and the Human Obsession With Falling* (New York, 2003), pp. 72–3.
25 Ibid., p. 206.
26 Ibid., p. 219.
27 Ibid., p. 9.

five: Equipment

1 Roland Barthes, *What Is Sport?* trans. Richard Howard (New Haven, CT, and London, 2007), pp. 59, 63.
2 Martin Heidegger, *Being and Time*, trans. John Macquarrie and Edward Robinson (Oxford, 1962), pp. 96–7.
3 Warren P. Fraleigh, 'The Moving "I"', in *The Philosophy of Sport: A Collection of Original Essays*, ed. Robert G. Osterhoudt (Carbondale, IL, 1973), p. 114.
4 Sigmund Freud, *Gesammelte Werke*, vol. xv: *Neue Folge der Vorlesungen zur Einführung in die Psychoanalyse* (London, 1940), p. 86.
5 Michel Serres, *Variations sur le corps* (Paris, 1999), pp. 152–3 (my translation).
6 Ibid., pp. 151–2.
7 Harry Vardon, *The Complete Golfer*, 9th edn (London, 1908), p. 174.
8 Lucien Lévy-Bruhl, *How Natives Think*, trans. Lillian A. Clare (Princeton, NJ, 1985), p. 76.
9 P. A. Vaile, *The New Golf* (New York, 1917), pp. 26, 25–6.
10 James Braid and Harry Vardon, *How to Play Golf* (New York, 1914), p. 45.
11 Ludwig Wittgenstein, *Philosophical Investigations*, 4th edn, trans. G.E.M. Anscombe, P.M.S. Hacker and Joachim Schulte (Chichester, 2009), § 68–71, pp. 37e–38e.

12 Sigmund Freud, *Beyond the Pleasure Principle* in *The Standard Edition of the Psychological Works of Sigmund Freud*, vol. XVIII, trans. James Strachey et al. (London, 1955), p. 38.

13 Robert W. Henderson, *Ball, Bat and Bishop: The Origin of Ball Games* (New York, 1947), p. 19.

14 Michel Serres, *The Parasite*, trans. Lawrence R. Schehr (Baltimore, MD, and London, 1982), p. 227.

15 Fintan Lane, *Long Bullets: A History of Road Bowling in Ireland* (Cork, 2005).

16 John Newbery, *A Little Pretty Pocket-Book, Intended for the Instruction and Amusement of Little master Tommy, and Pretty Miss Polly* (London, 1760), sig. C4v.

17 Freud, *Beyond the Pleasure Principle*, p. 15.

18 Ibid., p. 16.

19 H. A. Harris, *Sport in Greece and Rome* (London, 1972), pp. 79–80; Nigel B. Crowther, *Sport in Ancient Times* (Westport, CT and London, 2007), pp. 157–8.

20 Christopher Thacker, *The History of Gardens* (Berkeley and Los Angeles, 1979), pp. 230–33.

21 Francisco Xavier Clavigero, *The History of Mexico*, trans. Charles Cullen, 2 vols (London, 1787), vol. I, p. 403.

22 P. G. Tait and W. J. Steele, *A Treatise on the Dynamics of a Particle*, 2nd edn (Cambridge, 1865), p. 288.

23 Serres, *Variations sur le corps*, pp. 179–80.

24 Galen (Claudius Galenus), 'Galen's Treatise on the Small Ball', trans. F. A. Wright, in F. A. Wright, *Greek Athletics* (London, 1925), p. 115.

25 Richard Carew, *The Survey of Cornwall* (London, 1602), sigs V3r–V3v.

26 James Shirley, *The Bird in a Cage: A Comedie* (London, 1633), sig. G2v.

27 St Thomas Aquinas, *Summa Theologica*, trans. the Fathers of the English Dominican Province, 5 vols (Westminster, MD, 1981), Supplement, question 80.3, vol. V, p. 2883.

28 Janet and Peter Phillips, 'History From Below: Women's Underwear and the Rise of Women's Sport', *Journal of Popular Culture*, XXVII (1993), pp. 129–48.

29 Phil Pilley, ed., *The Story of Bowls: From Drake to Bryant* (London, 1987), pp. 50–51.

30 Bernard Adams, *The Badminton Story* (London, 1980), p. 18.

31 Ibid., p. 17.

32 Aristides Quintilianus, *On Music: In Three Books*, ed. and trans. Thomas J. Mathiesen (New Haven, CT, and London, 1983), p. 152.

six: Rules

1 Jean Baudrillard, 'Forget Baudrillard: An Interview With Sylvère Lotringer', in *Forget Foucault*, trans. Nicole Dufresne (New York, 1987), p. 92.

2 Ken Bray, *How to Score: Science and the Beautiful Game* (London, 2006), pp. 21–6.
3 Tim Harris, *Sport: Almost Everything You Ever Wanted to Know* (London, 2007), p. 243.
4 Peter Sloterdijk, *Schäume: Sphären*, vol. III: *Plurale Sphärologie* (Frankfurt, 2004), p. 87.
5 Robert Coover, *The Universal Baseball Association, Inc. J. Henry Waugh, Prop.* (New York and Scarborough, Ontario, 1971), p. 45.
6 Centre for Notational Analysis, *Notational Analysis of Sport I and II* (Cardiff, 1997).
7 Gerulamo Cardano, *A Book on Games of Chance*, trans. Sydney Henry Gould, in Ostein One, *Cardano: The Gambling Scholar* (New York, 1953).
8 Galileo Galileo, 'Sopra le scoperte dei dadi', trans. E. H. Thorne, in F. N. David, *Gods, Games, and Gambling: The Origins and History of Probability and Statistical Ideas from the Earliest Times to the Newtonian Era* (London, 1962), pp. 192–5.
9 Carl Friedrich Gauss, *Theory of the Motion of the Heavenly Bodies Moving About the Sun in Conic Sections*, trans. Charles Henry Davies (Boston, MA, 1857); Stephen M. Stigler, *Statistics on the Table: The History of Statistical Concepts and Methods* (Cambridge, MA, 1999), pp. 178–80.
10 Deborah J. Bennett, *Randomness* (Cambridge, MA and London, 1998), p. 62.
11 Leonard Mlodinow *The Drunkard's Walk: How Randomness Rules Our Lives* (London, 2008), pp. 50–51.
12 Jean-Paul Sartre, *Being and Nothingness: An Essay on Phenomenological Ontology*, trans. Hazel E. Barnes (London, 1984), p. 309.
13 Simon Barnes, 'The Team Who Conquered the Continent By Accident', *The Times* (25 May 2007), p. 106.
14 Marshall Swain and Myles Brand, 'The True Nature of Cheating', in *Football and Philosophy: Going Deep*, ed. Michael W. Austin (Lexington, KY, 2008), p. 93.
15 Horace Traubel, *With Walt Whitman in Camden*, vol. V: *April 8–September 14, 1889*, ed. Gertrude Traubel (Carbondale, IL, 1964), p. 145.
16 Brian Wilkins, *The Bowler's Art: Understanding Spin, Swing, and Swerve* (London, 1991), p. 165.
17 Scott Ostler, *How To Cheat in Sports* (London, 2008), p. 80.
18 Graham McFee, *Sport, Rules, and Values: Philosophical Investigations Into the Nature of Sport* (London, 2004), p. 45.

seven: Winning

1 William Somerville, *The Chace. A Poem* (London, 1735), p. 2.
2 William Somerville, *Field-Sports. A Poem* (London, 1742), p. 5.

3 Phillip Stubbes, *The Anatomie of Abuses Contayning a Discouerie, or Briefe Summarie of Such Notable Vices and Imperfections, as Now Raigne in Many Christian Countreyes of the Worlde* . . . (London, 1583), sigs. P7r–P8r.

4 Eric Dunning, *Sport Matters: Sociological Studies of Sport, Violence and Civilization* (London and New York, 1999), p. 81.

5 Richard Baxter, *The Saints Everlasting Rest, or, A Treatise of the Blessed State of the Saints in their Enjoyment of God in Glory* . . . (London, 1650), p. 818.

6 Richard Baxter, *A Saint or a Brute the Certain Necessity and Excellency of Holiness* . . . (London, 1662), p. 233.

7 John Milton, *Poems*, ed. John Carey and Alistair Fowler (London, 1968), p. 134.

8 Sigmund Freud, *Jokes and their Relation to the Unconscious, The Standard Edition of the Complete Psychological Works of Sigmund Freud*, trans. James Strachey et al., vol. VIII (London, 1955), pp. 118.

9 Roger Caillois, *Man, Play and Games*, trans. Meyer Barash (Urbana, IL, 2001), pp. 74–5, 97.

10 Emmanuel Levinas, *Entre Nous: On Thinking-of-the-Other* (New York, 1998), p. 148.

11 Caillois, *Man, Play and Games*, p. 109.

12 Anthony Julius, *Trails of the Diaspora: A History of Anti-Semitism in England* (Oxford, 2010), pp. 3, 6–11.

13 G.W.F. Hegel, *The Phenomenology of Mind*, trans. J. B. Baillie, 2 vols (London, 1910), vol. I, p. 366.

14 Ibid.

15 Ibid., vol. I, pp. 16–17.

16 Ibid., vol. I, p. 184.

17 Sigmund Freud, *Civilization and its Discontents*, in *The Standard Edition of the Complete Psychological Works of Sigmund Freud*, vol. XXI (London, 1964), p. 114.

18 Peter Sloterdijk, *God's Zeal: The Battle of the Three Monotheisms*, trans. Wieland Hoban (Cambridge and Malden, MA, 2009), p. 130.

19 Freud, *Civilization and Its Discontents*, p. 114.

20 Henry A. Kissinger, 'The Viet Nam Negotiations', *Foreign Affairs*, XLVII (1969), p. 214.

21 Sigmund Freud, 'Some Character-Types Met with in Psycho-Analytic Work', *The Standard Edition of the Complete Psychological Works of Sigmund Freud*, ed. and trans. James Strachey et al., vol. XIV (London, 1955), pp. 315–30.

22 Martin Heidegger, *Being and Time*, trans. John Macquarrie and Edward Robinson (Oxford, 1962), pp. 304–11.

23 Ludwig Wittgenstein, *Tractatus Logico-Philosophicus*, trans. D. F. Pears and B. F. McGuinness (London, 1963), p. 147.

24 Elias Ashmore, *Making Sense of Sport*, 4th edn (London and New York, 2005), p. 136.

25 R. C. Sipes, 'War, Sports and Aggression: An Empirical Test of Two Rival Theories', *American Anthropologist*, LXXV (1973), p. 80.

26 J. A. Mangan, ed., *Militarism, Sport, Europe: War Without Weapons* (London and Portland, OR, 2003).
27 George Orwell, 'The Sporting Spirit', in *I Belong to the Left: The Complete Works of George Orwell*, vol. XVII: *1945* (London, 1998), p. 442.
28 Ibid., p. 441.
29 Ibid., p. 442.
30 Norbert Elias and Eric Dunning, eds, *Quest for Excitement: Sport and Leisure in the Civilizing Process* (Oxford, 1986) pp. 50–51.
31 Ibid., p. 34.
32 Ibid., p. 51.
33 Ibid., p. 44.
34 Hazel Hartley, *Sport, Physical Recreation and the Law* (London and New York, 2009), pp. 69–92.
35 Ibid., p. 103.
36 Caillois, *Man, Play and Games*, p. 167.
37 Ibid., p. 97.
38 Angela Patmore, *Playing On Their Nerves: The Sport Experiment* (London, 1979), pp. 12–13.
39 Ibid., p. 24.
40 Arnold R. Beisser, *The Madness in Sports*, 2nd edn (Bowie, ML, 1977), p. 159.
41 *Calendar of the Close Rolls* 1910, pp. 181–2, quoted Elias and Dunning, *Quest for Excitement*, p. 176.
42 Ibid.
43 Peter Sloterdijk, *Rage and Time: A Psychopolitical Investigation*, trans. Mario Wenning (New York, 2010).
44 Caillois, *Man, Play and Games*, p. 110.
45 Gilles Deleuze, *Negotiations 1972–1990*, trans. Martin Joughin (New York, 1995), p. 119.
46 Gunnar Breivik, 'Being-in-the-Void: A Heideggerian Analysis of Skydiving', *Journal of the Philosophy of Sport*, XXXVII (2010), p. 42.
47 Jean-Paul Sartre, *Being and Nothingness: An Essay on Phenomenological Ontology*, trans. Hazel E. Barnes (London, 1984), p. 585.
48 Ibid., p. 584.
49 Ibid.
50 Ibid., p. 585.
51 Andy Martin, *Walking on Water* (London, 1992), p. 102.
52 Ibid.
53 Andy Martin, *Stealing the Wave: The Epic Struggle Between Ken Bradshaw and Mark Foo* (London, 2007).
54 Martin, *Walking on Water*, p. 23.
55 Gerard Manley Hopkins, *Poems*, 4th edn, ed. W. H. Gardner and N. H. Mackenzie (Oxford, 1970), p. 69.
56 Sartre, *Being and Nothingness*, pp. 591–2.
57 Michel Serres, *La Guerre mondiale* (Paris, 2008), pp. 67–9.
58 Michel Serres, *The Natural Contract*, trans. Elizabeth MacArthur and William Paulson (Ann Arbor, MI, 1995), p. 3.

Index